NICOMACHEAN ETHICS

The Library of Liberal Arts
OSKAR PIEST, FOUNDER

NICOMACHEAN ETHICS

ARISTOTLE

Translated, with introduction and notes, by
MARTIN OSTWALD

The Library of Liberal Arts
published by

Bobbs-Merrill Educational Publishing
Indianapolis

The Bobbs-Merrill Company, Inc.
4300 West 62nd Street
Indianapolis, Indiana 46268

First Edition
Ninteenth Printing—1980

Library of Congress Catalog Card Number 62-15690
ISBN 0-672-60256-3 (pbk.)

PREFACE

The present annotated translation of Aristotle's *Nicoma-chean Ethics* is, like most translations, primarily intended for those who know little or no Greek; its aim is to introduce the modern reader to Aristotle's most important contribution to ethical theory. I consequently have tried to make the text as readable as possible within the demand for a faithful and accurate rendering of the original.

Since Aristotle created rather than perpetuated a consistent philosophical vocabulary, I felt justified in abandoning the conventional translations of certain key words and concepts, hallowed though they are by tradition. To speak, for example, of "profligacy," "continence," or "temperance" in the twentieth century is either to distort Aristotle's meaning or to establish a block between him and ourselves; "self-indulgence," "moral strength," and "self-control" have more meaning for us as equivalents of *akolasia, enkrateia,* and *sōphrosynē.* While this kind of modernization may blur Aristotle's influence, through Latin translations, on the development of a philosophical vocabulary in the Middle Ages, and thus on our own time, the gain of bringing him closer to modern modes of expression seems to offset this loss. In addition, a Glossary of Greek terms is provided to serve as a bridge, as it were, between conventional translations of important terms and our own.

The footnotes are intended (*a*) to explain references which are likely to puzzle the modern reader; (*b*) to elucidate passages which can be understood only in the light of other Aristotelian works or which reveal, in some important way, the influence of earlier thinkers, especially Plato, upon Aristotle; and (*c*) to explain, in conjunction with the Glossary, the precise meanings of concepts for which no single satisfactory equivalent could be found in English.

The most pleasant task remains, that of expressing my

cordial thanks to Professors Glenn R. Morrow of the University of Pennsylvania and Charles H. Kahn of Columbia University for having read the entire manuscript most meticulously, and for having offered numerous suggestions for improving the Introduction, the translation, and the notes; to Mr. Oskar Piest, founder of the Liberal Arts Press, for his constant encouragement; to Professor Heinrich Brinkmann of Swarthmore College for help with mathematical terminology; to the Faculty Research Committee of Swarthmore College for grants to defray the cost of secretarial work; and to the University of Chicago Press for permission to quote from Richmond Lattimore's translation of Homer's *Iliad,* and the University of Michigan Press for permission to quote from Richmond Lattimore's translation of Hesiod.

M. O.

Swarthmore College
November 1962

CONTENTS
· · · · · · · · · · · · · · · ·

NICOMACHEAN ETHICS

Book Seven

Book Eight

INTRODUCTION

1. THE LIFE OF ARISTOTLE [1]

In 384 B.C. Aristotle was born in Stagirus (later called Stagira), a little town situated in the north-east corner of the Chalcidice peninsula. His father, Nicomachus, a physician who spent some time at the Macedonian court at Pella, died early, and Aristotle was brought up by relatives at Atarneus in Asia Minor. At the age of seventeen, in 367/66 B.C., he went to Athens to study at Plato's Academy. In Plato's absence in Sicily at that time, the distinguished mathematician and astronomer Eudoxus of Cnidus was presiding over the Academy, and his thought has left some traces in the *Nicomachean Ethics*.[2]

After Plato's death in 348/47 B.C., Aristotle left Athens, and together with Xenocrates, who had been a colleague of his at the Academy, accepted an invitation from the ruler Hermias of Atarneus to settle there. Two other former members of the Academy, Erastus and Coriscus, joined Aristotle and Xenocrates at Atarneus, and after an initial stay with Hermias, were given land to start a new school at Assos. For reasons unknown to us, Aristotle left Assos in 345/44 B.C. to found a new school at Mytilene on the island of Lesbos.

But his stay at Mytilene turned out to be of short duration: after two years, in 343/42 B.C., he was invited by Philip of Macedon to come to Pella to be the tutor of Alexander, then thirteen years of age. Three years later, the active part which Alexander was called upon to take in Macedonian affairs put

1 For a recent edition and discussion of the ancient and medieval evidence of Aristotle's biography, see Ingemar Düring, *Aristotle in the ancient biographical tradition* (Göteborg, 1957), especially Part IV, "From Hermippus to Ptolemy: A brief summary of results and conclusions," pp. 459-76.

2 For Eudoxus' influence, see I. 12, 1101b27-31, and X. 2.

an end to Aristotle's tutorship. Aristotle changed his residence
to his native Stagirus, which had been destroyed eight years
before but rebuilt in Aristotle's honor by Philip and Alexander, and in 335/34 B.C. he moved back to Athens. There he
spent the next twelve years teaching and writing at the
Lyceum. His activities came to an abrupt end after the death
of Alexander in June 323 B.C. When the news of Alexander's
death reached Athens a month later, an open revolt broke out.
Aristotle, because of his connections with the monarch, became
a *persona non grata,* and a certain Eurymedon brought an
indictment for impiety against him—the same charge on which
Socrates had been condemned to death—for having conferred
divine honors on a mortal in a hymn he had written in memory of his friend Hermias of Atarneus. But before the matter
came to trial, Aristotle decided to leave Athens in order, as
one tradition has it, not to give the Athenians an opportunity
to commit a second sin against philosophy. Together with his
family he fled to Chalcis, the birthplace of his mother, where
he soon died in November 322 B.C. at the age of sixty-two.

Aristotle's earliest works, especially his dialogues, are now
lost and only a few fragments survive. What we do have of his
writings are summaries of the lectures he delivered at various
times on subjects ranging from rhetoric to metaphysics, biology to politics, poetry to psychology, and so forth. These summaries of lecture courses were in almost every case revised—
probably even revised several times—partly by Aristotle himself and partly by his successors in the Peripatos [3] or by later
editors, and were deposited in Aristotle's library to be con-
sulted by teachers and students. This means in effect that
many works were originally not written in the form in which
they have come down to us: works such as the *Metaphysics,*
Physics, Politics, and *Nicomachean Ethics* (so called because
Aristotle's son Nicomachus is said to have edited the work after

[3] Peripatos is the name usually given to the school founded by the successors of Aristotle in Athens. The word, derived from the Greek verb
peripateō (I walk about), rose from the teachers' practice of delivering
lectures while walking.

his father's death) now contain in a more or less homogeneous juxtaposition part of the original courses of lectures plus their later revisions and additions. As a result, one of the tasks of modern philological scholarship has been to try to separate early from later layers both within individual works of Aristotle, and in the relation of the different works to one another.[4]

2. THE PLACE OF ETHICS IN ARISTOTLE'S PHILOSOPHY

Despite the changes and modifications which Aristotle's philosophical views underwent in the course of his life, there is, in the extant works at least, a consistent picture of the place occupied by the different intellectual disciplines in relation to scientific knowledge (*epistēmē*) as such. It is here that we find the most striking difference between Aristotle and his master Plato. For while Plato's work is characterized by a passionate conviction of the unity and interdependence of all branches of human knowledge, Aristotle with his sharp analytical mind is more concerned with finding what differentiates one branch of learning from the other and what is peculiar to each. In order to understand his analysis we have to begin by stating a few fundamental points.

For Aristotle, as for Plato, man possesses *logos,* the power of speech and reasoning. This does not mean that everything man does is rational; it simply means that man alone of all animals possesses reason, which gives him the capacity of organizing his various activities by means of thought in a way no other animal can. Moreover, since this power differentiates him from the other animals, it constitutes the essential element in his definition, and only insofar as man acts rationally can he be said to act as a human being at all. In other words, Aristotle— and Plato before him—believed that acting like a human being

---

[4] The pioneering study in the establishment of an Aristotelian chronology is Werner Jaeger's *Aristoteles* (Berlin, 1923; English tr. by R. Robinson in 1934, 2nd edn. 1948). A comprehensive account of the present state of scholarship in this respect is in R. A. Gauthier and J. Y. Jolif, *L'Éthique à Nicomaque,* I (Louvain, 1958), 26*-36*.

is tantamount to acting like a rational human being, and acting like a rational human being is the same thing as acting like
a good human being.

Aristotle recognizes three major areas of human activity,
that is, three areas in which man's rational faculty is displayed,
and he accordingly divides all scientific knowledge (*epistēmē*)
or thought (*dianoia*)—the terms are used interchangeably in
this context—into three groups: [5] theoretical (*theōrētikē*),
productive (*poiētikē*), and practical (*praktikē*) science, and together these three cover all possible activities of man as a
rational animal.

The highest form of knowledge is theoretical science, since
it involves the use of reason at its purest. It has no ulterior
motive, but simply wants to study truth for its own sake and to
understand the workings of reality and the universe without
desiring to effect any change in the objects which it studies.
What are the objects of theoretical science? Aristotle recognizes
three different kinds and, therefore, subdivides theoretical
science into three branches or *philosophiai*. The first and most
sovereign of these is what has, since Aristotle's time, come to
be called "metaphysics," because the earliest ancient editor of
Aristotle's works, Andronicus of Rhodes, who lived in the
first century B.C., placed Aristotle's treatises on this subject
"after" (*meta*) the treatises on natural science (*ta physika*).
Aristotle himself uses at various times three different names for
metaphysics: sometimes he refers to it as "first philosophy"
(*prōtē philosophia*), sometimes as *theologia,* and occasionally
he speaks of it simply as *sophia* or "intellectual wisdom." The
province of this science is reality as such, i.e., it investigates the
fundamental principles of all being *qua* being. In one sense,
therefore, it is concerned with such eternal and changeless
entities as the First Unmoved Mover, which exist separate
from matter and are all form; and inasmuch as metaphysics
takes this as its object, it can equally well be called "theology."
But metaphysics may also deal with the degree of "reality" or
"being" inherent in the matter-form combinations which we

[5] See *Metaphysics* E. 1 and K. 7.

encounter in the sublunary sphere in which we live. This means that it studies the axioms of science inasmuch as these are essential attributes of all "being," and from this point of view metaphysics is the "first," i.e., the most basic, philosophy.

The second theoretical science, physics (*physikē*) is also concerned with reality but not with reality in itself, as metaphysics is. Its province is the study of reality insofar as it is subject to motion, i.e., it examines the principles of motion and rest, growth and decay as they are found in the matter-form combinations of the animal and vegetable world around us. The *Physics* is of course Aristotle's most fundamental work concerned with this science; but in addition, such biological and physiological treatises as *De Caelo, Metereologica, De Partibus Animalium, Historia Animalium, De Anima,* and several more belong to it.

Mathematics, the third theoretical science, differs from physics in that its objects—number, magnitude, figure, etc.—are abstracted from matter and not considered as embodied in the matter-form combinations with which physics deals. The difference between mathematics and metaphysics is harder to see, especially in view of the metaphysical importance attached to mathematics by the Pythagoreans and by Plato. The abstract—and therefore eternal—nature of mathematics, which made it so attractive to Plato, meant to Aristotle only that it possesses less reality than the other theoretical sciences: lines, numbers, angles, and so forth have for him no existence separate from the particular objects of sense perception in which they are found. Therefore, mathematics, in Aristotle's view, does not deal with things as "realities" but as continuous entities that have dimension; it deals with a particular aspect of being and not with being as such, and thus loses to metaphysics the general significance which Aristotle's predecessors had attributed to it.[6]

In the productive and the practical sciences, reason is put to the service of man's most immediate needs. The objects with which both these branches of knowledge or thought are con-

6 *Ibid.,* K. 4, 1061b17-27.

cerned are not the "divine," eternal, and separate entities of theoretical science, but entities which depend on the human being who produces or acts respectively. Man himself is the initiating principle (*archē*) and the results of action and production depend on the active exercise (*energeia*) of faculties (*dynameis*) inherent in him. What we find in these two branches of knowledge, therefore, is reason dealing with what is changeable and with what "can be other than it is," for the objects of both production and action become what the individual producing or acting wants them to become. This, in turn, makes the productive and the practical sciences something peculiar to man. For while Aristotle attributes study and contemplation (*theōria*) also to the gods, he denies them production and moral action. The First Unmoved Mover of *Metaphysics* Λ and *Physics* VIII, for example, being eternal and unchangeable, is an immaterial being who imparts motion to the outer sphere of the Universe: he is not a creator in the sense in which that term is used of the God of Genesis. Moreover, we learn from the *Nicomachean Ethics* [7] that the gods have no need of action (*praxis*), since they already possess that happiness which is the end of all action. Accordingly, being confined to man, the productive and the practical sciences differ from the theoretical in that they have an ulterior motive and in that their objects are not eternal and changeless.

This is especially evident in the productive sciences. Here the end to which reason is employed is the production of a given product, which is, in its turn, intended to serve some human need. The producer's task ends as soon as the product is made; he is not concerned with the use to which it is put afterward. The rational faculty (*dynamis*) which produces the product is the art or skill (*technē*) of the producer, and its possession enables him to ensure that the product will be good and usable. It is a "know-how" rather than "knowledge" in some intellectual sense. These characteristics set off productive from both theoretical and practical science. A sculptor, for example, insofar as he is seriously engaged in his proper activity, will

[7] X. 8, 1178b8-18.

not study rocks in the way a theoretical scientist, e.g., a mineralogist or geologist, studies them. He will deal with them only as the raw material of the particular work he wishes to execute, and he chooses a particular stone in order to obtain the right texture for the statue he wants to produce; he does not choose it because he is interested in the stone as such. If this distinguishes the productive from the theoretical scientist, a further consideration shows how he differs from the practical scientist. The sculptor's end is attained as soon as the statue, the end product, is completed. Productive science does not tell him what to do with the product once it is finished. To determine that is the end of practical science.

For it is practical science that deals with the use of reason for the organization of life itself, or better, for living a good life. This means that the practical sciences, ethics and politics, resemble the productive in that the initiating motive (*archē*) is in man himself and not external to him, as it is in the theoretical sciences. But in the practical sciences man is a moral agent rather than a producer. His end is not the creation of a product which will exist independent of him once it is completed, but rather the living of a certain kind of life. In other words, in the practical sciences the end is neither the study (*theōria*) or knowledge (*gnōsis*) of something external to man as it is in the theoretical sciences, nor is it the creation of a product that will exist apart from him as soon as it is completed. It is the very activity of living a good life that is in itself the end. Since our main concern here is with ethics, which together with politics constitutes the realm of practical science, we shall now turn our attention to some salient points in Aristotle's ethical doctrine.

3. Some Observations on Aristotle's Ethical System

Of the three treatises on ethics that have come down to us under the name of Aristotle, the *Nicomachean Ethics* is the only one whose genuineness has never been doubted. The *Magna Moralia,* though doubtless a work of the Peripatetic

School, is no longer attributed to Aristotle,[8] and the *Eudemian Ethics* was for a long time ascribed to Eudemus of Rhodes not only as editor (which he probably was) but even as author. However, since the appearance of Kapp's [9] and Jaeger's [10] works, there is no longer any doubt that Aristotle is the author of both *Eudemian* and *Nicomachean Ethics* and that the former is based on a course of lectures given—probably at Assos—some fifteen years earlier than the courses which underlie the *Nicomachean Ethics.*

This is not the place to review in detail the arguments which establish the authenticity and priority of the *Eudemian Ethics.*[11] Suffice it to say that the *Eudemian Ethics* is much closer to the *Protrepticus,* which is admittedly early, and to some of the late works of Plato, such as the *Philebus,* than are the treatments of the same problems in the *Nicomachean Ethics.* Of especial interest in this connection is the double treatment of pleasure in the *Nicomachean Ethics,* (*a*) in Book VII, chapters 11-14, and (*b*) in Book X, chapters 1-5.[12] It is now certain that the first of these is earlier than the second; [13] moreover, since (*a*) leans heavily on the *Philebus,* while (*b*) is rather critical of it, and since (*a*) belongs to a section of the *Nicomachean Ethics,* viz., Books V-VII, which is identical with Books IV-VI of the *Eudemian Ethics,* we have here a good example of part of an earlier work embodied—either by Aristotle himself or by one of his editors—in a later one. So we find that to a certain extent old and new exist side by side in the *Nicomachean Ethics.* Yet it is also true that wherever there are differences in the

8 The problem is most recently discussed by G. Lieberg, *Die Lehre von der Lust in den Ethiken des Aristoteles,* "Zetemata" XIX (Munich, 1958), pp. 16-20.

9 Ernst Kapp, *Das Verhältnis der eudemischen zur nikomachischen Ethik* (diss., Freiburg, 1912).

10 See above, p. xiii and note 4.

11 See R. Robinson's translation of Jaeger's work, pp. 228-58, together with the good, though often extreme, criticism of Gauthier and Jolif, I, 26*-30*.

12 See below, p. 203, note 59.

13 See A. J. Festugière, *Aristote: Le Plaisir* (Paris, 1936), and Lieberg.

treatment of a given problem between the two works, the *Nicomachean Ethics* represents a more mature view than the *Eudemian*. In other words, in basing our discussion on the *Nicomachean Ethics* alone, we shall in fact discuss the main points of Aristotle's ethical system as a whole.

We pointed out in the preceding section that ethics is a practical science which in aim as well as in method differs from the theoretical sciences. For while the aim of the theoretical sciences is study and contemplation, the aim of ethics is to act in a certain way: it is not scientific knowledge but action. How, then, is it possible to discuss ethics in a philosophical way at all? How can one theorize about something which, according to Aristotle, is so radically different from theory?

That Aristotle was aware of this problem is indicated in a number of ways in the *Nicomachean Ethics*. He points out repeatedly that in ethics theory must always be subordinate to practice,[14] he stresses that moral behavior is acquired by habituation,[15] and that therefore only those can be admitted as students of ethics whose character is already formed sufficiently by habit to accept without argument the fact that moral behavior is good.[16] For rules of moral conduct cannot be defined as rigorously as the objects of the theoretical sciences. The latter are the changeless and eternal realities, given as such by nature; their "principle of motion and of rest" (*archē*) is, as we have seen, in the objects and not in man. In the practical sciences, on the other hand, where man as agent initiates action, the rules are less precise, since they depend on human will and human choice. Here is what Aristotle has to say about them:

> Problems of what is noble and just, which politics examines, present so much variety and irregularity that some people believe that they exist only by convention and not by nature.

---

[14] I. 3, 1095a5-6; II. 2, 1103b26-31; cf. also I. 6, 1096b32-35, and *Eudemian Ethics* I. 5, 1216a37-b25.
[15] II. 1, 1103a17-25.
[16] I. 3. 1095a2-11; 4, 1095b1-8.

The problem of the good, too, presents a similar kind of irregularity, because in many cases good things bring harmful results. There are instances of men ruined by wealth and others by courage. Therefore, in a discussion of such subjects, which has to start from a basis of this kind, we must be satisfied to indicate the truth with a rough and general sketch: when the subject and the basis of a discussion consist of matters that hold good only as a general rule, but not always, the conclusions reached must be of the same order. The various points that are made must be received in the same spirit. For a well-schooled man is one who searches for that degree of precision in each kind of study which the nature of the subject at hand admits: it is obviously just as foolish to accept arguments of probability from a mathematician as to demand strict demonstrations from an orator.[17]

The problem is thus to find principles as lucid and rigorous as possible on which a discussion of moral problems can be based. In other words, we must find for the practical sciences a basis as firm—comparatively speaking—as are the phenomena and realities studied in the theoretical sciences. In order to arrive at a basis for his discussion, Aristotle usually examines the beliefs current (*endoxa*) about a given problem. Such "current beliefs," he states in the *Topics*,[18] are "the views of all men, or of most men, or of the wise; in the latter case the view may be held by all wise men or by most of them, or by the most renowned and respected." Once these views have been collected and juxtaposed, it will become clear that many contradict each other, and the next step will be to balance different judgments against one another. It must be noted here that Aristotle's attitude toward traditional views, both popular and philosophical, is one of great respect: "Some of these views are expressed by many people and have come down from antiquity, some by a few men of high prestige, and it is not reasonable to assume that both groups are altogether wrong; the presumption is rather that they are right in at least one or even in most respects." [19] By juxtaposing them and by reveal-

[17] I. 3, 1094b14-27; cf. also 7, 1098a26-32, and II. 2, 1103b34-1104a10.
[18] *Topics* I. 1, 100b21-23.
[19] *Nic. Eth.* I. 8, 1098b27-29.

ing their contradictions, Aristotle focusses attention on the
intricacies of the problem he is about to discuss; and by proceeding as he does to criticize each opinion, he sharpens what
true perception is inherent in each and appropriates its truth,
until he reaches the point when a new truth will emerge which
contains all the valid elements of the opinions discussed. The
best example of this procedure in the *Nicomachean Ethics* is
afforded by the beginning of Book VII. The theme of this
book is moral weakness. Aristotle does not attempt to define it
until chapter 3; but he devotes the second half of chapter 1
(1145b2-20) first to an explicit statement of his method and
next to the enumeration of some six beliefs about moral weakness which, he thinks, deserve consideration; after that, the
views enumerated in the first chapter are discussed in the second.

But the discussion of current beliefs, both popular and
philosophical, is only a starting point (*archē*) in the sense of
being a first step in the analysis of particular goods; for the
decisive starting points or first principles of a system of ethics
are *archai* in a different and more profound sense. They are
certain propositions about the purpose of man, his place in
society, and what is good for him.

Aristotle's ethical theory is teleological in this sense, and the
larger part of the very first book of the *Nicomachean Ethics*
(chapters 4-12) is devoted to establishing the proposition that
happiness is the good at which all human action (*praxis*) aims,
and toward the end of the work (X. 6-7), the supremacy of happiness is asserted once again. It is important to note that happiness is for Aristotle not a fleeting, momentary phenomenon
which we may enjoy one day and lose the next, but a general
condition which encompasses the whole of a man's life, inasmuch as that life displays "activities in conformity with virtue." [20] Thus happiness is for Aristotle synonymous with "living well" (*eu zēn, kalōs zēn*) or "acting well" (*eu prattein,
eupraxia*), and "acting well" is in the Greek of any period the
same as "faring well."

20 *Ibid*. I. 10, 1100b10.

Although comments on the key concepts of Aristotle's ethical system will be found in the Glossary, we shall here single out a few of the most crucial and untranslatable for special consideration. The first of these is *aretē*, the word usually translated by "virtue," which, as we just saw, is an important element in the definition of happiness as "activities in conformity with virtue." The somewhat strait-laced and prudish connotations which "virtue" so often has in English are totally absent from the Greek. The word denotes a *functional* excellence or virtue not only in Aristotle's usage but throughout ancient Greek literature, and it implies in Plato and Aristotle that there is a set of qualities which will make man fulfill his function as a man properly and well in much the same way as a different set of qualities makes a good horse fulfill its own proper functions. There is thus nothing mysterious or divine about the concept of *aretē*: when "virtue" is predicated of a person, it simply means that he is fulfilling his proper task well, and if happiness is accepted as the proper goal of human life, it is clear that without "virtue" this or any other proper goal cannot be attained.[21]

Aristotle shares this basic view of *aretē* with his predecessors. But he goes beyond them in explicitly stating what it involves. A virtuous action is not merely any action which, somehow or other, will lead to happiness. We do not display virtue when we do something that happens to be good, but we must act with a deliberate desire to perform our function as human beings properly, that is, to perform it voluntarily and in full awareness of the fact that there are possible alternatives, which, however, we reject in deciding to act the way we will. The Greek word Aristotle uses for this process is *proairesis*, which literally means "forechoice," "a choosing ⟨one thing⟩ before, i.e., rather than ⟨another⟩," and without it no action can have moral value. Aristotle's final definition of the concept at the end of his discussion in III. 2-3 is "a deliberate desire for things that are within our power: we arrive at a decision on the basis of deliberation, and then let the deliberation guide

21 See also Glossary.

our desire." [22] It is, in other words, a thoughtful organization of our desires—not of all desires, but only of those which we are capable of fulfilling through our own efforts—without which no action can be termed "virtuous." [23]

But in order to have virtue it is not sufficient to exercise this *proairesis* or "choice" of acting well only on a number of isolated occasions. Virtue is, for Aristotle, a *hexis* (literally, "a having," "a holding," "a being in a certain condition"), something so deeply ingrained in a person by constant habit that he will almost automatically make the morally right choices on every occasion, rejecting at the same time and equally automatically all the alternatives as wrong. Virtue will thus be a firmly established characteristic of the person, and the aggregate of all his characteristics will constitute his character.[24]

If the fact that it is a *hexis* or "characteristic" explains the nature of virtue in relation to the agent, Aristotle's doctrine of the mean explains it in relation to the objects with which ethics is concerned. This doctrine is Aristotle's most original contribution to moral theory. It is stated at length in Book II, chapters 5-9, and the long passage from III. 6 to the end of Book V is devoted to applying it to the analysis of particular virtues and vices. The basis of the doctrine of the mean is the observation that the virtues are concerned with actions and emotions. When we are faced with a given situation which demands action, we may react too strongly, not strongly enough, or to a proper degree, and as a result we may want to do too much, too little, or the right amount to cope with it. In order to act virtuously, our actions and reactions must of course have the proper degree. But Aristotle goes further than that and characterizes as vice any act which exceeds or falls short of the proper degree. If, then, the intensity of re-action (Aristotle uses the word *pathos*, "emotion") to a situation be represented by a straight line, one end would represent

22 III. 3, 1113a10-12.
23 See also Glossary, *proairesis*.
24 See also Glossary, *hexis*, and II. 5.

deficiency and the other excess. Both of these constitute vice.
But at what point between the two do we find virtue? Aristotle
takes great pains to point out that the mean which is virtue
is not arithmetical: "if ten pounds of food is much for a man
to eat and two pounds little, it does not follow that the trainer
will prescribe six pounds, for this may in turn be much or
little for him to eat." [25] On the contrary, the mean must be
determined in relation to the agent. If his natural bent is to
follow one of the extremes—say, deficiency—the mean will for
him lie closer to the excess than it will for a person who naturally tends toward the excess. Accordingly, the mean, and with
it virtue, is not one fixed point, the same for all; it is a median
which is fixed absolutely only in that it lies between the extremes of excess and deficiency, but within which proper al-
lowance is made for differences between individuals.

It may seem peculiar to us that Aristotle opens and ends the
Nicomachean Ethics by emphasizing that ethics is part of the
larger science of politics, and a few words of explanation may
be in order. It is of course true that for Aristotle man is a
zōon politikon, a social and political being,[26] who realizes his
nature fully only in the city-state. But it is also true that moral
action is impossible outside human society, for actions are virtuous or not when they are performed in relation to one's
fellow men; a hermit is incapable of acting virtuously. For the
Greeks society and the state were identical. There was no society apart from the city-state and, interestingly enough, the
Greek language does not even have a word other than *polis*
to express what we mean by "society." And just as we regard
the creation of the right kind of "social climate" as one of the
preconditions of a healthy moral development, so Aristotle
realized that ethics is inseparable from the master science of
politics.

MARTIN OSTWALD

[25] *Nic. Eth.* II. 6, 1106a36-b3.
[26] I. 7, 1097b11, and *Politics* I. 2, 1253a3.

BIBLIOGRAPHY

WORKS CITED IN THE NOTES

Apelt, O. *Aristotelis Ethica Nicomachea.* 3rd edn. Leipzig, 1912.

Burnet, J. *The Ethics of Aristotle.* London, 1900.

Bywater, I. *Contributions to the Textual Criticism of Aristotle's Nicomachean Ethics.* Oxford, 1892.

Diehl, E. *Anthologia Lyrica Graeca.* 3rd edn. Leipzig, 1949-1952. (Diehl³)

Diels, H. *Die Fragmente der Vorsokratiker.* 3 vols. 6th edn. by W. Kranz. Berlin, 1951-1952. (DK⁶)

Dirlmeier, F. (tr.). *Aristoteles: Nikomachische Ethik.* Darmstadt, 1956.

Düring, Ingemar. *Aristotle in the Ancient Biographical Tradition.* ("Studia Graeca et Latina Gothoburgensia" V.) Göteborg, 1957.

Ehrenberg, Victor. *The Greek State.* Oxford, 1960.

Festugière, A. J. *Aristote: Le Plaisir.* Paris, 1936.

Gauthier, R. A. and J. Y. Jolif. *L'Éthique à Nicomaque.* 3 vols. Louvain, 1958-1959.

Glotz, G. *La solidarité de la famille dans le droit criminel en Grèce.* Paris, 1904.

Grant, Sir Alexander. *The Ethics of Aristotle.* 2 vols. 4th edn. London, 1885.

Grube, G. M. A. (tr.). Aristotle: *On Poetry and Style.* ("Library of Liberal Arts," No. 68.) New York, 1958.

Heath, T. L. *A History of Greek Mathematics.* 2 vols. Oxford, 1921.

Jaeger, Werner. *Aristoteles.* Berlin, 1923.

―――. *Aristotle.* Tr. R. Robinson. 2nd edn. Oxford, 1948.

Joachim, H. H. *Aristotle: The Nicomachean Ethics.* Oxford, 1951.

Kaibel, G. (ed.). *Comicorum Graecorum Fragmenta.* Berlin, 1899. (Kaibel)

Kapp, Ernst. *Das Verhältnis der eudemischen zur nikomachischen Ethik.* Diss., Freiburg, 1912.

Kock, T. (ed.). *Comicorum Atticorum Fragmenta.* 3 vols. Leipzig, 1880-1888. (Kock)

Lattimore, Richmond (tr.). *The Iliad of Homer.* Chicago, 1951.

———— (tr.). Hesiod: *The Works and Days; Theogony; The Shield of Herakles.* Ann Arbor, 1959.

Léonard, J. *Le bonheur chez Aristote.* Brussels, 1948.

Lieberg, G. *Die Lehre von der Lust in den Ethiken des Aristoteles.* ("Zetemata" XIX.) Munich, 1958.

Lobel, E. and D. Page (eds.). *Poetarum Lesbiorum Fragmenta.* Oxford, 1955. (L-P)

Nauck, A. *Tragicorum Graecorum Fragmenta.* 2nd edn. Leipzig, 1926. (Nauck[2])

Nuyens, F. *L'évolution de la psychologie d'Aristote.* Louvain, 1948.

Rackham, H. (tr.). Aristotle: *The Nicomachean Ethics.* London, and Cambridge, Mass., 1947.

Ramsauer, G. *Aristotelis Ethica Nicomachea.* Leipzig, 1878.

Rassow, H. *Forschungen über die Nikomachische Ethik des Aristoteles.* Weimar, 1874.

Ross, W. D. (tr.). *Ethica Nicomachea.* ("The Works of Aristotle," ed. W. D. Ross, Vol. IX.) Oxford, 1925.

Stewart, J. A. *Notes on the Nicomachean Ethics.* 2 vols. Oxford, 1892.

Susemihl, F. *Aristotelis Ethica Nicomachea.* Leipzig, 1880.

NOTE ON THE TEXT

This translation is based on the text of I. Bywater in the "Oxford Classical Texts," and any divergence from it is indicated in a footnote. Wherever available, the "Oxford Classical Texts" have also been used for references to other authors. For the Presocratic philosophers, H. Diels, *Die Fragmente der Vorsokratiker* (3 vols.; 6th edn. by W. Kranz, Berlin, 1951-52) has been used, and for the Greek lyric poets, E. Diehl's *Anthologia Lyrica Graeca* (3rd edn., Leipzig, 1949-52). Abbreviations for these and for other works are indicated in the Bibliography.

References to Aristotle's works are conventionally based on the first modern edition by I. Bekker, commissioned by the Prussian Academy (Berlin, 1831). Each page in Bekker's text is printed in two parallel columns, the left of which is called "a" and the right "b." We have followed the usual practice of indicating Bekker's page, column, and line numbers in the margin.

Caret brackets are used to indicate any additions made by myself for the sake of obtaining clarity of thought or style. I have also supplied the chapter headings, all footnotes, and have translated all quotations, unidentified as to translator, from classical sources.

M. O.

NICOMACHEAN ETHICS

BOOK I

1. *The good as the aim of action*

Every art or applied science [1] and every systematic investiga-   1094a
tion, and similarly every action and choice,[2] seem to aim at some
good; the good, therefore, has been well defined as that at
which all things aim.[3] But it is clear that there is a difference
in the ends at which they aim: in some cases the activity [4] is
the end, in others the end is some product [5] beyond the activity. In cases where the end lies beyond the action the product   5
is naturally superior to the activity.

Since there are many activities, arts, and sciences,[6] the number of ends is correspondingly large: of medicine the end is
health, of shipbuilding a vessel, of strategy, victory, and of
household management, wealth. In many instances several such
pursuits are grouped together under a single capacity: [7] the   10
art of bridle-making, for example, and everything else pertaining to the equipment of a horse are grouped together under
horsemanship; horsemanship in turn, along with every other
military action, is grouped together under strategy; and other
pursuits are grouped together under other capacities. In all
these cases the ends of the master sciences are preferable to   15
the ends of the subordinate sciences, since the latter are

---

1 See Glossary, *technē*, and VI. 4.
2 See Glossary, *proairesis;* Introduction, pp. xxii-xxiii; and III. 2.
3 We do not know who first gave this definition of the good. It is
certainly implied in the Platonic dialogues, especially in *Republic* VI;
but the most likely candidate for the formulation here is Eudoxus, for
whom see below, X. 2, 1172b9-15. But it is clear from this passage, from
X. 2, 1172b35-36, and from *Rhetoric* I. 6, 1362a23 that Aristotle himself
subscribed to this definition.
4 See Glossary, *energeia.*
5 See Glossary, *ergon.*
6 See Glossary, *epistēmē*, and VI. 3 and 6.
7 See Glossary, *dynamis.*

3

pursued for the sake of the former. This is true whether the ends of the actions lie in the activities themselves or, as is the case in the disciplines just mentioned, in something beyond the activities.

2. *Politics as the master science of the good*

Now, if there exists an end in the realm of action which we desire for its own sake, an end which determines all our other desires; if, in other words, we do not make all our
20 choices for the sake of something else—for in this way the process will go on infinitely so that our desire would be futile and pointless—then obviously this end will be the good, that is, the highest good. Will not the knowledge of this good, consequently, be very important to our lives? Would it not better equip us, like archers who have a target to aim at, to hit the proper mark? If so, we must try to comprehend in
25 outline at least what this good is and to which branch of knowledge or to which capacity it belongs.

This good, one should think, belongs to the most sovereign and most comprehensive master science, and politics 8 clearly fits this description. For it determines which sciences ought to exist in states, what kind of sciences each group of citizens
1094b must learn, and what degree of proficiency each must attain. We observe further that the most honored capacities, such as strategy, household management, and oratory, are contained in politics. Since this science uses the rest of the sciences,
5 and since, moreover, it legislates what people are to do and what they are not to do, its end seems to embrace the ends of the other sciences. Thus it follows that the end of politics is the good for man. For even if the good is the same for the individual and the state, the good of the state clearly is the

---

8 *Politikē* is the science of the city-state, the *polis*, and its members, not merely in our narrow 'political' sense of the word but also in the sense that a civilized human existence is, according to Plato and Aristotle, only possible in the *polis*. Thus *politikē* involves not only the science of the state, 'politics,' but of our concept of 'society' as well.

greater and more perfect thing to attain and to safeguard. The attainment of the good for one man alone is, to be sure, a source of satisfaction; yet to secure it for a nation and for states is nobler and more divine. In short, these are the aims of our investigation, which is in a sense an investigation of social and political matters.

3. The limitations of ethics and politics

Our discussion will be adequate if it achieves clarity within the limits of the subject matter. For precision cannot be expected in the treatment of all subjects alike, any more than it can be expected in all manufactured articles. Problems of what is noble and just, which politics examines, present so much variety and irregularity that some people believe that they exist only by convention and not by nature. The problem of the good, too, presents a similar kind of irregularity, because in many cases good things bring harmful results. There are instances of men ruined by wealth, and others by courage. Therefore, in a discussion of such subjects, which has to start from a basis of this kind, we must be satisfied to indicate the truth with a rough and general sketch: when the subject and the basis of a discussion consist of matters that hold good only as a general rule, but not always, the conclusions reached must be of the same order. The various points that are made must be received in the same spirit. For a well-schooled man is one who searches for that degree of precision in each kind of study which the nature of the subject at hand admits: it is obviously just as foolish to accept arguments of probability from a mathematician as to demand strict demonstrations from an orator.

Each man can judge competently the things he knows, and of these he is a good judge. Accordingly, a good judge in each particular field is one who has been trained in it, and a good judge in general, a man who has received an all-round schooling. For that reason, a young man is not equipped to be a student of politics; for he has no experience in the actions

10

15

20

25

1095a

which life demands of him, and these actions form the basis and subject matter of the discussion. Moreover, since he fol-
5 lows his emotions,[9] his study will be pointless and unprofitable, for the end of this kind of study is not knowledge but action. Whether he is young in years or immature in character makes no difference; for his deficiency is not a matter of time but of living and of pursuing all his interests under the influence of his emotions. Knowledge brings no benefit to this kind of person, just as it brings none to the morally weak.
10 But those who regulate their desires and actions by a rational principle [10] will greatly benefit from a knowledge of this subject. So much by way of a preface about the student, the limitations which have to be accepted, and the objective before us.

4. *Happiness is the good, but many views are held about it*

To resume the discussion: since all knowledge and every
15 choice is directed toward some good, let us discuss what is in our view the aim of politics, i.e., the highest good attainable by action. As far as its name is concerned, most people would probably agree: for both the common run of people and cultivated men call it happiness, and understand by "being happy" the same as "living well" and "doing well." But when
20 it comes to defining what happiness is, they disagree, and the account given by the common run differs from that of the philosophers. The former say it is some clear and obvious good, such as pleasure, wealth, or honor; some say it is one thing and others another, and often the very same person identifies it with different things at different times: when he

9 See Glossary, *pathos.*

10 The fundamental meaning of *logos* is 'speech,' 'statement,' in the sense of a coherent and rational arrangement of words; but it can apply to a rational principle underlying many things, and may be translated in different contexts by 'rational account,' 'explanation,' 'argument,' 'treatise,' or 'discussion.' In chaps. 7 and 13 below, *logos* is used in a normative sense, describing the human faculty which comprehends and formulates rational principles and thus guides the conduct of a good and reasonable man.

is sick he thinks it is health, and when he is poor he says it is wealth; and when people are conscious of their own igno- 25 rance, they admire those who talk above their heads in accents of greatness. Some thinkers used to believe that there exists over and above these many goods another good, good in itself and by itself, which also is the cause of good in all these things. An examination of all the different opinions would perhaps be a little pointless, and it is sufficient to concentrate on those which are most in evidence or which seem to make 30 some sort of sense.

Nor must we overlook the fact that arguments which proceed from fundamental principles [11] are different from arguments that lead up to them. Plato, too, rightly recognized this as a problem and used to ask whether the discussion was proceeding from or leading up to fundamental principles, just as in a race course there is a difference between running from the judges to the far end of the track and running back again.[12] 1095b Now, we must start with the known. But this term has two connotations: "what is known to us" and "what is known" pure and simple. Therefore, we should start perhaps from what is known to us. For that reason, to be a competent stu- 5 dent of what is right and just, and of politics generally, one must first have received a proper upbringing in moral conduct. The acceptance of a fact as a fact is the starting point, and if this is sufficiently clear, there will be no further need to ask why it is so. A man with this kind of background has or can easily acquire the foundations from which he must start. But if he neither has nor can acquire them, let him lend an ear to Hesiod's words:

That man is all-best who himself works out 10
    every problem. . . .
That man, too, is admirable who follows one
    who speaks well.

11 See Glossary, *archē*.
12 A Greek race course was U-shaped with the starting line at the open end, which is also where the judges would have their place. The race was run around a marker set up toward the opposite end of the U, and back again to the starting line.

He who cannot see the truth for himself, nor,
   hearing it from others,
store it away in his mind, that man
  is utterly useless.[13]

5. *Various views on the highest good*

But to return to the point from which we digressed.[14] It is
not unreasonable that men should derive their concept of the
15   good and of happiness from the lives which they lead. The
common run of people and the most vulgar identify it with
pleasure, and for that reason are satisfied with a life of enjoyment. For the most notable kinds of life are three: the life
just mentioned, the political life, and the contemplative life.

The common run of people, as we saw, betray their utter
20   slavishness in their preference for a life suitable to cattle; but
their views seem plausible because many people in high places
share the feelings of Sardanapallus.[15] Cultivated and active
men, on the other hand, believe the good to be honor, for
honor, one might say, is the end of the political life. But this
is clearly too superficial an answer: for honor seems to depend
25   on those who confer it rather than on him who receives it,
whereas our guess is that the good is a man's own possession
which cannot easily be taken away from him. Furthermore,
men seem to pursue honor to assure themselves of their own
worth; at any rate, they seek to be honored by sensible men
and by those who know them, and they want to be honored
on the basis of their virtue or excellence.[16] Obviously, then,

---

[13] Hesiod, *Works and Days* 293, 295-297, as translated by Richmond
Lattimore in *Hesiod: The Works and Days; Theogony; The Shield of
Herakles* (Ann Arbor: University of Michigan Press, 1959).

[14] The "digression" is the last paragraph of chap. 4 above.

[15] Sardanapallus is the Hellenized name of the Assyrian king Ashur-
banipal (669-626 B.C.). Many stories about his sensual excesses were current in antiquity.

[16] *Aretē* denotes the functional excellence of any person, animal, or
thing—that quality which enables the possessor to perform his own
particular function well. Thus the *aretai* (plural) of man in relation to
other men are his qualities which enable him to function well in society.

excellence, as far as they are concerned, is better than honor. 30
One might perhaps even go so far as to consider excellence
rather than honor as the end of political life. However, even
excellence proves to be imperfect as an end: for a man might
possibly possess it while asleep or while being inactive all his
life, and while, in addition, undergoing the greatest suffering   1096a
and misfortune. Nobody would call the life of such a man
happy, except for the sake of maintaining an argument. But
enough of this: the subject has been sufficiently treated in our
publications addressed to a wider audience.[17] In the third
place there is the contemplative life, which we shall examine 5
later on. As for the money-maker, his life is led under some
kind of constraint: clearly, wealth is not the good which we
are trying to find, for it is only useful, i.e., it is a means to
something else. Hence one might rather regard the aforemen-
tioned objects as ends, since they are valued for their own
sake. But even they prove not to be the good, though many
words have been wasted to show that they are. Accordingly,
we may dismiss them.   10

6. *Plato's view of the Good*

But perhaps we had better examine the universal good and
face the problem of its meaning, although such an inquiry is

The translation 'virtue' often seems too narrow, and accordingly 'excellence' and 'goodness,' or a combination of these, will also be used. See
Glossary for a more complete explanation.

17 The exact meaning of *ta enkyklia* has been the subject of much
controversy. The basic sense of the term is 'common,' 'ordinary,' 'run-of-
the-mill,' and Aristotle seems to use it in reference to his more popular
treatises, such as the *Eudemus, Protrepticus, On Kingship,* etc., some of
which were written in the form of dialogues. These writings, now largely
lost, were addressed to a wider public and not exclusively to Aristotle's
pupils in the Lyceum. Moreover, it is likely that *ta enkyklia* refers to the
same publications as *hoi exōterikoi logoi* (cf. below, chap. 13, 1102a26-27,
and VI. 4, 1140a3), literally: 'outside discussions or treatises,' i.e., non-
technical philosophical writings addressed to an audience 'outside' the
circle of Aristotle's students proper. For a recent discussion of the problem,
see R. A. Gauthier and J. Y. Jolif, *L'Éthique à Nicomaque,* Vol. I
(Louvain, 1958), pp. 36*-40*.

repugnant, since those who have introduced the doctrine of
Forms [18] are dear to us. But in the interest of truth, one
should perhaps think a man, especially if he is a philosopher,
15 had better give up even ⟨theories that once were⟩ his own and
in fact must do so. Both are dear to us, but it is our sacred
duty to honor truth more highly ⟨than friends⟩.[19]

The proponents of this theory did not make Forms out of
those classes within which they recognized an order involving
priority and posteriority; for that reason they made no pro-
vision, either, for a Form comprising all numbers.[20] However,

[18] The reference is of course to Plato's theory of *eidē* or *ideai* and
especially the Form of the Good, which is Aristotle's chief target here.
Aristotle gives us his own understanding of that theory in two important
passages. The first is above, chap. 4, 1095a26-28: "Some thinkers used to
believe that there exists over and above these many goods [*sc.* pleasure,
wealth, honor, etc.] another good, good in itself, which is also the cause
of good in all these things." The second is in *Eudemian Ethics* I. 8,
1217b2-16:

> For they say that the Good itself is the best of all ⟨good things⟩, and
> that the Good itself has the attribute of being the first of the goods and
> of being by its presence the cause of goodness in the other goods. Both
> these attributes, they say, inhere in the Form of the Good. . . . For the
> Good is most truly defined in terms of the Form of the Good ⟨since all
> other goods are good ⟨only⟩ in terms of participating in it or resembling
> it⟩, and it is the first of the goods: for if that in which things participate
> were to be destroyed, the things participating in the Form would also
> be destroyed, viz., the things which derive their definition from their
> participation in the Form. Now, this is the relation existing between
> the first and the later ⟨members of a series⟩. Hence the Good itself is the
> Form of the Good, for it exists separate from the things which partici-
> pate in it, just as the other Forms do.

See also H. H. Joachim's remarks on this passage in his *Aristotle: The
Nicomachean Ethics* (Oxford, 1951), pp. 31-33.

[19] It is often taken for granted that the proverb *amicus Plato, sed
magis amica veritas* stems from this passage. However, while the sentiment expressed here is at least as old as Plato himself (cf. *Republic* X.
595b-c and 607c), the proverb itself is probably based on a thirteenth-
century Latin translation of an older Greek biography of Aristotle.

[20] Since for Plato and his followers the Forms are absolute being, in
which there is no room for becoming or any kind of development, they
do not recognize a Form of a developing series, in which each successive
member implies the preceding members of the same series. But, as

the term "good" is used in the categories of substance, of quality, and of relatedness alike; but a thing-as-such, i.e., a sub-   20
stance, is by nature prior to a relation into which it can enter:
relatedness is, as it were, an offshoot or logical accident of substance. Consequently, there cannot be a Form common to the
good-as-such and the good as a relation.

Secondly, the term "good" has as many meanings as the
word "is": it is used to describe substances, e.g., divinity and
intelligence are good; qualities, e.g., the virtues are good;   25
quantities, e.g., the proper amount is good; relatedness, e.g.,
the useful is good; time, e.g., the right moment is good; place,
e.g., a place to live is good; and so forth. It is clear, therefore,
that the good cannot be something universal, common to all
cases, and single; for if it were, it would not be applicable in
all categories but only in one.

Thirdly, since the things which are included under one
Form are the subject matter of a single science, there should   30
be a single science dealing with all good things. But in actual
fact there are many sciences dealing even with the goods that
fall into a single category. To take, for example, the right moment: in war it is the proper concern of strategy, whereas in
treating a disease it is part of the study of medicine. Or to take
the proper amount: in food it is the subject of medicine; in
physical training, of gymnastics.

One might even (go further and) raise the question what

Aristotle proceeds to show, the term "good" belongs to such a developing series: if we call a certain quality, e.g., blueness, "good," we have to
assume first that there is such a thing as blueness, i.e., we have to predicate it in the category of substance before we can predicate it in the
category of quality.

A few words ought to be said here about Aristotle's "categories." The
categories constitute a list of the general types of predicates that can
be assigned to any subject. The first and most basic category is that of
substance or being: this includes all predicates which attempt to answer
the question, "what is it?" Examples would be: "a man," "an animal,"
"a mountain." After we have identified what the thing is (substance), we
may say how large it is (quantity), what sort of thing it is (quality), in
what relation it stands to something else (relatedness), and so forth. The
matter is treated in detail in Aristotle's *Categories*.

35   exactly they mean by a "thing-as-such"; for the selfsame defini-
1096b   tion of "man" applies to both "man-as-such" and a particular
man. For inasmuch as they refer to "man," there will be no
difference between the two; and if this is true, there will be no
difference, either, between "good-as-such" and "good," since
both are good. Nor indeed will the "good-as-such" be more of
a good because it is everlasting: after all, whiteness which lasts
for a long time is no whiter than whiteness which lasts only
for a day.

5   The argument of the Pythagoreans on this point seems to
be more convincing. They give unity a place in the column of
goods; and indeed even Speusippus seems to follow them. But
more about this elsewhere.[21]

An objection might be raised against what we have said on
the ground that the ⟨Platonic⟩ doctrine does not refer to every
kind of good, and that only things which are pursued and
10   loved for their own sake are called "good" by reference to one
single Form. That which produces good or somehow guarantees its permanence, ⟨the Platonists argue,⟩ or that which
prevents the opposite of a good from asserting itself is called
"good" because it is conducive to the intrinsically good and in
a different sense. Now, the term "good" has obviously two
different meanings: (1) things which are intrinsically good, and
(2) things which are good as being conducive to the intrinsically good. Let us, therefore, separate the intrinsically good
15   things from the useful things and examine whether they are
called "good" by reference to a single Form.

What sort of things could be called intrinsically good? Are
they the goods that are pursued without regard to additional
benefits, such as thought, sight, certain pleasures and honors?
For even if we pursue these also for the sake of something else,
one would still classify them among things intrinsically good.
20   Or is nothing good except the Form of Good? If that is the
case, the Form will be pointless. But if, on the contrary,

21 For the Pythagorean table of opposites, see *Metaphysics* A. 986a22-26.
Speusippus was a disciple of Plato and succeeded him as head of the
Academy.

thought, sight, etc. also belong to the group of intrinsically good things, the same definition of "good" will have to be manifested in all of them, just as, for example, the definition of whiteness is the same in snow and in white paint. But in actual fact, the definitions of "good" as manifested in honor, thought, and pleasure are different and distinct. The good, therefore, is not some element common to all these things as   25 derived from one Form.

What, then, is the meaning of "good" (in these different things)? Surely, it is not that they merely happen to have the same name. Do we call them "good" because they are derived from a single good, or because they all aim at a single good? Or do we rather call them "good" by analogy, e.g., as sight is good in the body, so intelligence is good in the soul, and so other things are good within their respective fields?

But perhaps this subject should be dismissed for the present,   30 because a detailed discussion of it belongs more properly to a different branch of philosophy, (namely, first philosophy). The same applies to the Form (of the Good): for, assuming that there is some single good which different things possess in common, or that there exists a good absolutely in itself and by itself, it evidently is something which cannot be realized in action or attained by man. But the good which we are now seeking must be attainable.

Perhaps one may think that the recognition of an absolute   35 good will be advantageous for the purpose of attaining and realizing in action the goods which can be attained and real-   1097a ized. By treating the absolute good as a pattern, (they might argue,) we shall gain a better knowledge of what things are good for us, and once we know that, we can achieve them. This argument has, no doubt, some plausibility; however, it does not tally with the procedure of the sciences. For while all   5 the sciences aim at some good and seek to fulfill it, they leave the knowledge of the absolute good out of consideration. Yet if this knowledge were such a great help, it would make no sense that all the craftsmen are ignorant of it and do not even attempt to seek it. One might also wonder what benefit a weaver or a carpenter might derive in the practice of his own art from a knowledge of the absolute Good, or in what way a physician who has contemplated the Form of the Good will

10 become more of a physician or a general more of a general. For actually, a physician does not even examine health in this fashion; he examines the health of man, or perhaps better, the health of a particular man, for he practices his medicine on particular cases. So much for this.

7. The good is final and self-sufficient; happiness is defined

15 Let us return again to our investigation into the nature of the good which we are seeking. It is evidently something different in different actions and in each art: it is one thing in medicine, another in strategy, and another again in each of the other arts. What, then, is the good of each? Is it not that for the sake of which everything else is done? That means it is health in the case of medicine, victory in the case of strategy,

20 a house in the case of building, a different thing in the case of different arts, and in all actions and choices it is the end. For it is for the sake of the end that all else is done. Thus, if there is some one end for all that we do, this would be the good attainable by action; if there are several ends, they will be the goods attainable by action.

Our argument has gradually progressed to the same point at

25 which we were before,[22] and we must try to clarify it still further. Since there are evidently several ends, and since we choose some of these—e.g., wealth, flutes, and instruments generally—as a means to something else, it is obvious that not all ends are final. The highest good, on the other hand, must be something final.[23] Thus, if there is only one final end, this will be the good we are seeking; if there are several, it will be

30 the most final and perfect of them. We call that which is pursued as an end in itself more final than an end which is pursued for the sake of something else; and what is never chosen

22 The reference is to the beginning of chap. 2 above.
23 See Glossary, teleios.

as a means to something else we call more final than that
which is chosen both as an end in itself and as a means to
something else. What is always chosen as an end in itself and
never as a means to something else is called final in an unqualified sense. This description seems to apply to happiness
above all else: for we always choose happiness as an end in it-   1097b
self and never for the sake of something else. Honor, pleasure,
intelligence, and all virtue we choose partly for themselves—
for we would choose each of them even if no further advantage would accrue from them—but we also choose them partly
for the sake of happiness, because we assume that it is through
them that we will be happy. On the other hand, no one   5
chooses happiness for the sake of honor, pleasure, and the like,
nor as a means to anything at all.

   We arrive at the same conclusion if we approach the question from the standpoint of self-sufficiency. For the final and
perfect good seems to be self-sufficient. However, we define
something as self-sufficient not by reference to the "self" alone.
We do not mean a man who lives his life in isolation, but a
man who also lives with parents, children, a wife, and friends   10
and fellow citizens generally, since man is by nature a social
and political being.[24] But some limit must be set to these relationships; for if they are extended to include ancestors, descendants, and friends of friends, they will go on to infinity.
However, this point must be reserved for investigation later.[25]
For the present we define as "self-sufficient" that which taken
by itself makes life something desirable and deficient in noth-   15
ing. It is happiness, in our opinion, which fits this description.
Moreover, happiness is of all things the one most desirable,
and it is not counted as one good thing among many others.
But if it were counted as one among many others, it is obvious that the addition of even the least of the goods would
make it more desirable; for the addition would produce an
extra amount of good, and the greater amount of good is always more desirable than the lesser. We see then that happi-

24 Cf. *Politics* I. 2, 1253a3, and Glossary, *politikē*.
25 See below, chaps. 10 and 11, and IX. 10.

20   ness is something final and self-sufficient and the end of our
     actions.

     To call happiness the highest good is perhaps a little trite,
     and a clearer account of what it is, is still required. Perhaps
     this is best done by first ascertaining the proper function [26] of
     man. For just as the goodness and performance of a flute
25   player, a sculptor, or any kind of expert, and generally of any-
     one who fulfills some function or performs some action, are
     thought to reside in his proper function, so the goodness and
     performance of man would seem to reside in whatever is his
     proper function. Is it then possible that while a carpenter and a
     shoemaker have their own proper functions and spheres of ac-
     tion, man as man has none, but was left by nature a good-for-
30   nothing without a function? [27] Should we not assume that just
     as the eye, the hand, the foot, and in general each part of the
     body clearly has its own proper function, so man too has some
     function over and above the functions of his parts? What can
     this function possibly be? Simply living? He shares that even
     with plants, but we are now looking for something peculiar to
1098a man. Accordingly, the life of nutrition and growth must be
     excluded.[28] Next in line there is a life of sense perception. But
     this, too, man has in common with the horse, the ox, and every
     animal. There remains then an active life of the rational ele-
     ment. The rational element has two parts: one is rational in
     that it obeys the rule of reason, the other in that it possesses
     and conceives rational rules. Since the expression "life of the
5   rational element" also can be used in two senses, we must make
     it clear that we mean a life determined by the activity,[29] as

26 See Glossary, *ergon.*

27 The translation here has to be more explicit than the Greek: *argon*
is a *double-entendre,* which means literally 'without function' or 'doing
no work' but was also used colloquially to denote a 'loafer.'

28 Cf. Aristotle's later work, the *De Anima* II. 2, 413a20 ff., where the
different kinds of life are elaborated to include the life of nutrition, of
sense perception, of thought, and of movement, to which desire is added
in II. 3, 414a31. See also below, p. 30, note 47.

29 See Glossary, *energeia.*

opposed to the mere possession, of the rational element. For
the activity, it seems, has a greater claim to be the function of
man.

The proper function of man, then, consists in an activity of
the soul in conformity with a rational principle or, at least,
not without it. In speaking of the proper function of a given
individual we mean that it is the same in kind as the function
of an individual who sets high standards for himself: [30] the
proper function of a harpist, for example, is the same as the
function of a harpist who has set high standards for himself.
The same applies to any and every group of individuals: the   10
full attainment of excellence must be added to the mere function. In other words, the function of the harpist is to play the
harp; the function of the harpist who has high standards is to
play it well. On these assumptions, if we take the proper function of man to be a certain kind of life, and if this kind of
life is an activity of the soul and consists in actions performed
in conjunction with the rational element, and if a man of high
standards is he who performs these actions well and properly,
and if a function is well performed when it is performed in
accordance with the excellence appropriate to it; we reach the   15
conclusion that [31] the good of man is an activity of the soul in
conformity with excellence or virtue, and if there are several
virtues, in conformity with the best and most complete.

But we must add "in a complete life." For one swallow does

[30] This is the first occurrence in the *Nic. Eth.* of the *spoudaios* (literally, 'serious man'), whom Aristotle frequently invokes for purposes similar
to those which make modern laws invoke the "reasonable man." However,
Aristotle's stress is less on the reasonableness of a man under particular
circumstances than on a person who has a sense of the importance of
living his life well and of fulfilling his function in society in accordance
with the highest standards.

[31] There is no good reason to follow Bywater in bracketing lines 12-16
("if we take the proper function of man . . . we reach the conclusion
that") on the grounds that they merely repeat the preceding argument.
On the contrary, they provide an excellent summary and should be retained.

not make a spring, nor does one sunny day; similarly, one day or a short time does not make a man blessed [32] and happy.

20   This will suffice as an outline of the good: for perhaps one ought to make a general sketch first and fill in the details afterwards. Once a good outline has been made, anyone, it seems, is capable of developing and completing it in detail, and time is a good inventor or collaborator in such an effort. Advances

25   in the arts,[33] too, have come about in this way, for anyone can fill in gaps. We must also bear in mind what has been said above, namely that one should not require precision in all pursuits alike, but in each field precision varies with the matter under discussion and should be required only to the extent to which it is appropriate to the investigation. A carpenter and a geometrician both want to find a right angle, but they

30   do not want to find it in the same sense: the former wants to find it to the extent to which it is useful for his work, the latter, wanting to see truth, ⟨tries to ascertain⟩ what it is and what sort of thing it is. We must, likewise, approach other subjects in the same spirit, in order to prevent minor points from assuming a greater importance than the major tasks.

1098b Nor should we demand to know a causal explanation in all matters alike; in some instances, e.g., when dealing with fundamental principles, it is sufficient to point out convincingly that such-and-such is in fact the case. The fact here is the primary thing and the fundamental principle. Some fundamental principles can be apprehended by induction, others by sense perception, others again by some sort of habituation,[34] and

---

[32] The distinction Aristotle seems to observe between *makarios*, 'blessed' or 'supremely happy,' and *eudaimōn*, 'happy,' is that the former describes happiness insofar as it is god-given, while the latter describes happiness as attained by man through his own efforts.

[33] For the Greek sense of "art," *technē*, see Glossary.

[34] This, according to Aristotle, is the way in which the fundamental principles of ethics are learned, and for that reason a person must be mature in order to be able to study ethics properly. It is most important for the modern reader to note that Aristotle is not trying to persuade his listener of the truth of these principles, but takes it for granted that he has learned them at home. Cf. also above, chap. 3, 1095a2-11, and II. 1.

others by still other means. We must try to get at each of them
in a way naturally appropriate to it, and must be scrupulous　5
in defining it correctly, because it is of great importance for
the subsequent course of the discussion. Surely, a good beginning is more than half the whole, and as it comes to light, it
sheds light' on many problems.

8. *Popular views about happiness confirm our position*

We must examine the fundamental principle with which we
are concerned, ⟨happiness,⟩ not only on the basis of the logical
conclusion we have reached and on the basis of the elements
which make up its definition, but also on the basis of the views　10
commonly expressed about it. For in a true statement, all the
facts are in harmony; in a false statement, truth soon intro-
duces a discordant note.

Good things are commonly divided into three classes: (1)
external goods, (2) goods of the soul, and (3) goods of the
body. Of these, we call the goods pertaining to the soul goods
in the highest and fullest sense. But in speaking of "soul," we
refer to our soul's actions and activities.[35] Thus, our definition　15
tallies with this opinion which has been current for a long
time and to which philosophers subscribe. We are also right in
defining the end as consisting of actions and activities; for in
this way the end is included among the goods of the soul and
not among external goods.

Also the view that a happy man lives well and fares well　20
fits in with our definition: for we have all but defined happiness as a kind of good life and well-being.

Moreover, the characteristics which one looks for in happiness
are all included in our definition. For some people think that
happiness is virtue, others that it is practical wisdom, others
that it is some kind of theoretical wisdom; [36] others again believe it to be all or some of these accompanied by, or not de-　25
void of, pleasure; and some people also include external pros-

35 See Glossary, *energeia.*
36 See Glossary, *phronēsis* and *sophia.*

perity in its definition.[37] Some of these views are expressed by
many people and have come down from antiquity, some by a
few men of high prestige, and it is not reasonable to assume
that both groups are altogether wrong; the presumption is
rather that they are right in at least one or even in most
respects.

Now, in our definition we are in agreement with those who
30   describe happiness as virtue or as some particular virtue, for
our term "activity in conformity with virtue" implies virtue.
But it does doubtless make a considerable difference whether
we think of the highest good as consisting in the possession or
in the practice of virtue, viz., as being a characteristic [38] or an
activity. For a characteristic may exist without producing any
1099a good result, as for example, in a man who is asleep or incapac-
itated in some other respect. An activity, on the other hand,
must produce a result: ⟨an active person⟩ will necessarily act
and act well. Just as the crown at the Olympic Games is not
awarded to the most beautiful and the strongest but to the
5   participants in the contests—for it is among them that the vic-
tors are found—so the good and noble things in life are won by
those who act rightly.

The life of men active in this sense is also pleasant in itself.
For the sensation of pleasure belongs to the soul, and each
man derives pleasure from what he is said to love: a lover of
horses from horses, a lover of the theater from plays, and in
10   the same way a lover of justice from just acts, and a lover of

[37] It is possible to identify the proponents of some of the views mentioned here with a fair degree of assurance. The view that virtue alone
constitutes happiness was espoused by Antisthenes and the Cynics (and
later by the Stoics); in VI. 13, 1144b17-21, the doctrine that all virtues
are forms of *phronēsis* or 'practical wisdom' is attributed to Socrates;
theoretical wisdom as virtue may perhaps be attributed to Anaxagoras
and his doctrine of *Nous;* the view that pleasure must be added to virtue
and wisdom is that of Plato's *Philebus* 27d, 60d-e, and 63e; and the ancient commentators on this passage identify Xenocrates, Plato's pupil and
later head of the Academy, as regarding external goods as essential for
the good life.

[38] See Glossary, *hexis,* and II. 5.

virtue in general from virtuous acts. In most men, pleasant acts
conflict with one another because they are not pleasant by
nature, but men who love what is noble derive pleasure from
what is naturally pleasant. Actions which conform to virtue
are naturally pleasant, and, as a result, such actions are not
only pleasant for those who love the noble but also pleasant
in themselves. The life of such men has no further need of   15
pleasure as an added attraction, but it contains pleasure
within itself. We may even go so far as to state that the man
who does not enjoy performing noble actions is not a good
man at all. Nobody would call a man just who does not enjoy
acting justly, nor generous who does not enjoy generous   20
actions, and so on. If this is true, actions performed in conformity with virtue are in themselves pleasant.

Of course it goes without saying that such actions are good
as well as noble, and they are both in the highest degree, if
the man of high moral standards displays any right judgment
about them at all; and his judgment corresponds to our description. So we see that happiness is at once the best, noblest,
and most pleasant thing, and these qualities are not separate, 25
as the inscription at Delos makes out:

> The most just is most noble, but health is the best,
> and to win what one loves is pleasantest.

For the best activities encompass all these attributes, and it is
in these, or in the best one of them, that we maintain happi-   30
ness consists.

Still, happiness, as we have said, needs external goods as
well. For it is impossible or at least not easy to perform noble
actions if one lacks the wherewithal. Many actions can only be
performed with the help of instruments, as it were: friends,   1099b
wealth, and political power. And there are some external
goods the absence of which spoils supreme happiness, e.g.,
good birth, good children, and beauty: for a man who is very
ugly in appearance or ill-born or who lives all by himself and
has no children cannot be classified as altogether happy; even
less happy perhaps is a man whose children and friends are   5

worthless, or one who has lost good children and friends through death. Thus, as we have said,[39] happiness also requires well-being of this kind, and that is the reason why some classify good fortune with happiness, while others link it to virtue.

9. How happiness is acquired

This also explains why there is a problem whether happiness is acquired by learning, by discipline, or by some other kind of training, or whether we attain it by reason of some divine dispensation or even by chance. Now, if there is anything at all which comes to men as a gift from the gods, it is reasonable to suppose that happiness above all else is god-given; and of all things human it is the most likely to be god-given, inasmuch as it is the best. But although this subject is perhaps more appropriate to a different field of study, it is clear that happiness is one of the most divine things, even if it is not god-sent but attained through virtue and some kind of learning or training. For the prize and end of excellence and virtue is the best thing of all, and it is something divine and blessed.[40] Moreover, if happiness depends on excellence, it will be shared by many people; for study and effort will make it accessible to anyone whose capacity for virtue is unimpaired. And if it is better that happiness is acquired in this way rather than by chance, it is reasonable to assume that this is the way in which it is acquired. For, in the realm of nature, things are naturally arranged in the best way possible—and the same is also true of the products of art and of any kind of causation, especially the highest. To leave the greatest and noblest of things to chance would hardly be right.

A solution of this question is also suggested by our earlier definition, according to which the good of man, happiness, is some kind of activity of the soul in conformity with virtue.[41] All the other goods are either necessary prerequisites for

39 See above, 1098b26-29.
40 See p. 18, note 32.
41 See above, chap. 7, 1098a16-17.

happiness, or are by nature co-workers with it and useful instruments for attaining it. Our results also tally with what we said at the outset: [42] for we stated that the end of politics is the best of ends; and the main concern of politics is to 30 engender a certain character in the citizens and to make them good and disposed to perform noble actions.

We are right, then, when we call neither a horse nor an ox nor any other animal happy, for none of them is capable of participating in an activity of this kind. For the same reason, 1100a a child is not happy, either; for, because of his age, he cannot yet perform such actions. When we do call a child happy, we do so by reason of the hopes we have for his future. Happiness, as we have said, requires completeness in virtue as well as a complete lifetime. Many changes and all kinds of con- 5 tingencies befall a man in the course of his life, and it is possible that the most prosperous man will encounter great misfortune in his old age, as the Trojan legends tell about Priam. When a man has met a fate such as his and has come to a wretched end, no one calls him happy.

10. Can a man be called "happy" during his lifetime?

Must we, then, apply the term "happy" to no man at all 10 as long as he is alive? Must we, as Solon would have us do, wait to see his end? [43] And, on this assumption, is it also true that a man is actually happy after he is dead? Is this not simply absurd, especially for us who define happiness as a kind of activity? Suppose we do not call a dead man happy, and interpret Solon's words to mean that only when a man is 15 dead can we safely say that he has been happy, since he is now beyond the reach of evil and misfortune—this view, too, is open to objection. For it seems that to some extent good and evil really exist for a dead man, just as they may exist for a

---

[42] See above, chap. 2, 1094a27-b7.

[43] This is one of the main points made by Solon, Athenian statesman and poet of the early sixth century B.C., in his conversation with the Lydian king, Croesus, in Herodotus I. 32.

man who lives without being conscious of them, for example,
20 honors and disgraces, and generally the successes and failures
of his children and descendants.[44] This presents a further
problem. A man who has lived happily to his old age and has
died as happily as he lived may have many vicissitudes befall
his descendants: some of them may be good and may be
25 granted the kind of life which they deserve, and others may
not. It is, further, obvious that the descendants may conceiv-
ably be removed from their ancestors by various degrees.
Under such circumstances, it would be odd if the dead man
would share in the vicissitudes of his descendants and be
happy at one time and wretched at another. But it would also
be odd if the fortunes of their descendants did not affect the
30 ancestors at all, not even for a short time.

But we must return to the problem raised earlier, for
through it our present problem perhaps may be solved. If one
must look to the end and praise a man not as being happy but
as having been happy in the past, is it not paradoxical that
at a time when a man actually is happy this attribute, though
35 true, cannot be applied to him? We are unwilling to call the
1100b living happy because changes may befall them and because
we believe that happiness has permanence and is not amenable to changes under any circumstances, whereas fortunes
revolve many times in one person's lifetime. For obviously, if

---

[44] The comment on this passage by J. Burnet, *The Ethics of Aristotle*
(London, 1900), p. 49, is worth quoting:

There is no question here as to the departed being aware of what goes
on in this world. On the contrary, the point is that what happens after
a man's death may affect our estimate of his life in just the same way
as what happens in his lifetime without his being aware of it. Neither
makes any difference to the man himself, but the popular belief is . . .
that it must affect our estimate of it. We cannot call that life a success
which leads to failure, even though the man himself may never know
of his failure, or may die in time to escape it. So with the fortunes of
children. Even now we say 'what would his father think, if he were
alive?'

It should be added, however, that the Greeks had a much stronger feeling
for the cohesion of the family than we do; cf. G. Glotz, *La solidarité de la
famille dans le droit criminel en Grèce* (Paris, 1904).

we are to keep pace with a man's fortune, we shall frequently
have to call the same man happy at one time and wretched 5
at another and demonstrate that the happy man is a kind of
chameleon, and that the foundations ⟨of his life⟩ are unsure.
Or is it quite wrong to make our judgment depend on fortune? Yes, it is wrong, for fortune does not determine whether
we fare well or ill, but is, as we said, merely an accessory to
human life; activities in conformity with virtue constitute 10
happiness, and the opposite activities constitute its opposite.

The question which we have just discussed further confirms
our definition. For no function of man possesses as much
stability as do activities in conformity with virtue: these seem
to be even more durable than scientific knowledge. And the
higher the virtuous activities, the more durable they are, be- 15
cause men who are supremely happy spend their lives in
these activities most intensely and most continuously, and
this seems to be the reason why such activities cannot be forgotten.

The happy man will have the attribute of permanence
which we are discussing, and he will remain happy throughout his life. For he will always or to the highest degree both
do and contemplate what is in conformity with virtue; he will
bear the vicissitudes of fortune most nobly and with perfect 20
decorum under all circumstances, inasmuch as he is truly
good and "four-square beyond reproach." [45]

But fortune brings many things to pass, some great and
some small. Minor instances of good and likewise of bad luck
obviously do not decisively tip the scales of life, but a number 25
of major successes will make life more perfectly happy; for,
in the first place, by their very nature they help to make life
attractive, and secondly, they afford the opportunity for noble
and good actions. On the other hand, frequent reverses can
crush and mar supreme happiness in that they inflict pain
and thwart many activities. Still, nobility shines through even 30
in such circumstances, when a man bears many great misfor-

[45] A quotation from a poem of Simonides (*ca.* 556-468 B.C.), which is
discussed by Socrates and Protagoras in Plato's *Protagoras* 338e-318a.

tunes with good grace not because he is insensitive to pain but because he is noble and high-minded.

If, as we said, the activities determine a man's life, no supremely happy man can ever become miserable, for he will

35 never do what is hateful and base. For in our opinion, the

1101a man who is truly good and wise will bear with dignity whatever fortune may bring, and will always act as nobly as circumstances permit, just as a good general makes the most strategic use of the troops at his disposal, and a good shoe-

5 maker makes the best shoe he can from the leather available, and so on with experts in all other fields. If this is true, a happy man will never become miserable; but even so, supreme happiness will not be his if a fate such as Priam's befalls him. And yet, he will not be fickle and changeable; he will not be

10 dislodged from his happiness easily by any misfortune that comes along, but only by great and numerous disasters such as will make it impossible for him to become happy again in a short time; if he recovers his happiness at all, it will be only after a long period of time, in which he has won great distinctions.

Is there anything to prevent us, then, from defining the happy man as one whose activities are an expression of com-

15 plete virtue, and who is sufficiently equipped with external goods, not simply at a given moment but to the end of his life? Or should we add that he must die as well as live in the manner which we have defined? For we cannot foresee the future, and happiness, we maintain, is an end which is absolutely final and complete in every respect. If this be granted, we shall define as "supremely happy" those living men who fulfill and

20 continue to fulfill these requirements, but blissful only as human beings. So much for this question.

11. *Do the fortunes of the living affect the dead?*

That the fortunes of his descendants and of all those near and dear to him do not affect the happiness of a dead man

at all, seems too unfeeling a view and contrary to the prevailing opinions. Many and different in kind are the accidents that can befall us, and some hit home more closely than others. It would, therefore, seem to be a long and endless task to make detailed distinctions, and perhaps a general outline will be sufficient. Just as one's own misfortunes are sometimes momentous and decisive for one's life and sometimes seem comparatively less important, so the misfortunes of our various friends affect us to varying degrees. In each case it makes a considerable difference whether those who are affected by an event are living or dead; much more so than it matters in a tragedy whether the crimes and horrors have been perpetrated before the opening of the play or are part of the plot. This difference, too, must be taken into account and perhaps still more the problem whether the dead participate in any good or evil. These considerations suggest that even if any good or evil reaches them at all, it must be something weak and negligible (either intrinsically or in relation to them), or at least something too small and insignificant to make the unhappy happy or to deprive the happy of their bliss. The good as well as the bad fortunes of their friends seem, then, to have some effect upon the dead, but the nature and magnitude of the effect is such as not to make the happy unhappy or to produce any similar changes.

12. *The praise accorded to happiness*

Now that we have settled these questions, let us consider whether happiness is to be classified among the things which we praise or rather among those which we honor; for it is clear that it is not a potential ⟨but an actual good⟩.[46]

---

[46] Cf. *Magna Moralia* I. 2, 1183b20-30:
Some things are goods we honor, others things we praise, and others again are potential goods. By goods we honor I mean things such as the divine; things which are better ⟨than the ordinary⟩, such as the soul or the intelligence; things which are older ⟨than most⟩, such as the original source and the like. . . . By goods we praise I mean, for

The grounds on which we bestow praise on anything evidently are its quality and the relation in which it stands to other things. In other words, we praise a just man, a courageous man, and in general any good man, and also his virtue
15 or excellence, on the basis of his actions and achievements; moreover, we praise a strong man, a swift runner, and so forth, because he possesses a certain natural quality and stands in a certain relation to something good and worth while. Our feelings about praising the gods provide a further illustration of this point. For it is ridiculous to refer the gods to our stand-
20 ards; but this is precisely what praising them amounts to, since praise, as we said, entails a reference to something else. But if praise is appropriate only for relative things, it is clear that the best things do not call for praise but for something greater and better, as indeed is generally recognized: for we call the gods "blessed" and "happy" and use these terms also for the
25 most godlike man. The same is true of good things: no one praises happiness in the same sense in which he praises justice, but he exalts its bliss as something better and more nearly divine.

Eudoxus, too, seems to have used the right method for advocating that pleasure is the most excellent, for he took the fact that pleasure, though a good, is not praised as an indica-
30 tion of its superiority to the things that are praised, as god and the good are, for they are the standards to which we refer everything else.

Praise is proper to virtue or excellence, because it is excellence that makes men capable of performing noble deeds. Eulogies, on the other hand, are appropriate for achievements of the body as well as of the mind. However, a detailed analysis of this subject is perhaps rather the business of those who have

---

example, the virtues, since actions done in conformity with them bring praise; and potential goods are, for instance, political power, wealth, strength, and beauty, for a man of high moral principles has the capacity to use these well and a bad man to use them badly. Therefore such goods are called potential.

made a study of eulogies. For our present purposes, we may 35
draw the conclusion from the preceding argument that happiness is one of the goods that are worthy of honor and are 1102a
final. This again seems to be due to the fact that it is a starting
point or fundamental principle, since for its sake all of us do
everything else. And the source and cause of all good things
we consider as something worthy of honor and as divine.

13. *The psychological foundations of the virtues*

Since happiness is a certain activity of the soul in conformity 5
with perfect virtue, we must now examine what virtue or excellence is. For such an inquiry will perhaps better enable us
to discover the nature of happiness. Moreover, the man who is
truly concerned about politics seems to devote special attention to excellence, since it is his aim to make the citizens good
and law-abiding. We have an example of this in the lawgivers 10
of Crete and Sparta and in other great legislators. If an examination of virtue is part of politics, this question clearly fits
into the pattern of our original plan.

There can be no doubt that the virtue which we have to
study is human virtue. For the good which we have been seeking is a human good and the happiness a human happiness. 15
By human virtue we do not mean the excellence of the body,
but that of the soul, and we define happiness as an activity of
the soul. If this is true, the student of politics must obviously
have some knowledge of the workings of the soul, just as the
man who is to heal eyes must know something about the
whole body. In fact, knowledge is all the more important for 20
the former, inasmuch as politics is better and more valuable
than medicine, and cultivated physicians devote much time
and trouble to gain knowledge about the body. Thus, the student of politics must study the soul, but he must do so with his
own aim in view, and only to the extent that the objects of his
inquiry demand: to go into it in greater detail would perhaps 25
be more laborious than his purposes require.

Some things that are said about the soul in our less technical discussions [47] are adequate enough to be used here, for instance, that the soul consists of two elements, one irrational and one rational. Whether these two elements are separate, like the parts of the body or any other divisible thing, or
30 whether they are only logically separable though in reality indivisible, as convex and concave are in the circumference of a circle, is irrelevant for our present purposes.

Of the irrational element, again, one part seems to be common to all living things and vegetative in nature: I mean that part which is responsible for nurture and growth. We must assume that some such capacity of the soul exists in everything
1102b that takes nourishment, in the embryonic stage as well as when the organism is fully developed; for this makes more sense than to assume the existence of some different capacity at the latter stage. The excellence of this part of the soul is, therefore, shown to be common to all living things and is not exclusively human. This very part and this capacity seem to be
5 most active in sleep. For in sleep the difference between a good man and a bad is least apparent—whence the saying that for half their lives the happy are no better off than the wretched. This is just what we would expect, for sleep is an inactivity of the soul in that it ceases to do things which cause it to be called good or bad. However, to a small extent some bodily movements do penetrate to the soul in sleep, and in this sense
10 the dreams of honest men are better than those of average people. But enough of this subject: we may pass by the nutritive part, since it has no natural share in human excellence or virtue.

In addition to this, there seems to be another integral ele-

[47] See p. 9, note 17. It is interesting to note that in this connection Aristotle does not mention the extant *De Anima*, which differs considerably from his remarks here and even contradicts them, but refers instead to an earlier work now lost, perhaps the *Protrepticus*. The reason for this is presumably that the *De Anima* was written later than this section of the *Nic. Eth.*; cf. F. Nuyens, *L'évolution de la psychologie d'Aristote* (Louvain, 1948), pp. 189-93. The same is probably true also of the discussion of the soul in VI. 1, 1139a3-17.

ment of the soul which, though irrational, still does partake of
reason in some way. In morally strong and morally weak men
we praise the reason that guides them and the rational element of the soul, because it exhorts them to follow the right   15
path and to do what is best. Yet we see in them also another
natural strain different from the rational, which fights and resists the guidance of reason. The soul behaves in precisely the
same manner as do the paralyzed limbs of the body. When we
intend to move the limbs to the right, they turn to the left,   20
and similarly, the impulses of morally weak persons turn in
the direction opposite to that in which reason leads them.
However, while the aberration of the body is visible, that of
the soul is not. But perhaps we must accept it as a fact, nevertheless, that there is something in the soul besides the rational
element, which opposes and reacts against it. In what way the
two are distinct need not concern us here. But, as we have   25
stated, it too seems to partake of reason; at any rate, in a morally strong man it accepts the leadership of reason, and is perhaps more obedient still in a self-controlled [48] and courageous
man, since in him everything is in harmony with the voice of
reason.

　　Thus we see that the irrational element of the soul has
two parts: the one is vegetative and has no share in reason
at all, the other is the seat of the appetites and of desire in   30
general and partakes of reason insofar as it complies with
reason and accepts its leadership; it possesses reason in the
sense that we say it is "reasonable" to accept the advice of a
father and of friends, not in the sense that we have a "rational" understanding of mathematical propositions. That the
irrational element can be persuaded by the rational is shown
by the fact that admonition and all manner of rebuke and
exhortation are possible. If it is correct to say that the appeti-   1103a
tive part, too, has reason, it follows that the rational element
of the soul has two subdivisions: the one possesses reason in

---

[48] The problems involved in self-control and in moral strength are
discussed in III. 10-12, and VII, respectively. For the distinction between
sōphrōn, 'self-controlled,' and *enkratēs*, 'morally strong,' see the Glossary.

the strict sense, contained within itself, and the other possesses reason in the sense that it listens to reason as one would listen to a father.

Virtue, too, is differentiated in line with this division of the soul. We call some virtues "intellectual" and others "moral": theoretical wisdom, understanding, and practical wisdom are intellectual virtues, generosity and self-control moral virtues. In speaking of a man's character, we do not describe him as wise or understanding, but as gentle or self-controlled; but we praise the wise man, too, for his characteristic, and praiseworthy characteristics are what we call virtues.

BOOK II

1. *Moral virtue as the result of habits*

Virtue, as we have seen, consists of two kinds, intellectual virtue and moral virtue. Intellectual virtue or excellence owes 15
its origin and development chiefly to teaching, and for that reason requires experience and time. Moral virtue, on the other hand, is formed by habit, *ethos,* and its name, *ēthikē,* is therefore derived, by a slight variation, from *ethos.* This shows, too, that none of the moral virtues is implanted in us by nature, for nothing which exists by nature can be changed by habit. For example, it is impossible for a stone, which has 20
a natural downward movement, to become habituated to moving upward, even if one should try ten thousand times to inculcate the habit by throwing it in the air; nor can fire be made to move downward, nor can the direction of any nature-given tendency be changed by habituation. Thus, the virtues are implanted in us neither by nature nor contrary to nature: we are by nature equipped with the ability to receive them, and habit brings this ability to completion and ful- 25
fillment.[1]

Furthermore, of all the qualities with which we are endowed by nature, we are provided with the capacity first, and display the activity afterward.[2] That this is true is shown by the senses: it is not by frequent seeing or frequent hearing that we

1 What we get in this paragraph is Aristotle's answer to the problem raised at the opening of Plato's *Meno* (70a) whether excellence is acquired by teaching, by practice, or by nature. This problem, also hinted at by Aristotle at the beginning of I. 3 above, is fully articulated in *Eudemian Ethics* I. 1, 1214a14 ff.

2 See Glossary, *energeia* and *dynamis.* For Aristotle, the *dynamis* ('capacity,' 'ability,' 'potentiality') remains latent until it is developed into an *energeia* ('actuality,' 'activity'), i.e., into an actual result or achievement.

33

acquired our senses, but on the contrary we first possess and
30 then use them; we do not acquire them by use. The virtues,
on the other hand, we acquire by first having put them into
action, and the same is also true of the arts.[3] For the things
which we have to learn before we can do them we learn by
doing: men become builders by building houses, and harpists
by playing the harp. Similarly, we become just by the practice
1103b of just actions, self-controlled by exercising self-control, and
courageous by performing acts of courage.

This is corroborated by what happens in states. Lawgivers
make the citizens good by inculcating ⟨good⟩ habits in them,
and this is the aim of every lawgiver; if he does not succeed
5 in doing that, his legislation is a failure. It is in this that a
good constitution differs from a bad one.

Moreover, the same causes and the same means that produce any excellence or virtue can also destroy it, and this is
also true of every art. It is by playing the harp that men become both good and bad harpists, and correspondingly with
10 builders and all the other craftsmen: a man who builds well
will be a good builder, one who builds badly a bad one. For
if this were not so, there would be no need for an instructor,
but everybody would be born as a good or a bad craftsman.
The same holds true of the virtues: in our transactions with
15 other men it is by action that some become just and others unjust, and it is by acting in the face of danger and by developing
the habit of feeling fear or confidence that some become
brave men and others cowards. The same applies to the appetites and feelings of anger: by reacting in one way or in
another to given circumstances some people become self-con-
20 trolled and gentle, and others self-indulgent and short-tempered. In a word, characteristics [4] develop from corresponding
activities. For that reason, we must see to it that our activities
are of a certain kind, since any variations in them will be
reflected in our characteristics. Hence it is no small matter

---

[3] For the meaning of *technē* ('art'), see Glossary.
[4] See Glossary, *hexis*.

whether one habit or another is inculcated in us from early
childhood; on the contrary, it makes a considerable difference,
or, rather, all the difference.   25

2. Method in the practical sciences

The purpose of the present study is not, as it is in other
inquiries, the attainment of theoretical knowledge: [5] we are
not conducting this inquiry in order to know what virtue is,
but in order to become good, else there would be no advantage
in studying it. For that reason, it becomes necessary to examine the problem of actions, and to ask how they are to be
performed. For, as we have said, the actions determine what   30
kind of characteristics are developed.

That we must act according to right reason is generally
conceded and may be assumed as the basis of our discussion.
We shall speak about it later [6] and discuss what right reason
is and examine its relation to the other virtues. But let us
first agree that any discussion on matters of action cannot be 1104a
more than an outline and is bound to lack precision; for as
we stated at the outset,[7] one can demand of a discussion only
what the subject matter permits, and there are no fixed data
in matters concerning action and questions of what is beneficial, any more than there are in matters of health. And if
this is true of our general discussion, our treatment of par-   5
ticular problems will be even less precise, since these do not
come under the head of any art which can be transmitted by
precept, but the agent must consider on each different occasion
what the situation demands, just as in medicine and in navigation. But although such is the kind of discussion in which we   10
are engaged, we must do our best.

First of all, it must be observed that the nature of moral
qualities is such that they are destroyed by defect and by

5 See Glossary, theōria.
6 See VI. 13.
7 See I. 3.

excess. We see the same thing happen in the case of strength
and of health, to illustrate, as we must, the invisible by means
15 of visible examples: [8] excess as well as deficiency of physical
exercise destroys our strength, and similarly, too much and
too little food and drink destroys our health; the proportionate amount, however, produces, increases, and preserves it.
The same applies to self-control, courage, and the other
20 virtues: the man who shuns and fears everything and never
stands his ground becomes a coward, whereas a man who
knows no fear at all and goes to meet every danger becomes
reckless. Similarly, a man who revels in every pleasure and
abstains from none becomes self-indulgent, while he who
avoids every pleasure like a boor becomes what might be
25 called insensitive. Thus we see that self-control and courage
are destroyed by excess and by deficiency and are preserved by
the mean.

Not only are the same actions which are responsible for
and instrumental in the origin and development of the virtues
also the causes and means of their destruction, but they will
also be manifested in the active exercise of the virtues. We can
30 see the truth of this in the case of other more visible qualities,
e.g., strength. Strength is produced by consuming plenty of
food and by enduring much hard work, and it is the strong
man who is best able to do these things. The same is also true
of the virtues: by abstaining from pleasures we become self-
controlled, and once we are self-controlled we are best able
35 to abstain from pleasures. So also with courage: by becoming
1104b habituated to despise and to endure terrors we become courageous, and once we have become courageous we will best
be able to endure terror.

3. Pleasure and pain as the test of virtue

An index to our characteristics is provided by the pleasure
or pain which follows upon the tasks we have achieved. A

8 This looks like a direct reference to Anaxagoras' statement (frg. B 21a
DK⁹): "Appearances are a glimpse of the unseen."

man who abstains from bodily pleasures and enjoys doing so 5
is self-controlled; if he finds abstinence troublesome, he is
self-indulgent; a man who endures danger with joy, or at
least without pain, is courageous; if he endures it with pain,
he is a coward. For moral excellence is concerned with pleasure and pain; it is pleasure that makes us do base actions and 10
pain that prevents us from doing noble actions. For that
reason, as Plato says,[9] men must be brought up from childhood to feel pleasure and pain at the proper things; for this
is correct education.

Furthermore, since the virtues have to do with actions and
emotions, and since pleasure and pain are a consequence of
every emotion and of every action, it follows from this point 15
of view, too, that virtue has to do with pleasure and pain.
This is further indicated by the fact that punishment is inflicted by means of pain. For punishment is a kind of medical
treatment and it is the nature of medical treatments to take
effect through the introduction of the opposite of the disease.[10]
Again, as we said just now,[11] every characteristic of the soul
shows its true nature in its relation to and its concern with 20
those factors which naturally make it better or worse. But it
is through pleasures and pains that men are corrupted, i.e.,
through pursuing and avoiding pleasures and pains either
of the wrong kind or at the wrong time or in the wrong
manner, or by going wrong in some other definable respect.
For that reason some people [12] define the virtues as states of
freedom from emotion and of quietude. However, they make
the mistake of using these terms absolutely and without add- 25
ing such qualifications as "in the right manner," "at the right
or wrong time," and so forth. We may, therefore, assume as
the basis of our discussion that virtue, being concerned with
pleasure and pain in the way we have described, makes us

9 See Plato, *Republic* III. 12, 401e-402a; *Laws* II. 653a-654d.
10 The idea here evidently is that the pleasure of wrongdoing must be
cured by applying its opposite, i.e., pain.
11 At the end of chap. 2, 1104a27-29.
12 Probably Speusippus is meant here. See p. 12, note 21.

act in the best way in matters involving pleasure and pain, and that vice does the opposite.

The following considerations may further illustrate that virtue is concerned with pleasure and pain. There are three
30 factors that determine choice and three that determine avoidance: the noble, the beneficial, and the pleasurable, on the one hand, and on the other their opposites: the base, the harmful, and the painful. Now a good man will go right and a bad man will go wrong when any of these, and especially when pleasure is involved. For pleasure is not only common to man
35 and the animals, but also accompanies all objects of choice:
1105a in fact, the noble and the beneficial seem pleasant to us. Moreover, a love of pleasure has grown up with all of us from infancy. Therefore, this emotion has come to be ingrained in our lives and is difficult to erase. Even in our actions we use, to a greater or smaller extent, pleasure and pain as a criterion.
5 For this reason, this entire study is necessarily concerned with pleasure and pain; for it is not unimportant for our actions whether we feel joy and pain in the right or the wrong way. Again, it is harder to fight against pleasure than against anger, as Heraclitus says; [13] and both virtue and art are always concerned with what is harder, for success is better when it is
10 hard to achieve. Thus, for this reason also, every study both of virtue and of politics must deal with pleasures and pains, for if a man has the right attitude to them, he will be good; if the wrong attitude, he will be bad.

We have now established that virtue or excellence is concerned with pleasures and pains; that the actions which pro-
15 duce it also develop it and, if differently performed, destroy it; and that it actualizes itself fully in those activities to which it owes its origin.

4. *Virtuous action and virtue*

However, the question may be raised what we mean by saying that men become just by performing just actions and

[13] Heraclitus, frg. B 85 DK⁰: "To fight against anger is hard; for it buys what it wants at the price of the soul."

self-controlled by practicing self-control. For if they perform just actions and exercise self-control, they are already just and self-controlled, in the same way as they are literate and   20 musical if they write correctly and practice music.[14]

But is this objection really valid, even as regards the arts? No, for it is possible for a man to write a piece correctly by chance or at the prompting of another: but he will be literate only if he produces a piece of writing in a literate way, and that means doing it in accordance with the skill of literate   25 composition which he has in himself.

Moreover, the factors involved in the arts and in the virtues are not the same. In the arts, excellence lies in the result itself, so that it is sufficient if it is of a certain kind. But in the case of the virtues an act is not performed justly or with self-control if the act itself is of a certain kind, but only if in addi-   30 tion the agent has certain characteristics as he performs it: first of all, he must know what he is doing; secondly, he must choose to act the way he does, and he must choose it for its own sake; and in the third place, the act must spring from a firm and unchangeable character. With the exception of knowing what one is about, these considerations do not enter into the mastery of the arts; for the mastery of   1105b the virtues, however, knowledge is of little or no importance, whereas the other two conditions count not for a little but are all-decisive, since repeated acts of justice and self-control result in the possession of these virtues. In other words, acts are called just and self-controlled when they are   5 the kind of acts which a just or self-controlled man would perform; but the just and self-controlled man is not he who performs these acts, but he who also performs them in the way just and self-controlled men do.

Thus our assertion that a man becomes just by performing just acts and self-controlled by performing acts of self-control   10

---

[14] It is difficult to find an exact English equivalent for *mousikē*. For although the concept includes music, its meaning is wide enough to encompass all those artistic and intellectual activities over which the Muses preside. Accordingly, it ranges from the writing and reciting of poetry to dancing, astronomy, etc.

is correct; without performing them, nobody could even be on the way to becoming good. Yet most men do not perform such acts, but by taking refuge in argument they think that they are engaged in philosophy and that they will become good in this way. In so doing, they act like sick men who

15 listen attentively to what the doctor says, but fail to do any of the things he prescribes. That kind of philosophical activity will not bring health to the soul any more than this sort of treatment will produce a healthy body.

5. *Virtue defined: the genus*

The next point to consider is the definition of virtue or excellence. As there are three kinds of things found in the

20 soul: (1) emotions, (2) capacities, and (3) characteristics, virtue must be one of these. By "emotions" I mean appetite, anger, fear, confidence, envy, joy, affection, hatred, longing, emulation, pity, and in general anything that is followed by pleasure or pain; by "capacities" I mean that by virtue of which we are said to be affected by these emotions, for example, the capacity

25 which enables us to feel anger, pain, or pity; and by "characteristics" I mean the condition, either good or bad, in which we are, in relation to the emotions: for example, our condition in relation to anger is bad, if our anger is too violent or not violent enough, but if it is moderate, our condition is good; and similarly with our condition in relation to the other emotions.

Now the virtues and vices cannot be emotions, because we

30 are not called good or bad on the basis of our emotions, but on the basis of our virtues and vices. Also, we are neither praised nor blamed for our emotions: a man does not receive praise for being frightened or angry, nor blame for being angry pure and simple, but for being angry in a certain way.

1106a Yet we are praised or blamed for our virtues and vices. Furthermore, no choice is involved when we experience anger or fear, while the virtues are some kind of choice or at least involve choice. Moreover, with regard to our emotions we are

said to be "moved," but with regard to our virtues and vices   5
we are not said to be "moved" but to be "disposed" in a certain way.

For the same reason, the virtues cannot be capacities, either,
for we are neither called good or bad nor praised or blamed
simply because we are capable of being affected. Further, our
capacities have been given to us by nature, but we do not
by nature develop into good or bad men. We have discussed   10
this subject before.[15] Thus, if the virtues are neither emotions
nor capacities, the only remaining alternative is that they are
characteristics.[16] So much for the genus of virtue.

6. Virtue defined: the differentia

It is not sufficient, however, merely to define virtue in
general terms as a characteristic: we must also specify what
kind of characteristic it is. It must, then, be remarked that   15
every virtue or excellence (1) renders good the thing itself of
which it is the excellence, and (2) causes it to perform its function well. For example, the excellence of the eye makes both the
eye and its function good, for good sight is due to the excellence of the eye. Likewise, the excellence of a horse makes it
both good as a horse and good at running, at carrying its   20
rider, and at facing the enemy. Now, if this is true of all
things, the virtue or excellence of man, too, will be a characteristic which makes him a good man, and which causes him to
perform his own function well. To some extent we have al-

15 See above, chap. 1.

16 For this peculiar argument, which defines virtue as a characteristic
by a process of elimination of alternatives, see the discussion of quality in
Categories 8, 8b25-11a38, where Aristotle distinguishes four types of quality: (a) characteristic and disposition (hexis, diathesis), (b) capacity and
incapacity (dynamis, adynamia), (c) affective quality and emotion (pathētikē
poiotēs, pathos), and (d) shape and form (schēma, morphē). These and
none other are the only possible types of quality, and since (d) shape and
form obviously have nothing to do with the qualities (i.e., virtues) of the
soul, only the first three are dealt with here. For a fuller treatment, see
H. H. Joachim, pp. 81-85. Cf. also Glossary, hexis.

ready stated how this will be true; [17] the rest will become
25   clear if we study what the nature of virtue is.

Of every continuous entity that is divisible into parts it is
possible to take the larger, the smaller, or an equal part, and
these parts may be larger, smaller, or equal [18] either in relation to the entity itself, or in relation to us. The "equal" part
is something median between excess and deficiency. By the
30   median of an entity I understand a point equidistant from
both extremes, and this point is one and the same for everybody. By the median relative to us I understand an amount
neither too large nor too small, and this is neither one nor the
same for everybody. To take an example: if ten is many and
two is few, six is taken as the median in relation to the entity,
for it exceeds and is exceeded by the same amount, and is thus
35   the median in terms of arithmetical proportion. But the median
relative to us cannot be determined in this manner: if ten
1106b pounds of food is much for a man to eat and two pounds little,
it does not follow that the trainer will prescribe six pounds,
for this may in turn be much or little for him to eat; it may
be little for Milo [19] and much for someone who has just begun
to take up athletics. The same applies to running and wres-
5   tling. Thus we see that an expert in any field avoids excess and
deficiency, but seeks the median and chooses it—not the median of the object but the median relative to us.

If this, then, is the way in which every science perfects its
work, by looking to the median and by bringing its work up
to that point—and this is the reason why it is usually said of a
10   successful piece of work that it is impossible to detract from
it or to add to it, the implication being that excess and deficiency destroy success while the mean safeguards it (good
craftsmen, we say, look toward this standard in the perform-

---

17 See above, chap. 2.

18 It is impossible to capture in English the overtone these three words
carry. They can also mean "too large," "too small," and "fair."

19 Milo of Croton, said to have lived in the second half of the sixth century B.C., was a wrestler famous for his remarkable strength.

ance of their work)—and if virtue, like nature, is more precise
and better than any art, we must conclude that virtue aims at   15
the median. I am referring to moral virtue: for it is moral
virtue that is concerned with emotions and actions, and it is
in emotions and actions that excess, deficiency, and the median
are found. Thus we can experience fear, confidence, desire,
anger, pity, and generally any kind of pleasure and pain either
too much or too little, and in either case not properly. But   20
to experience all this at the right time, toward the right objects, toward the right people, for the right reason, and in the
right manner—that is the median and the best course, the
course that is a mark of virtue.

Similarly, excess, deficiency, and the median can also be
found in actions. Now virtue is concerned with emotions and
actions; and in emotions and actions excess and deficiency miss   25
the mark, whereas the median is praised and constitutes success. But both praise and success are signs of virtue or excellence. Consequently, virtue is a mean in the sense that it aims
at the median. This is corroborated by the fact that there are
many ways of going wrong, but only one way which is right—
for evil belongs to the indeterminate, as the Pythagoreans
imagined, but good to the determinate. This, by the way, is   30
also the reason why the one is easy and the other hard: it is
easy to miss the target but hard to hit it. Here, then, is an
additional proof that excess and deficiency characterize vice,
while the mean characterizes virtue: for "bad men have many
ways, good men but one." [20]   35

We may thus conclude that virtue or excellence is a characteristic involving choice, and that it consists in observing
the mean relative to us, a mean which is defined by a rational
principle, such as a man of practical wisdom [21] would use to   1107a
determine it. It is the mean by reference to two vices: the
one of excess and the other of deficiency. It is, moreover, a

[20] The author of this verse is unknown.
[21] See Glossary, *phronēsis*. The concept will be discussed more fully in
VI. 5.

mean because some vices exceed and others fall short of what
5   is required in emotion and in action, whereas virtue finds
and chooses the median. Hence, in respect of its essence and
the definition of its essential nature virtue is a mean, but in
regard to goodness and excellence it is an extreme.

Not every action nor every emotion admits of a mean. There
are some actions and emotions whose very names connote
10   baseness, e.g., spite, shamelessness, envy; and among actions,
adultery, theft, and murder. These and similar emotions and
actions imply by their very names that they are bad; it is
not their excess nor their deficiency which is called bad. It is,
therefore, impossible ever to do right in performing them: to
15   perform them is always to do wrong. In cases of this sort, let
us say adultery, rightness and wrongness do not depend on
committing it with the right woman at the right time and in
the right manner, but the mere fact of committing such action
at all is to do wrong. It would be just as absurd to suppose
that there is a mean, an excess, and a deficiency in an unjust
or a cowardly or a self-indulgent act. For if there were, we
20   would have a mean of excess and a mean of deficiency, and an
excess of excess and a deficiency of deficiency. Just as there
cannot be an excess and a deficiency of self-control and courage—because the intermediate is, in a sense, an extreme—so
there cannot be a mean, excess, and deficiency in their respective opposites: their opposites are wrong regardless of how
25   they are performed; for, in general, there is no such thing as
the mean of an excess or a deficiency, or the excess and deficiency of a mean.

7. *Examples of the mean in particular virtues*

However, this general statement is not enough; we must
also show that it fits particular instances. For in a discussion
30   of moral actions, although general statements have a wider
range of application, statements on particular points have
more truth in them: actions are concerned with particulars

and our statements must harmonize with them. Let us now take particular virtues and vices from the following table.[22] In feelings of fear and confidence courage is the mean. As for the excesses, there is no name that describes a man who exceeds in fearlessness—many virtues and vices have no name; but a man who exceeds in confidence is reckless, and a man who exceeds in fear and is deficient in confidence is cowardly.   1107b

In regard to pleasures and pains—not all of them and to a lesser degree in the case of pains—the mean is self-control   5 and the excess self-indulgence. Men deficient in regard to pleasure are not often found, and there is therefore no name for them, but let us call them "insensitive."

In giving and taking money, the mean is generosity, the excess and deficiency are extravagance and stinginess. In these 10 vices excess and deficiency work in opposite ways: an extravagant man exceeds in spending and is deficient in taking, while a stingy man exceeds in taking and is deficient in spending. For our present purposes, we may rest content with an outline and a summary, but we shall later define these qualities 15 more precisely.[23]

There are also some other dispositions in regard to money: magnificence is a mean (for there is a difference between a magnificent and a generous man in that the former operates on a large scale, the latter on a small); gaudiness and vulgarity are excesses, and niggardliness a deficiency. These vices differ 20 from the vices opposed to generosity. But we shall postpone until later a discussion of the way in which they differ.[24]

As regards honor and dishonor, the mean is high-mindedness, the excess is what we might call vanity, and the deficiency small-mindedness. The same relation which, as we said, exists

---

[22] Aristotle evidently used a table here to illustrate graphically the various virtues and their opposite extremes. Probably the table mentioned here is the same as the "outline" given in *Eudemian Ethics* II. 3, 1220b38-1221a12, where the extremes and the mean are arranged in different parallel columns.

[23] In IV. 1.

[24] See IV. 2.

between magnificence and generosity, the one being distin-
25   guished from the other in that it operates on a small scale,
exists also between high-mindedness and another virtue: as
the former deals with great, so the latter deals with small
honors. For it is possible to desire honor as one should or
more than one should or less than one should: a man who exceeds in his desires is called ambitious, a man who is deficient
unambitious, but there is no name to describe the man in the
30   middle. There are likewise no names for the corresponding dispositions except for the disposition of an ambitious man which
is called ambition. As a result, the men who occupy the extremes
lay claim to the middle position. We ourselves, in fact, sometimes call the middle person ambitious and sometimes un-
1108a   ambitious; sometimes we praise an ambitious and at other
times an unambitious man. The reason why we do that will
be discussed in the sequel; [25] for the present, let us discuss the
rest of the virtues and vices along the lines we have indicated.

In regard to anger also there exists an excess, a deficiency,
5   and a mean. Although there really are no names for them,
we might call the mean gentleness, since we call a man who
occupies the middle position gentle. Of the extremes, let the
man who exceeds be called short-tempered and his vice a short
temper, and the deficient man apathetic and his vice apathy.

There are, further, three other means which have a certain
10   similarity with one another, but differ nonetheless one from
the other. They are all concerned with human relations in
speech and action, but they differ in that one of them is concerned with truth in speech and action and the other two with
pleasantness: (a) pleasantness in amusement and (b) pleasantness in all our daily life. We must include these, too, in our
15   discussion, in order to see more clearly that the mean is to
be praised in all things and that the extremes are neither
praiseworthy nor right, but worthy of blame. Here, too, most
of the virtues and vices have no name, but for the sake of
clarity and easier comprehension we must try to coin names
for them, as we did in earlier instances.

[25] See 1108a16-19, and IV. 4.

To come to the point; in regard to truth, let us call the man in the middle position truthful and the mean truthful- 20
ness. Pretense in the form of exaggeration is boastfulness and its possessor boastful, while pretense in the form of understatement is self-depreciation and its possessor a self-depreciator.[26]

Concerning pleasantness in amusement, the man in the middle position is witty and his disposition wittiness; the excess is called buffoonery and its possessor a buffoon; and the 25
deficient man a kind of boor and the corresponding characteristic boorishness.

As far as the other kind of pleasantness is concerned, pleasantness in our daily life, a man who is as pleasant as he should be is friendly and the mean is friendliness. A man who exceeds is called obsequious if he has no particular purpose in being pleasant, but if he is acting for his own material advantage, he is a flatterer. And a man who is deficient and unpleasant in every respect is a quarrelsome and grouchy kind of person.[27] 30

A mean can also be found in our emotional experiences and in our emotions. Thus, while a sense of shame is not a virtue, a bashful or modest man is praised. For even in these matters we speak of one kind of person as intermediate and of another as exceeding if he is terror-stricken and abashed at everything. On the other hand, a man who is deficient in shame or has none at all is called shameless, whereas the intermediate man 35
is bashful or modest.

Righteous indignation is the mean between envy and spite, 1108b
all of these being concerned with the pain and pleasure which we feel in regard to the fortunes of our neighbors. The righteously indignant man feels pain when someone prospers undeservedly; an envious man exceeds him in that he is pained when he sees anyone prosper; and a spiteful man is so deficient 5
in feeling pain that he even rejoices ⟨when someone suffers undeservedly⟩.

---

26 For an explanation of these qualities, see Glossary, *eirōneia*.

27 The recently discovered play of Menander, the *Dyskolos* or *The Grouchy Man* has this kind of person as its central character.

But we shall have an opportunity to deal with these matters again elsewhere.[28] After that, we shall discuss justice;
since it has more than one meaning, we shall distinguish the
10   two kinds of justice and show in what way each is a mean.[29]

8. *The relation between the mean and its extremes*

There are, then, three kinds of disposition: two are vices
(one marked by excess and one by deficiency), and one, virtue,
the mean. Now, each of these dispositions is, in a sense, opposed to both the others: the extremes are opposites to the
middle as well as to one another, and the middle is opposed to
15   the extremes. Just as an equal amount is larger in relation to
a smaller and smaller in relation to a larger amount, so, in
the case both of emotions and of actions, the middle characteristics exceed in relation to the deficiencies and are deficient in
relation to the excesses. For example, a brave man seems reckless in relation to a coward, but in relation to a reckless man
20   he seems cowardly. Similarly, a self-controlled man seems self-
indulgent in relation to an insensitive man and insensitive in
relation to a self-indulgent man, and a generous man extravagant in relation to a stingy man and stingy in relation to an
extravagant man. This is the reason why people at the extremes each push the man in the middle over to the other
25   extreme: a coward calls a brave man reckless and a reckless
man calls a brave man a coward, and similarly with the other
qualities.

However, while these three dispositions are thus opposed
to one another, the extremes are more opposed to one another
than each is to the median; for they are further apart from
one another than each is from the median, just as the large

28 In III. 6 through IV. 9.

29 In Book V. This sentence is followed in the manuscripts by the statement: "We shall deal in a similar fashion with the rational virtues." However, since the expression "*rational* virtue" occurs nowhere else in Aristotle, and since the treatment given to the intellectual virtues in Book VI
is not at all given "in a similar fashion," it seems best to regard this
sentence as spurious.

is further removed from the small and the small from the
large than either one is from the equal. Moreover, there ap-   30
pears to be a certain similarity between some extremes and
their median, e.g., recklessness resembles courage and extravagance generosity; but there is a very great dissimilarity between the extremes. But things that are furthest removed from
one another are defined as opposites, and that means that the
further things are removed from one another the more oppo-   35
site they are.

In some cases it is the deficiency and in others the excess   1109a
that is more opposed to the median. For example, it is not the
excess, recklessness, which is more opposed to courage, but
the deficiency, cowardice; while in the case of self-control it is
not the defect, insensitivity, but the excess, self-indulgence
which is more opposite. There are two causes for this. One   5
arises from the nature of the thing itself: when one of the
extremes is closer and more similar to the median, we do not
treat it but rather the other extreme as the opposite of the
median. For instance, since recklessness is believed to be more
similar and closer to courage, and cowardice less similar, it is
cowardice rather than recklessness which we treat as the oppo-   10
site of courage. For what is further removed from the middle
is regarded as being more opposite. So much for the first
cause which arises from the thing itself. The second reason is
found in ourselves: the more we are naturally attracted to
anything, the more opposed to the median does this thing appear to be. For example, since we are naturally more attracted
to pleasure we incline more easily to self-indulgence than to a   15
disciplined kind of life. We describe as more opposed to the
mean those things toward which our tendency is stronger; and
for that reason the excess, self-indulgence, is more opposed to
self-control than is its corresponding deficiency.

9. *How to attain the mean*

Our discussion has sufficiently established (1) that moral
virtue is a mean and in what sense it is a mean; (2) that it is   20

a mean between two vices, one of which is marked by excess and the other by deficiency; and (3) that it is a mean in the sense that it aims at the median in the emotions and in actions. That is why it is a hard task to be good; in every case it
25 is a task to find the median: for instance, not everyone can find the middle of a circle, but only a man who has the proper knowledge. Similarly, anyone can get angry—that is easy—or can give away money or spend it; but to do all this to the right person, to the right extent, at the right time, for the right reason, and in the right way is no longer something easy that anyone can do. It is for this reason that good conduct is rare, praiseworthy, and noble.

30   The first concern of a man who aims at the median should, therefore, be to avoid the extreme which is more opposed to it, as Calypso advises: "Keep clear your ship of yonder spray and surf." [30] For one of the two extremes is more in error than the other, and since it is extremely difficult to hit the mean,
35 we must, as the saying has it, sail in the second best way and
1109b take the lesser evil; and we can best do that in the manner we have described.

Moreover, we must watch the errors which have the greatest attraction for us personally. For the natural inclination of one man differs from that of another, and we each come to recognize our own by observing the pleasure and pain produced in us ⟨by the different extremes⟩. We must then draw ourselves away
5 in the opposite direction, for by pulling away from error we shall reach the middle, as men do when they straighten warped timber. In every case we must be especially on our guard against pleasure and what is pleasant, for when it comes to pleasure we cannot act as unbiased judges. Our attitude to-
10 ward pleasure should be the same as that of the Trojan elders was toward Helen, and we should repeat on every occasion

---

[30] Homer, *Odyssey* XII. 219-220. The advice was actually given not by Calypso but by Circe (XII. 108-110), and in the lines quoted here Odysseus is the speaker, relaying the advice to his helmsman. Aristotle's quotations from Homer are apparently made from memory, and are rarely exact.

the words they addressed to her.[31] For if we dismiss pleasure as they dismissed her, we shall make fewer mistakes.

In summary, then, it is by acting in this way that we shall best be able to hit the median. But this is no doubt difficult, especially when particular cases are concerned. For it is not easy to determine in what manner, with what person, on what occasion, and for how long a time one ought to be angry. There are times when we praise those who are deficient in anger and call them gentle, and other times when we praise violently angry persons and call them manly. However, we do not blame a man for slightly deviating from the course of goodness, whether he strays toward excess or toward deficiency, but we do blame him if his deviation is great and cannot pass unnoticed. It is not easy to determine by a formula at what point and for how great a divergence a man deserves blame; but this difficulty is, after all, true of all objects of sense perception: determinations of this kind depend upon particular circumstances, and the decision rests with our ⟨moral⟩ sense.

This much, at any rate, is clear: that the median characteristic is in all fields the one that deserves praise, and that it is sometimes necessary to incline toward the excess and sometimes toward the deficiency. For it is in this way that we will most easily hit upon the median, which is the point of excellence.

[31] The reference is to Homer, *Iliad* III. 156-160, tr. Richmond Lattimore (Chicago: University of Chicago Press, 1951):

'Surely there is no blame on Trojans and strong-greaved Achaians
if for long time they suffer hardship for a woman like this one.
Terrible is the likeness of her face to immortal goddesses.
Still, though she be such, let her go away in the ships, lest
she be left behind, a grief to us and our children.'

BOOK III

1. *Actions voluntary and involuntary*

30   Virtue or excellence is, as we have seen, concerned with emotions and actions. When these are voluntary we receive praise and blame; when involuntary, we are pardoned and sometimes even pitied. Therefore, it is, I dare say, indispensable for a student of virtue to differentiate between voluntary and involuntary actions, and useful also for lawgivers, to help them in meting out honors and punishments.[1]

35   It is of course generally recognized that actions done under constraint or due to ignorance are involuntary. An act is done

1110a under constraint when the initiative or source of motion comes from without. It is the kind of act in which the agent or the person acted upon contributes nothing. For example, a wind might carry a person somewhere ⟨he did not want to go⟩, or men may do so who have him in their power. But a problem arises in regard to actions that are done through fear of a greater evil or for some noble purpose, for instance, if a tyrant

5   were to use a man's parents or children as hostages in ordering him to commit a base deed, making their survival or death depend on his compliance or refusal. Are actions of this kind voluntary or involuntary? A similar problem also arises when a cargo is jettisoned in a storm. Considering the action itself,

10   nobody would voluntarily throw away property; but when it is a matter of saving one's own life and that of his fellow pas-

---

1 There is no clear equivalent in English to express *hekousion* and its opposite *akousion*, which form the theme of this chapter. An agent is described as *hekōn* when he has consented to perform the action which he is performing. This consent may range from mere passive acquiescence to intentional and deliberate conduct. The neuter *hekousion* is used to denote an action so performed. Conversely, an *akōn* is a man who has not given his consent to acting the way he does, regardless of whether he acts unconsciously, inadvertently, or even against his own will, and an *akousion* is an action performed by such a man.

sengers, any sensible man would do so. Actions of this kind are, then, of a mixed nature, although they come closer to being voluntary than to being involuntary actions. For they are desirable at the moment of action; and the end for which an action is performed depends on the time at which it is done. Thus the terms "voluntary" and "involuntary" are to be used with reference to the moment of action. In the cases just mentioned, the agent acts voluntarily, because the initiative in 15 moving the parts of the body which act as instruments rests with the agent himself; and where the source of motion is within oneself, it is in one's power to act or not to act. Such actions, then, are voluntary, although in themselves they are perhaps involuntary, since nobody would choose to do any one of them for its own sake.

⟨That actions of this kind are considered as voluntary is also shown by the fact that⟩ sometimes people are even praised for 20 doing them, for example, if they endure shameful or painful treatment in return for great and noble objectives. If the opposite is the case, reproach is heaped upon them, for only a worthless man would endure utter disgrace for no good or reasonable purpose. There are some instances in which such actions elicit forgiveness rather than praise, for example, when a man acts improperly under a strain greater than human na- 25 ture can bear and which no one could endure. Yet there are perhaps also acts which no man can possibly be compelled to do, but rather than do them he should accept the most terrible sufferings and death. Thus, the circumstances that compel Alcmaeon in Euripides' play to kill his own mother are patently absurd.[2] In making a choice, it is sometimes hard to decide what advantages and disadvantages should be weighed

[2] Euripides' play has not come down to us. According to the myth, Alcmaeon killed his mother, Eriphyle, to avenge the death of his father, Amphiaraus. Amphiaraus, foreknowing through his gift of prophecy that he would be doomed if he joined the expedition of the Seven against Thebes, refused to join it until compelled to do so by his wife, who had been bribed by the gift of a necklace to make him join. An ancient commentator on this passage tells us that Alcmaeon's motive for killing his mother in Euripides' play was to escape the curse of his father.

30   against one another, and what losses we should endure to gain
what we want; but it is even harder to abide by a decision
once it is made. For as a rule, what we look forward to is painful and what we are forced to do is base. It is because of this
difficulty that praise or blame depends on whether or not a
man successfully resists compulsion.

1110b   What kind of actions can we say, then, are done under constraint? To state the matter without qualification, are all actions done under constraint of which the cause is external and
to which the agent contributes nothing? On the other hand,
actions which are in themselves involuntary, yet chosen under
given circumstances in return for certain benefits and performed on the initiative of the agent—although such actions
are involuntary considered in themselves, they are nonetheless
5   voluntary under the circumstances, and because benefits are
expected in return. In fact, they have a greater resemblance
to voluntary actions. For actions belong among particulars,
and the particular act is here performed voluntarily. But it is
not easy to lay down rules how, in making a choice, two alternatives are to be balanced against one another; there are many
differences in the case of particulars.

⟨There is a conceivable objection to this definition of "voluntary."⟩ Suppose someone were to assert that pleasant and
noble acts are performed under constraint because the pleasant
10   and the noble are external to us and have a compelling power.
But on this view, all actions would be done under constraint:
for every man is motivated by what is pleasant and noble in
everything he does. Furthermore, it is painful to act under
constraint and involuntarily, but the performance of pleasant
and noble acts brings pleasure. Finally, it is absurd to blame
external circumstances rather than oneself for falling an easy
prey to such attractions, and to hold oneself responsible for
15   noble deeds, while pleasure is held responsible for one's base
deeds.

It appears, thus, that an act done under constraint is one in
which the initiative or source of motion comes from without,
and to which the person compelled contributes nothing.

Turning now to acts due to ignorance, we may say that all
of them are non-voluntary, but they are involuntary only
when they bring sorrow and regret in their train: a man who
has acted due to ignorance and feels no compunction whatso-
ever for what he has done was not a voluntary agent, since he   20
did not know what he was doing, nor yet was he involuntary,
inasmuch as he feels no sorrow. There are, therefore, two distinct types of acts due to ignorance: a man who regrets what
he has done is considered an involuntary agent, and a man
who does not may be called a non-voluntary agent; for as the
two cases are different, it is better to give each its own name.

There also seems to be a difference between actions *due to*   25
ignorance and acting *in* ignorance. A man's action is not considered to be due to ignorance when he is drunk or angry, but
due to intoxication and anger, although he does not know
what he is doing and is in fact acting in ignorance.

Now every wicked man is in a state of ignorance as to what
he ought to do and what he should refrain from doing, and
it is due to this kind of error that men become unjust and, in
general, immoral. But an act can hardly be called involuntary   30
if the agent is ignorant of what is beneficial. Ignorance in
moral choice does not make an act involuntary—it makes it
wicked; nor does ignorance of the universal, for that invites
reproach; rather, it is ignorance of the particulars 3 which constitute the circumstances and the issues involved in the action.

3 A few remarks ought to be made about the practical syllogism involved in this passage. Reasoning on matters of conduct involves two
premises, one major and one minor. The major premise is always universal, e.g., "to remove by stealth another person's property is stealing,"
and the minor premise particular, e.g., "this horse is another person's
property," so that the conclusion would be: "To remove this horse by
stealth is stealing." What Aristotle says here is that ignorance of the
major premise produces an immoral act, while ignorance of the minor
premise produces an involuntary act which may be pitied or pardoned.
Thus it is a moral defect for a man not to know that to remove by stealth
another person's property is stealing. In an involuntary act, on the other
hand, the agent does know the universal premise, but is ignorant of the
particular, i.e., that this horse is the property of another. We shall hear
more about the practical syllogism later, especially in VII. 3.

1111a   It is on these that pity and pardon depend, for a person who acts in ignorance of a particular circumstance acts involuntarily.

It might, therefore, not be a bad idea to distinguish and enumerate these circumstances. They are: ignorance of (1) who the agent is, (2) what he is doing, (3) what thing or person is affected, and sometimes also (4) the means he is using, e.g.,
5   some tool, (5) the result intended by his action, e.g., saving a life, and (6) the manner in which he acts, e.g., gently or violently.

Now no one except a madman would be ignorant of all these factors, nor can he obviously be ignorant of (1) the agent; for how could a man not know his own identity? But a person might be ignorant of (2) what he is doing. For example, he might plead that something slipped out of his mouth, or that he did not know that he was divulging a secret, as
10   Aeschylus said when he was accused of divulging the Mysteries; 4 or again, as a man might do who discharges a catapult, he might allege that it went off accidentally while he only wanted to show it. Moreover, (3) someone might, like Merope, mistake a son for an enemy; 5 or (4) he might mistake a pointed spear for a foil, or a heavy stone for a pumice stone. Again, (5) someone might, in trying to save a man by giving him something to drink, in fact kill him; or, (6) as in sparring,
15   a man might intend merely to touch, and actually strike a blow.

4 The details of this story are preserved only in some late, but ancient, authors: Clement of Alexandria, *Stromateis* II. 14. 60, and Aelian, *Variae Historiae* V. 19. The Mysteries were a secret form of religious worship whose doctrines and rites were revealed only to the initiated; Aeschylus was accused before the Areopagus of having divulged some of the secrets of the Eleusinian Mysteries. These particular Mysteries, celebrated at Eleusis in Attica, were administered for the Athenian state by certain Eleusinian families, and honored Demeter, goddess of corn and patroness of agriculture, and her daughter Persephone. Aeschylus pleaded that he had not known the matter was secret and was acquitted.

5 In a lost play of Euripides, Merope was about to slay her son Cresphontes, believing him to be an enemy. Cf. *Poetics* 1454a5.

As ignorance is possible with regard to all these factors which constitute an action, a man who acts in ignorance of any one of them is considered as acting involuntarily, especially if he is ignorant of the most important factors. The most important factors are the thing or person affected by the action and the result. An action upon this kind of ignorance is called involuntary, provided that it brings also sorrow and regret in   20 its train.

Since an action is involuntary when it is performed under constraint or through ignorance, a voluntary action would seem to be one in which the initiative lies with the agent who knows the particular circumstances in which the action is performed.

⟨This implies that acts due to passion and appetite are voluntary.⟩ For it is perhaps wrong to call involuntary those acts which are due to passion and appetite. For on that assumption   25 we would, in the first place, deny that animals or even children are capable of acting voluntarily. In the second place, do we perform none of the actions that are motivated by appetite and passion voluntarily? Or do we perform noble acts voluntarily and base acts involuntarily? The latter alternative is ridiculous, since the cause in both cases is one and the same. But it is no doubt also absurd to call those things which we ought to desire "involuntary." For in some cases we should   30 be angry and there are some things for which we should have an appetite, as for example, health and learning. Moreover, we think of involuntary actions as painful, while actions that satisfy our appetite are pleasant. And finally, what difference is there, as far as involuntariness is concerned, between a wrong committed after calculation and a wrong committed in a fit of passion? Both are to be avoided; but the irrational emotions are considered no less a part of human beings than   1111b reasoning is, and hence, the actions of a man which spring from passion and appetite ⟨are equally a part of him⟩. It would be absurd, then, to count them as involuntary.

2. Choice

After this definition of voluntary and involuntary actions,
5 our next task is to discuss choice.[6] For choice seems to be very
closely related to virtue and to be a more reliable criterion for
judging character than actions are.

Choice clearly seems to be something voluntary, but it is
not the same as voluntariness; voluntariness is a wider term.
For even children and animals have a share in the voluntary,
but not in choice. Also, we can describe an act done on the
10 spur of the moment as a voluntary act, but not the result of
choice.

It seems to be a mistake to identify choice, as some people
do,[7] with appetite, passion, wish, or some form of opinion.
For choice is not shared by irrational creatures, whereas appetite and passion are. Moreover, the acts of a morally weak
person are accompanied by appetite, but not by choice, while
15 a morally strong[8] person acts from choice, but not from appetite. Also, appetite can be opposed to choice, but not appetite
to appetite. Again, appetite deals with what is pleasant and
painful, while choice deals neither with the pleasant nor with
the painful. The resemblance between choice and passion is
even slighter. For an act due to passion hardly seems to be
based on choice.

Choice is not even the same as wish, although the two seem
20 to be close to one another. For choice does not have the impossible as its object, and if anyone were to assert that he
was *choosing* the impossible, he would be considered a fool.
But wish can be for the impossible, e.g., immortality.[9] Wish

6 See Glossary, *proairesis*.

7 We do not know whom Aristotle had in mind.

8 On 'morally strong' and 'morally weak,' see under *sōphrōn* in the
Glossary.

9 This statement must not be regarded as a rejection on Aristotle's part
of a doctrine of immortality. What he is asserting here is merely a reflec-
tion of the common Greek distinction between "mortal" men and "immortal" gods: it is impossible to choose to live forever, but it is possible

has as its objects also those things which cannot possibly be attained through our own agency. We might, for instance, wish for the victory of a particular actor or a particular athlete. But no one chooses such things, for we choose only what 25 we believe might be attained through our own agency. Furthermore, wish is directed at the end rather than the means, but choice at the means which are conducive to a given end. For example, we *wish* to be healthy and *choose* the things that will give us health. Similarly, we say that we *wish* to be happy and describe this as our wish, but it would not be fitting to say that we *choose* to be happy. In general, choice seems to be concerned with the things that lie within our power. 30

Again, choice cannot be identified with opinion. For opinion may refer to any matter, the eternal and the impossible no less than things within our power. Also, opinions are characterized by their truth or falsity, not by their moral goodness or badness, as choices are.

Now, perhaps no one identifies choice with opinion in general; but it would not even be correct to identify it with some 1112a particular opinion. For our character is determined by our choosing good or evil, not by the opinions we hold. We choose to take or avoid a good or an evil, but we hold opinions as to what a thing is, whom it will benefit, or how: but ⟨the decision⟩ to take or avoid is by no means an opinion. Also, a 5 choice is praised for being directed to the proper object or for being correctly made, but opinions are praised for being true. Moreover, we make a choice of things which we definitely know to be good, whereas we form opinions about what we do not quite know. Nor does it seem that the same people make the best choices and also hold the best opinions: some hold rather good opinions, but because of a moral depravity they 10 do not make the right choice. Whether opinion precedes or follows choice is immaterial; for we are not concerned with this problem, but only whether choice is to be identified with some form of opinion.

---

to wish it. To a certain extent Aristotle does believe in the possibility of human immortality, see X. 7, 1177b26 ff. and *De Anima* III. 5, 430a22-25.

Since choice, then, is none of the things mentioned, what is
it or what kind of thing? As we have said, it clearly seems to
be something voluntary, but not everything voluntary is the
15 object of choice. Could it be the result of preceding deliberation? ⟨This is probably correct,⟩ for choice involves reason and
thought. The very name "choice" [10] seems to suggest that it is
something "chosen before" other things.

3. Deliberation

⟨To turn to deliberation:⟩ do people deliberate about everything? And is everything an object of deliberation? Or are
there some things about which one cannot deliberate? Perhaps
we ought to say that an object of deliberation is what a sensi-
20 ble man would deliberate about, but not a fool or madman.
Now, nobody deliberates about the eternal, such as the order
of the universe or the incommensurability of the diagonal and
the side of the square. Nor, on the other hand, do we deliberate about things that are in motion if they always occur in the
same way, whether by sheer necessity, by nature, or by some
25 other cause: for example, we do not deliberate about solstices
and sunrises. Neither do we deliberate about irregular occur-
rences, such as drought or rain, nor about chance events, such
as the discovery of a treasure. We do not even deliberate about
anything and everything that concerns man: no Spartan deliberates about what form of government would be best for
30 the Scythians. For none of these things can happen through
our agency.
But what we do deliberate about are things that are in our
power and can be realized in action; in fact, these are the only
things that remain to be considered. For in addition to nature,
necessity, and chance, we regard as causal principles intelligence and anything done through human agency. But of
course different groups of people deliberate only about what is
attainable by their own actions. Also, there can be no deliber-
1112b ation in any science that is exact and self-contained, such as

10 *Proairesis*, literally 'fore-choice' or 'preference.'

writing the letters of the alphabet: we have no differences of opinion as to how they are to be written.[11] Rather, we deliberate about matters which are done through our own agency, though not always in the same manner, e.g., about questions of medicine or of acquiring wealth. We deliberate more about navigation than about physical training, because navigation is 5 less exact as a discipline. The same principle can also be applied to the other branches of knowledge. But we deliberate more about the arts than about the sciences, since we have more differences of opinion about them. Deliberation, then, operates in matters that hold good as a general rule, but whose outcome is unpredictable, and in cases in which an indeterminate element is involved. When great issues are at stake, we distrust our own abilities as insufficient to decide 10 the matter and call in others to join us in our deliberations.

We deliberate not about ends but about the means to attain ends: no physician deliberates whether he should cure, no orator whether he should be convincing, no statesman whether he should establish law and order, nor does any expert deliberate about the end of his profession. We take the end for granted, and then consider in what manner and by what 15 means it can be realized. If it becomes apparent that there is more than one means by which it can be attained, we look for the easiest and best; if it can be realized by one means only, we consider in what manner it can be realized by that means, and how that means can be achieved in its turn. We continue that process until we come to the first link in the chain of causation, which is the last step in order of discovery. For when a man deliberates, he seems to be seeking something 20

11 Aristotle's meaning here is elucidated by the corresponding passage in the *Eudemian Ethics* II. 10, 1226a33-b2, where the difference between a physician and a writer is taken as the example. In his deliberations, a physician is liable to two kinds of mistakes: (1) he may adopt the wrong kind of treatment or (2) he may give the right treatment to the wrong particular case. In writing, on the other hand, only the second kind of mistake is possible: the writer always knows how the letters should be written, but he may place a correctly drawn letter where it does not belong.

and to be analyzing his problem in the manner described, as he would a geometrical figure: the last step in the analysis is at once the first in constructing the figure.[12] (By the way, it seems that not all investigation is deliberation—mathematical investigation is not—though every deliberation is an investigation.) Moreover, if in the process of investigation we encounter

25 an insurmountable obstacle, for example, if we need money and none can be procured, we abandon our investigation; but if it turns out to be possible, we begin to act. By "possible" I mean those things which can be realized through our own agency: for even what our friends do for us is, in a way, done through our own agency, since the initiative is our own. Sometimes the object of our investigation is to find the instruments we need and sometimes to discover how to use them. The

30 same is true of other matters, too: sometimes we have to find what the means are, and sometimes how they are to be used or through whom they can be acquired. To sum up our conclusions: (1) man is the source of his actions; (2) deliberation is concerned with things attainable by human action; and (3) actions aim at ends other than themselves. For we cannot deliberate about ends but about the means by which ends can be attained. Nor can we deliberate about particular facts, e.g.,

1113a whether this is a loaf of bread or whether this loaf of bread has been properly baked: such facts are the object of sense perception. And if we continue deliberating each point in turn, we shall have to go on to infinity.

The object of deliberation and the object of choice are identical, except that the object of choice has already been determined, since it has been decided upon on the basis of deliberation.

5 ation. For every man stops inquiring how he is to act when he has traced the initiative of action back to himself and to the

12 Aristotle is thinking of the steps followed in constructing a geometrical figure. We first assume the completed figure as constructed and then proceed by analysis to see, one by one, what the various steps are by which it was constructed. These steps reveal the constituent parts of the completed figure, i.e., the means by which the end—here the figure—is attained. We thus begin our analysis with the completed figure, but begin our construction with the last part analyzed.

dominant part of himself: it is this part that exercises choice. This may be illustrated by the ancient political systems represented in Homer, where the kings would make a choice and then proclaim it to the people.

Since, then, the object of choice is something within our power which we desire as a result of deliberation, we may define choice as a deliberate desire for things that are within our power: we arrive at a decision on the basis of deliberation, and then let the deliberation guide our desire. So much for an outline of choice, its objects, and the fact that it is concerned with means rather than ends.

4. *Wish*

That wish is concerned with the end has already been stated.[13] Now, some people think that its object is the good, and others think that it is what seems good.[14] Those who maintain that it is the good are faced with the conclusion that a man who makes a wrong choice does not really wish what he wishes: for if it is the object of his wish it must be good, while in the case in question it is actually bad. On the other hand, those who assert that the object of wish is what seems good must conclude that nothing is by nature the object of wish, but only what seems good to a particular individual. Yet different, and in many instances opposite things seem good to different individuals.

If these consequences are unacceptable, must we not admit that in an unqualified sense and from the standpoint of truth the object of wish is the good, but that for each individual it is whatever seems good to him?[15] (This distinction solves the

13 In chap. 2 above.

14 Socrates, Plato and the Academy are probably the former and some of the Sophists the latter. Cf. Plato, *Gorgias* 466e ff., and also Protagoras' famous dictum that man is the measure of all things as cited in Plato, *Theaetetus* 152a.

15 This seemingly trivial sentence is, in fact, one of the most important in the *Ethics*. It seems trivial in that it hinges on the double meaning inherent in the Greek verbal adjective *boulēton* (here translated as 'object

problem.⟩ Thus, what seems good to a man of high moral
25 standards is truly the object of wish, whereas a worthless man
wishes anything that strikes his fancy. It is the same with
the human body: people whose constitution is good find those
things wholesome which really are so, while other things are
wholesome for invalids, and similarly their opinions will vary
as to what is bitter, sweet, hot, heavy, and so forth. ⟨Just as
a healthy man judges these matters correctly, so in moral
questions⟩ a man whose standards are high judges correctly,
30 and in each case what is truly good will appear to him to be
so. Thus, what is good and pleasant differs with different
characteristics or conditions, and perhaps the chief distinction
of a man of high moral standards is his ability to see the truth
in each particular moral question, since he is, as it were, the
standard and measure for such questions. The common run
of people, however, are misled by pleasure. For though it is
1113b not the good, it seems to be, so that they choose the pleasant
in the belief that it is good and avoid pain thinking that it is
evil.

5. Man as responsible agent

Now, since the end is the object of wish, and since the
means to the end are the objects of deliberation and choice,
it follows that actions concerned with means are based on
5 choice and are voluntary actions. And the activities in which
the virtues find their expression deal with means. Conse-

---

of wish'), which means (1) an actual object of wish, something wished as
a matter of fact; and (2) something intrinsically wishable, the true object
of wish as an ethical norm. But behind this linguistic ambiguity lies the
whole question of the factual and the normative in ethical choices. Aristotle's solution is to recognize "whatever seems good to a particular individual" as the factual object of all wishes and choice, but at the same
time to insist upon the existence of a normative object of wish, which is
"by nature the object of wish" and which he defines as the end actually
wished and chosen by the good man. This shows in what sense the man
of high moral standards is for Aristotle the "standard and measure," who
makes the actual and the normative coincide.

quently, virtue or excellence depends on ourselves, and so does
vice. For where it is in our power to act, it is also in our power
not to act, and where we can say "no," we can also say "yes."
Therefore, if we have the power to act where it is noble to act,
we also have the power not to act where not to act is base;
and conversely, if we have the power not to act where inaction   10
is noble, we also have the power to act where action is base.
But if we have the power to act nobly or basely, and likewise
the power not to act, and if such action or inaction constitutes
our being good and evil, we must conclude that it depends on
us whether we are decent or worthless individuals. The saying, "No one is voluntarily wicked nor involuntarily happy,"   15
seems to be partly false and partly true. That no one is involuntarily happy is true, but wickedness is voluntary. If we
do not accept that, we must contradict the conclusions at
which we have just arrived, and must deny that man is the
source and begetter of his actions as a father is of his children.
But if our conclusions are accepted, and if we cannot trace
back our actions to starting points other than those within   20
ourselves, then all actions in which the initiative lies in ourselves are in our power and are voluntary actions.

These conclusions are corroborated by the judgment of
private individuals and by the practice of lawgivers. They
chastise and punish evildoers, except those who have acted
under constraint or due to some ignorance for which they are
not responsible, but honor those who act nobly; their inten-   25
tion seems to be to encourage the latter and to deter the
former. Yet nobody encourages us to perform what is not
within our power and what is not voluntary: there would be
no point in trying to stop by persuasion a man from feeling
hot, in pain, or hungry, and so forth, because we will go on
feeling these conditions no less for that.

Even ignorance is in itself no protection against punishment   30
if a person is thought to be responsible for his ignorance. For
example, the penalty is twice as high if the offender acted in
a state of drunkenness, because the initiative is his own: he
had the power not to get drunk, and drunkenness was respon-

sible for his ignorance. Moreover, punishment is inflicted for offenses committed in ignorance of such provisions of the law as the offender ought to have known or might easily have

1114a known. It is also inflicted in other cases in which ignorance seems to be due to negligence: it was in the offender's power not to be ignorant, it is argued, and he could have made sure had he wanted to.

But, it might be objected, carelessness may be part of a man's character. We counter, however, by asserting that a man is himself responsible for becoming careless, because he

5 lives in a loose and carefree manner; he is likewise responsible for being unjust or self-indulgent, if he keeps on doing mischief or spending his time in drinking and the like. For a given kind of activity produces a corresponding character. This is shown by the way in which people train themselves for any kind of contest or performance: they keep on practicing for it. Thus, only a man who is utterly insensitive can be

10 ignorant of the fact that moral characteristics are formed by actively engaging in particular actions.

Moreover, it is unreasonable to maintain that a man who acts unjustly or self-indulgently does not wish to be unjust or self-indulgent. If a man is not ignorant of what he is doing when he performs acts which will make him unjust, he will of course become unjust voluntarily; nor again, can wishing any more make him stop being unjust and become just than it can make a sick man healthy. Let us assume the case of a

15 man who becomes ill voluntarily through living a dissolute life and disobeying doctors' orders. In the beginning, before he let his health slip away, he could have avoided becoming ill: but once you have thrown a stone and let it go, you can no longer recall it, even though the power to throw it was yours, for the initiative was within you. Similarly, since an unjust or a self-indulgent man initially had the possibilty not to be-

20 come unjust or self-indulgent, he has acquired these traits voluntarily; but once he has acquired them it is no longer possible for him not to be what he is.

There are some cases in which not only the vices of the soul, but also those of the body are voluntary and are accordingly criticized. Nobody blames a man for being ugly by nature; but we do blame those who become ugly through lack of exercise and through taking no care of their person. The same applies to infirmities and physical handicaps: every one 25 would pity rather than reproach a man who was blind by nature or whose blindness is due to disease or accident, but all would blame him if it were caused by drunkenness or some other form of self-indulgence. In other words, those bodily vices which depend on ourselves are blamed and those which do not are not blamed. This being so, we may conclude that other kinds of vice for which we are blamed also depend 30 upon ourselves.

But someone might argue as follows: "All men seek what appears good to them, but they have no control over how things appear to them; the end appears different to different 1114b men." If, we reply, the individual is somehow responsible for his own characteristics, he is similarly responsible for what appears to him (to be good). But if he is not so responsible, no one is responsible for his own wrongdoing, but everyone does wrong through ignorance of the proper end, since he believes that his actions will bring him the greatest good. However, the 5 aim we take for the end is not determined by the choice of the individual himself, but by a natural gift of vision, as it were, which enables him to make correct judgments and to choose what is truly good: to be well endowed by nature means to have this natural gift. For to be well and properly provided by nature with the greatest and noblest of gifts, a gift which can be got or learned from no one else, but which is one's possession in the form in which nature has given it: that is the 10 meaning of being well endowed by nature in the full and true sense of the word.

But if this theory is true, how will virtue be any more voluntary than vice? The end has been determined for, and appears to, a good man and a bad man alike by nature or something of that sort; and both will use the end thus de- 15 termined as the standard for any actions they may undertake. Thus, whether the end that appears (to be good) to a particular person, whatever it may be, is not simply given to him by

nature but is to some extent due to himself; or whether, though the end is given by nature, virtue is voluntary in the sense that a man of high moral standards performs the actions that lead up to the end voluntarily: in either case vice, too, is bound to be no less voluntary than virtue. For, like the good
20 man, the bad man has the requisite ability to perform actions through his own agency, even if not to formulate his own ends. If, then, our assertion is correct, viz., that the virtues are voluntary because we share in some way the responsibility for our own characteristics and because the ends we set up for ourselves are determined by the kind of persons we are, it follows that the vices, too, are voluntary; for the same is
25 true of them.

To sum up: we have described the virtues in general and have given an outline of the genus to which they belong, i.e., that they are means and that they are characteristics. We have stated that they spontaneously tend to produce the same kind of actions as those to which they owe their existence; that they are in our power and voluntary; and that they follow the
30 dictates of right reason. However, our actions and our characteristics are not voluntary in the same sense: we are in control of our actions from beginning to end, insofar as we know the particular circumstances surrounding them. But we control only the beginning of our characteristics: the particu-
1115a lar steps in their development are imperceptible, just as they are in the spread of a disease; yet since the power to behave or not to behave in a given way was ours in the first place, our characteristics are voluntary.

Let us resume our discussion of the various virtues: what are they? With what sort of thing do they deal? And how do
5 they operate? The answer to these questions will also tell us how many virtues there are.

6. *Courage and its sphere of operation*

First of all, courage: that it is a mean with respect to fear and confidence has already been shown. What we fear is obviously something fearful, and this is in general something evil. Hence it is that some people define fear as the expectation of evil.[16]

Now it is true that we fear all evils, e.g., disrepute, poverty, disease, friendlessness, death. But it does not seem that a courageous man is concerned with all of these. There are some evils, such as disrepute, which are proper and right for him to fear and wrong not to fear: a man who fears disrepute is decent and has a sense of shame, a man who does not fear it is shameless. Still, some people describe a man who fears no disrepute as courageous in a metaphorical sense, for he resembles a courageous man in that a courageous man, too, is fearless. Perhaps one should not fear poverty or disease or generally any evil that does not spring from vice or is not due to oneself. However, it is not the man who has no fear of these things who is courageous. But we call him so because of his resemblance to the courageous man. For some people who are cowards on the battlefield are generous and face the loss of money cheerfully. On the other hand, a man is not a coward if he fears insult to his wife and children, or if he fears envy or the like; nor is he courageous if he is of good cheer when he is about to be flogged.

What kind of fearful things, then, are the concern of the courageous man? No doubt those of the greatest moment: no person endures what is terrifying more steadfastly than he. Now, the most fearful thing of all is death; for it is the end, and once a man is dead it seems that there is no longer anything good or evil for him. But it would seem that not even death shows the courage of a man in all circumstances. For example, death by drowning or by disease does not. What kind of death, then, does bring out courage? Doubtless the noblest kind, and that is death in battle, for in battle a man is faced by the greatest and most noble of dangers. This is corroborated by the honors which states as well as monarchs bestow upon courage.

Properly speaking, therefore, we might define as courageous a man who fearlessly faces a noble death and any situations

[16] Aristotle is thinking of Plato, *Protagoras* 358d.

that bring a sudden death. Such eventualities are usually
35 brought about by war. But of course a courageous man is
1115b also fearless at sea and in illness, though not in the same way
as sailors are. Because of their experience, the sailors are opti-
mistic, while the courageous man has given up hope of saving
his life but finds the thought of such an ⟨inglorious⟩ death
revolting. Furthermore, circumstances which bring out courage
are those in which a man can show his prowess or where he
5 can die a noble death, neither of which is true of death by
drowning or illness.[17]

7. Courage: its nature and its opposites

Now, the same things are not fearful to all people, and
there are some things of which we say that they surpass human
endurance. The latter are fearful at least to every sensible
person. But terrors which are humanly bearable differ in
10 magnitude and degree, and so do the circumstances that inspire confidence. Now, the courageous man is dauntless as a
human being. Hence he will fear what is fearful; but he will
endure it in the right way and as reason directs for the sake of
acting nobly: that is the end of virtue. It is of course possible
to fear things to a greater or lesser degree, and also to fear
15 what is not fearful. Errors arise from fearing what one should
not, fearing in the wrong manner, fearing at the wrong time,
and so on, and similarly with events that inspire confidence.

Accordingly, he is courageous who endures and fears the
right things, for the right motive, in the right manner, and
at the right time, and who displays confidence in a similar
20 way. For a courageous man feels and acts according to the
merits of each case and as reason guides him. Now, the end
of every activity corresponds to the characteristic that produces
it. This also applies to a courageous man: courage is noble,[18]

---

[17] The preceding seems to be aimed at Plato, who in *Laches* 191d-e
argues that courage is displayed not only in war but also in the face of
death at sea and by disease.
[18] I adopt Rassow's reading: καὶ τῷ ἀνδρείῳ δέ· ἡ ⟨δ'⟩ ἀνδρεία καλόν.

and, accordingly, its end is noble, too; for a thing is defined by
its end. Thus it is for a noble end that a courageous man endures and acts as courage demands.

To turn to the types of excess. There is no name for a man
who exceeds in lack of fear. (We have stated earlier that many   25
qualities have no name.) [19] But he must be a madman or
immune to pain if he fears nothing, neither earthquake nor
flood, as they say of the Celts. He who exceeds in confidence
in a fearful situation is called reckless. A reckless man is
usually thought of as boastful and as someone who pretends
to have courage; at any rate, he wants to appear to behave in   30
a fearful situation as a courageous man really behaves. Therefore he imitates him whenever the situation enables him to do
so. Hence most reckless men are reckless cowards: they put on
a show of confidence when the situation permits, but do not
stand their ground when there is something to fear.

A man who exceeds in fear is a coward: he fears the wrong
things, in the wrong manner, and so forth, all the way down   35
the list. He is also deficient in confidence; but his excessive   1116a
fear in painful situations is more obvious. A coward is a
pessimistic sort of fellow, for he fears everything. But a courageous man is the very opposite, because confidence implies
optimism.

To sum up: a coward, a reckless man, and a courageous
man are all concerned with the same situations, but their   5
attitudes toward them are different. The former two show
excess and deficiency, while the courageous man keeps to the
median and behaves as he ought. Further, reckless men are
impetuous, and though they are eager before danger comes,
they keep out of it when it is there; courageous men, on the
other hand, are keen in the thick of action but calm beforehand.

Courage, as we have stated, is a mean concerning matters   10
that inspire confidence and fear, in the situations described.
It chooses and endures what it does because it is noble to do
so or base to refuse. But to seek death as an escape from

19 See II. 7.

poverty, love, or some other painful experience is to be a
coward rather than a man of courage. For to run away from
troubles is softness, and such a man does not endure death
15 because it is noble but because he is fleeing from evil.

8. Qualities similar to courage

So much for our discussion of what courage is. However,
there are five further types of character to which this name is
also applied. (1) There is, in the first place, because of its close
resemblance to true courage, the courage of the citizen soldier.
Citizens, it seems, endure dangers because the laws and customs penalize and stigmatize them if they do not, and honor
them if they do. Hence those peoples are considered the most
20 courageous among whom cowards are held in dishonor and
courageous men in honor. It is this very type of courage which
Homer describes in such characters as Diomedes and Hector:

Polydamas will be first to put a reproach upon me,[20]

and:

25   for some day Hektor will say openly before the Trojans:
"The son of Tydeus, running before me. . . ." [21]

This kind of courage bears the closest resemblance to the one
we have described earlier, in that it is motivated by virtue,
that is, by a sense of shame and by the desire for a noble object (to wit, honor) and avoidance of reproach as something
base.

30   We might include under this head also those who are forced
to act by their superiors. They are, however, inferior ⟨to the
previous case⟩ inasmuch as they are prompted not by a sense
of shame but by fear, and because what they try to avoid is not
baseness but pain. Their masters exert compulsion as Hector
does when he says:

20 Homer, *Iliad* XXII. 100, tr. Richmond Lattimore.
21 *Ibid.*, VIII. 148-149.

But if I shall see any man who cowers and stays out of
   battle,
Him nothing shall save to escape from the dogs.[22]   35

Field commanders do the selfsame thing when they beat their
troops if the latter retreat, and when they line them up with   1116b
a trench or something of the sort behind them: they all use
compulsion. But courageous action ought to be motivated not
by compulsion, but by the fact that it is noble.

(2) Secondly, experience in facing particular dangers is believed to be courage. Socrates for this very reason thought
courage was knowledge.[23] Different people exhibit this kind of   5
courage under different circumstances, but in warfare professional soldiers are especially noted for it. For they have the
best insight into the many false alarms which war seems to
⟨bring with it⟩. They give the impression of being courageous,
because the others do not know what is happening. Moreover,
their experience enables them to be efficient in attack and in
defense, for they are capable of using arms and are equipped   10
with the best for offensive as well as defensive purposes. Therefore, they fight with the advantage armed men have over un-
armed, or trained athletes over amateurs; for in athletic contests it is not the most courageous who are the best fighters,
but the strongest and those who are physically best conditioned. When the strain of danger becomes too great, however,   15
and when they are inferior in men and equipment, professional soldiers turn cowards: they are the first to run away,
while the citizen militia stand their ground and die, as happened at the temple of Hermes.[24] For citizens, flight is dis-

22 Although sentiments like these are also expressed by Hector in *Iliad*
XV. 348-351, the words cited here are closer to, though not identical with,
those spoken by Agamemnon in *Iliad* II. 391-393. Aristotle is evidently
quoting from memory.

23 See, for example, Plato, *Laches* 199a-b, though this is by no means
Socrates' final word on the matter.

24 This event took place during the Sacred War in 353 B.C. in the Boeo-
tian city of Coronea. Mercenaries, brought in by the Boeotians to defend
them against the Phocian Onomarchus, turned tail and left the citizen
troops to the mercy of the invader.

20   graceful and death preferable to saving one's life on these
     terms; but the professionals go to face danger from the very
     outset in the belief that they are stronger, and once they real-
     ize that they are mistaken they run away, fearing death more
     than disgrace. But this sort of thing is not courage.

        (3) Thirdly, a spirited temper is classified as courage. When
     men, in a fit of temper, become like wild beasts and turn on
25   those who have wounded them, they are considered coura-
     geous, because courageous men are spirited. For nothing makes
     a man as ready to encounter dangers as a spirited temper.
     That is why Homer is full of expressions like: "he put
     strength into his spirit" and "he aroused his might and spirit"
     and "bitter fierceness welled up through his nostrils" and "his
     blood boiled"; [25] for all such expressions seem to describe
30   spirited temper as it is aroused and goes into action. Now,
     courageous men act the way they do because it is noble, and a
     spirited temper gives them support. But wild beasts are moti-
     vated by pain. ⟨They attack only⟩ when they are wounded or
     scared, but not ⟨when they are left in peace⟩ in a forest. Thus
     they are not courageous, because they are spurred by pain and
35   a roused temper to rush into danger without foreseeing any
     of the perils that are in store for them: on this basis even asses
     would be courageous when they are hungry, for no beating
1117a can make them budge from their pasture. Adulterers, too, are
     prompted by lust to do many daring things.[26]

        However, the kind of courage that comes from a spirited
     temper seems to be the most natural and becomes true courage
5   when choice and purpose are added to it. Moreover, anger
     gives men pain and revenge pleasure; and although those who
     fight for these motives are good fighters, they are not coura-

     [25] For these phrases, see Homer, *Iliad* XI. 11; XIV. 151; XVI. 529; V.
     470; XV. 232 and 594; and *Odyssey* XXIV. 318-319. Only the last phrase
     is not Homeric, but it can be found in post-Aristotelian literature in
     Theocritus, *Idyll* XX. 15, and may well have appeared in some epic poem
     still known to Aristotle but lost to us.

     [26] The best extant manuscript of the *Nic. Eth.*, the Laurentian, does
     not contain the next sentence: "Thus we see that courage does not
     consist in being spurred into danger by pain and a roused temper."

geous, for it is not the incentive of what is noble that makes
them fight, and they are not guided by reason but by emotion.
However, they have something which closely resembles courage.

(4) Nor are optimists courageous, for they gain their con-   10
fidence in danger from having won many victories over many
people. They resemble courageous men in that both are confident; the confidence of courageous men, however, is inspired
by the motives discussed above, while the confidence of optimists is based upon their belief that they are the strongest and
will suffer no harm. People behave the same way when drunk:
drinking makes them optimists. But when things turn out con-   15
trary to their expectation they run away. On the other hand,
a courageous man, as we have seen, is characterized by the fact
that he endures what is fearful to man and what seems fearful
to him, because to do so is noble and to do otherwise is base.
For that reason it is a mark of even greater courage to be fearless and unruffled when suddenly faced with a terrifying situation than when the danger is clear beforehand. For the reac-
tion is more prone to be due to a characteristic, since it is less   20
dependent on preparation. When we see what is coming we
can make a choice based on calculation and guided by reason,
but when a situation arises suddenly our actions are determined by our characteristics.

(5) Finally, people who act in ignorance of their danger give
the impression of being courageous. In fact, they are not far
removed from the optimists, but they are inferior in that they
have none of the self-reliance which enables the optimists to
hold their ground for some time. Once the ignorant realize,
however, that the situation is not what they suspected it was,   25
they are deceived and run away. This is what happened to the
Argives when they encountered the Spartans and took them
for Sicyonians.[27]

---

[27] In the battle at the Long Walls of Corinth in 392 B.C., the Spartans
had armed themselves with shields captured from the Sicyonians and
defeated the Argives. The event is related in Xenophon, *Hellenica* IV.
4. 10.

So much for a description of the nature of the courageous man and of those who are believed to be courageous.

9. Courage: its relation to pleasure and pain

Although courage is concerned with feelings of confidence and of fear, it is not concerned with both to an equal extent,
30 but deals more with situations that inspire fear. For he who is unruffled in such situations and shows the right attitude toward them is more truly courageous than he who does so in situations that inspire confidence. In fact, as we have pointed out,[28] men are called courageous for enduring pain. Hence courage is a painful thing and is justly praised, because it is
35 more difficult to endure what is painful than to abstain from what is pleasant.

1117b   Nevertheless, it would seem that the end which courage aims at is pleasant, obscured though it is by the attendant circumstances. Take athletic contests, for example: for boxers the end is pleasant—the object for which they fight, the wreath and the honors—though the blows they receive hurt them (since they
5 are made of flesh and blood) and are painful, as is all their exertion. Since these painful elements are so great in number, the goal of the fight appears small and devoid of anything pleasant. If the same thing is also true of courage, death and wounds will be painful for a courageous man and he will suffer them unwillingly, but he will endure them because it is noble to do so or base to do otherwise. And the closer a man
10 is to having virtue or excellence in its entirety and the happier he is, the more pain will death bring him. Life is more worth living for such a man than for anyone else, and he stands to lose the greatest goods, and realizes that fact, and that is painful. But he is no less courageous for that, and perhaps rather more so, since he chooses noble deeds in war in return for suffering pain. Accordingly, only insofar as it attains its

[28] This had not been explicitly stated, but is implied by the beginning of chap. 7.

end is it true to say of every virtue that it is pleasant when 15
practiced.

But perhaps this does not mean to say that men of true
courage make the best professional soldiers. The best profes-
sionals are men who have less courage, but have nothing to
lose; for they are willing to face dangers and will sell their
lives for a small profit.

So much for our discussion of courage. On the basis of what 20
we have said, it is not difficult to comprehend at least in outline what it is.

10. *Self-control and its sphere of operation*

After courage let us discuss self-control,[29] for these two seem
to be virtues of our irrational part. We have stated earlier that
self-control is a mean in regard to pleasures[30] (for it is con- 25
cerned with pain only to a lesser extent and in a different
way), and self-indulgence, too, manifests itself in the same
situations. Therefore, let us now define with what kind of
pleasures it is concerned.

We must first differentiate between the pleasures of the soul
and the pleasures of the body. Take, for example, the pleasures of fulfilled ambition and love of learning: when the man
who has attained his ambition and the man who loves learning
finds joy in the thing he loves, it is not his body but rather his 30
thought that is affected. Men who indulge in these pleasures
are called neither self-controlled nor self-indulgent. Similarly,
these terms cannot be applied to men who indulge in any
pleasures other than those of the body: we call men who are
fond of hearing and of telling stories and who spend their days

29 Literally translated, the term *sōphrosynē* means 'soundness of mind,'
and describes the full knowledge of one's limitations in a positive as well
as a negative sense. In other words, the *sōphrōn* knows what he is capable
of, as well as what he is incapable of doing. Unfortunately, the translation 'self-control' is more negative than positive in modern usage; it
should be understood not merely as 'restraint' but also as 'mastery.'

30 See II. 7.

35   in trivialities gossipy, but not self-indulgent, nor do we call
1118a   self-indulgent those who feel pain at the loss of money or of
        friends.

        Self-control deals with the pleasures of the body, but not
        even with all of these. For people who find delight in visual
        objects such as colors, shapes, and pictures are called neither
5   self-controlled nor self-indulgent; still, even here it does seem
        possible to feel delight in the right manner as well as exces-
        sively or deficiently. The same is true of the objects of sound:
        no one terms those self-indulgent who take an excessive de-
        light in music or in the theater, or self-controlled those who
        enjoy it in the right manner. Nor do we apply these terms in
        connection with the sense of smell, except incidentally: those
10   who like the smell of fruit, roses, or incense we do not call
        self-indulgent, but rather those who like the smell of perfume
        or fine cooking. For it is in these things that self-indulgent
        people take delight, because they remind them of the objects
        of their appetite. True, one sees other people, too, finding de-
        light in the smell of food when they are hungry, but only the
15   self-indulgent is characterized by the delight he takes in such
        things, since to him they are the stimulants of appetite.

        Moreover, the lower animals derive no pleasure through these
        senses, unless it be incidentally. Dogs do not take delight in
        smelling hares but in eating them: the smell only makes them
20   perceive the hare. Nor does a lion enjoy the lowing of an ox but
        the devouring: the lowing merely makes him perceive that
        the ox is close by, and consequently he seems to enjoy it. In
        the same way, it is not the sight of "stag or mountain goat" [31]
        that gives him joy, but the prospect of a meal.

        Thus self-control and self-indulgence are concerned with
        such pleasures as we share with the other animals, and which
25   therefore appear slavish and bestial. These are the pleasures
        of touch and taste. But they evidently involve little or no use
        of taste at that: for the function of taste consists in the dis-
        crimination of flavors, and that is what wine tasters and chefs
        do when they prepare delicacies. Now, these people do not

        [31] Cited from Homer, *Iliad* III. 24.

find delight in discriminating flavors—or at any rate self-indulgent people do not—but in the actual enjoyment of them,   30
which comes about exclusively through touch in eating and in
drinking as well as in sexual intercourse. That is why a certain
gourmet prayed for a throat longer than a crane's, implying
that he derived his pleasure from touch.³² The senses involved
in self-indulgence are those most widely shared by living be-   1118b
ings. It seems that self-indulgence is considered reprehensible
for a good reason, for it inheres in us not as human beings but
as animals. Therefore, it is bestial to delight in such things
and to be inordinately fond of them. As a matter of fact, the
pleasures of touch in which free men most often indulge, such   5
as the massages and warm baths in the gymnasia, form an exception. For ⟨the pleasure⟩ of the self-indulgent is not ⟨pro-
duced by⟩ the touch of the whole body, but by the touch of
some specific parts.

11. *Self-control: its nature and its opposites*

There seem to be two kinds of appetite. The first is shared
by all, the second is peculiar to some individuals and is ad-
ventitious. For example, the appetite for nourishment is common to all and natural, since everyone who lacks food or   10
drink (or occasionally both) has an appetite for it; and also, as
Homer says,³³ everyone who is young and vigorous has an appetite for sexual intercourse. But when it comes to appetite for
some specific kind of food or sexual relation, not everybody
shares it, nor do all have appetite for the same things. This
appetite, therefore, is evidently more personal. Still, it has
something natural about it; for different people find different
things pleasant, and some things are extraordinarily pleasant
to everyone.

Now in the natural appetites few people go wrong, and that   15
in only one direction, namely excess. For to eat and to drink

---

³² The reference is to the famous and proverbial gourmand Philoxenus;
cf. *Eudemian Ethics* III. 2, 1231a15-17.
³³ See Homer, *Iliad* XXIV. 130-131.

anything until one is more than full is to exceed the natural amount, since natural appetite merely means filling a deficiency. For that reason, people who eat too much are called "belly-gorgers," inasmuch as they fill their stomach beyond
20   what is needed. Men who are all too slavish develop this trait.

On the other hand, in the pleasures peculiar to individuals many men go wrong and in many ways. For while people are said to be "partial" to something either because they find delight in things they should not, or because they find greater delight in them than most people do, or because they find them delightful in the wrong way, the self-indulgent exceed in
25   all three respects: they enjoy some things that they should not, because they are detestable things, and if there are any such things that ought to be enjoyed, they enjoy them more than they should or more than most people do.

It is thus evident that the excess in regard to pleasures is self-indulgence and that it is reprehensible. But as far as pain is concerned, there is a difference between self-control and courage. A man is not called "self-controlled" because he can
30   endure pain or "self-indulgent" because he cannot. He is called "self-indulgent" for feeling more pain than he should at not getting his pleasure (so that it is pleasure which makes him feel pain), and "self-controlled" for not feeling pain at the absence of or abstinence from his pleasure. A self-indul-
1119a gent man has appetite for everything pleasant or for what is most pleasant, and he is driven by his appetite to choose pleasant things at the cost of everything else. As a result, he feels pain both when he fails to get what he wants and when he has an appetite for it. His appetite is accompanied by pain,
5   although it seems strange to feel pain because of pleasure.

On the other hand, men deficient in regard to pleasures, who find less delight in them than they should, are scarcely ever found, for such insensitivity is not human. Even the animals discriminate between different kinds of food and enjoy some and not others. If there is someone to whom nothing is pleasant and who does not differentiate one thing from an-

other, he must be anything but a man. There is no name for 10
such a creature, since he is scarcely to be found.

A self-controlled man observes the mean in these matters.
He takes no pleasure in what is most pleasant to the self-
indulgent, but rather finds it disgusting; in general, he takes
no pleasure in what he should not, and no excessive pleasure in
touch and taste. He feels neither pain nor appetite, or only
moderately, when he does not have these pleasures: he feels
them no more than he should, nor when he should not, and 15
so forth. But all the pleasant things that contribute to his
health and well-being he desires moderately and in the way he
should, and also other pleasures as long as they are neither
detrimental to health and well-being nor incompatible with
what is noble nor beyond his means. A man who does not observe these standards loves such pleasures more than they are
worth. But a self-controlled man is of a different sort: he fol- 20
lows right reason.

12. Self-indulgence

Self-indulgence resembles voluntary ⟨action⟩ more than cowardice does. For it is motivated by pleasure, while cowardice
is motivated by pain, and pleasure is something we choose, and
pain something we avoid. Moreover, pain upsets and destroys
the nature of the man who experiences it, but pleasure does
nothing of the kind. Thus, self-indulgence is more voluntary
⟨than cowardice⟩. For the same reason, it is also more reprehensible. In fact, it is easier to habituate oneself to withstand 25
the attractions of pleasure, for life is full of them and habituation involves no danger; while the opposite is true of fearful
situations.

It would seem, however, that cowardice is more voluntary
than particular cowardly acts. For while cowardice itself is
free from pain, cowardly acts, through the pain they entail, so
upset a man that he throws away his arms and disgraces him- 30
self in other ways. Hence such acts are actually considered

as done under constraint. The opposite is true of a self-indulgent man. In his case, the particular acts are voluntary, inasmuch as they are done with appetite and desire, while the
general characteristics are less so. No one has the urge to be
self-indulgent.

We apply the word "self-indulgence" also to the naughtiness
of children,[34] for this bears some resemblance to the self-indulgence we have been discussing. It makes no difference for our
1119b   present purposes which of the two senses is derived from the
other, but obviously what comes later in life is named after
what comes earlier. The metaphor seems to be quite good: for
what desires the base and what grows wild needs to be
"checked" or "pruned," [35] and that is, above all, appetite and
5   a child. For, like self-indulgent men, children live as their
appetite directs them, and the desire for pleasure is especially
strong in them. So if appetite and desire do not obey and do
not subject themselves to the ruling element, they will go far
astray. For the desire for pleasure is insatiable in a senseless
creature and knows no bounds, and the active gratification of
appetite will increase the appetite with which we were born,
10   and if the appetites are great and intense, they push aside the
power of reasoning. They should, therefore, be moderate and
few in number, and should never oppose the guidance of reason: that is what we mean by "obedient" and "checked." And
just as a child must live as his tutor bids him live, so the appetitive element in us must be guided by the bidding of reason.
15   Consequently, the appetitive element of a self-controlled man
must be in harmony with the guidance of reason. For the aim
of both his appetite and his reason is to do what is noble. The
appetite of a self-controlled man is directed at the right objects, in the right way, and at the right time; and this is what
reason prescribes. So much for our discussion of self-control.

---

34 *Akolasia,* which we translate as 'self-indulgence,' literally means
'lack of chastisement.' The word was obviously used to describe naughty
children.
35 Both these ideas inhere in *kolazein,* the verb negated by *akolasia*
('self-indulgence').

BOOK IV

1. *Generosity, extravagance, and stinginess*

Next in order let us discuss generosity.[1] It seems to be the mean in the sphere of material goods. A man is praised as generous neither for what he does on the battlefield, nor in situations in which a person is praised as self-controlled, nor again in the making of judicial decisions. He is praised in matters involving the giving and taking of material goods, more particularly the giving. By "material goods" we understand everything whose value is measured in money.

There also exists in matters involving material goods extravagance and stinginess as excesses and deficiencies. We attach the label of stinginess always to those who are more intent on material goods than they should be; the term "extravagance," on the other hand, is sometimes used with wider implications, when we call moral weaklings and people who spend their money in indulging themselves "extravagant." They have so many vices all at once that they are regarded as the most worthless of all. But that is not proper usage; for "extravagant" denotes a person who has only one bad quality, namely, that of wasting his property. A man ruined by his own doing is a hopeless case [2] indeed; wasting one's property seems to be a kind of self-destruction, since property provides the means for living. This is, therefore, the sense in which we understand "extravagance."

Things meant for use can be used well and badly, and wealth is a useful thing. Now, any particular object is put to the best use by a man who possesses the virtue proper to that object. Accordingly, wealth will be put to best use by him who

25

30

1120a

5

1 See Glossary, *eleutheriotēs*.
2 It is impossible to reproduce the *double-entendre* in *asōtos* in English. Literally, it means a 'man who preserves nothing,' but Aristotle here gives it the sense of 'one for whom there is no preservation.'

possesses the excellence proper to material goods, and that is the
generous man. Use, we think, consists in spending and giving
material goods, while taking and keeping them is more properly called "possession." Therefore, a generous man is charac-
10 terized rather by giving to the right people than by taking
from the right and not taking from the wrong sources. For
excellence consists in doing good rather than in having good
done to one, and in performing noble actions rather than in
not performing base ones. It is fairly obvious that giving implies doing good and acting nobly, and that taking implies
15 having good done to one and not acting basely. Furthermore,
we show gratitude to him who gives, not to him who does not
take, and, what is more, we praise him. Also, it is easier not
to take than to give, for people are less liable to give away
what belongs to them than not to take what is another's.
Moreover, givers are called "generous," whereas those who do
20 not take are rather praised for their honesty and justice,[3] not
their generosity, and takers are not likely to be praised. Generous men are perhaps loved more than any other people who
are loved for their excellence, for they are helpful, and their
helpfulness consists in giving.

Virtuous actions are noble and are performed because they
are noble. Accordingly, a generous man, too, will give—and
give in the correct manner—because that is noble. He will give
25 to the right people, the right amount, at the right time, and
do everything else that is implied in correct giving. Moreover,
it will give him pleasure to do so, or ⟨at least⟩ no pain; for to
act in conformity with virtue is pleasant or painless, but certainly not painful. If he gives to the wrong people or for the
wrong motive, and not because it is noble to give, he will not
be called generous but something else. ⟨The same applies to
30 a man who finds giving⟩ painful. He would prefer material

---

3 These two expressions seem the best to render *dikaiosynē* in this
context. This virtue, to which Aristotle devotes the whole of Book
V of the *Nic. Eth.* and Plato the entire *Republic*, implies more than its
usual English translation 'justice' indicates. It regulates all the relations
within the state, and deals primarily not only with matters that are
settled before a law court.

goods to noble action, and that is not what marks a man as generous. Nor will a generous man take from the wrong source; that kind of taking is not characteristic of a man who holds material goods in low esteem. He is not likely to make requests, either: a person who does good is not one to accept good turns lightly. But he will take from the right source, from his own possessions, for example, not because it is noble   1120b to do so, but because it is necessary in order to have ⟨something⟩ to give. He will not, however, be careless of his personal possessions, since he wishes to use them as a means of helping others. He will not give to anybody and everybody, so that he may have ⟨something⟩ to give to the right people at the right time and where it is noble to do so. Still, a generous man has a strong tendency to go to such excess in giving   5 that he leaves too little for himself; for not to look out for himself is typical of a generous person.

We speak of generosity relative to a person's property. For a generous act does not depend on the amount given, but on the characteristic of the giver, and this makes him give relative to his property. In other words, it is quite possible that a man who gives less is more generous, if his gift comes from smaller   10 resources. Those who have not accumulated their own property but have inherited it are thought to be more generous, not only because they have never experienced want, but also because everyone has a greater love for what he has produced himself, as do parents and poets.[4] A generous man does not easily get rich, inasmuch as he is not a taker or a keeper, but   15 an openhanded spender who values material goods not for their own sake but for the sake of giving. That is also why fortune is blamed when the most worthy individuals are the least wealthy. And not without reason: one cannot have material goods or anything else without devoting care to getting them.

Still, ⟨a generous man⟩ will not give to the wrong people, at   20

4 Precisely the same point is made by Socrates in his conversation with Cephalus in Plato's *Republic* I. 330c, in words which suggest Aristotle's dependence on Plato here.

the wrong time, and so forth; for if he did, his actions would no longer be dictated by generosity, and if he spent his money on the wrong things, he would have none to spend on the right ones. For as we have said, a man is generous who spends relative to his property and on the right objects; he who ⟨spends⟩ to excess is extravagant. Therefore, we do not call
25 tyrants or absolute monarchs extravagant, for, it seems, the amounts they give and spend cannot very well be in excess of the amounts they possess.

Now, since generosity is the mean in giving and taking material goods, a generous person will give and spend the right amounts on the right objects, in small and great matters alike,
30 and he will derive pleasure from doing so. Also, he will take the right amounts from the right sources. For since the virtue is a mean both in giving and in taking, he will do both in the proper manner: honest taking goes with honest giving, and any other kind of taking is contrary to it. Now, the practices that belong together are found in the same individual, while contrary practices obviously are not. If he should happen to
1121a spend his money in a manner other than proper and noble, he will feel pain, but moderately and in the right way; for it is a mark of virtue or excellence to feel pleasure and pain at the right objects and in the right way. Moreover, a generous man is easy to get along with in business matters, for he can be
5 taken advantage of, since he sets no store by material goods and since he feels more vexation at not having made a proper expenditure, than pain at having made a wrong one; he is not a man to Simonides' liking.[5]

Here, too, an extravagant man goes completely wrong: he feels neither pleasure nor pain at the right objects and in the right manner. This will become more apparent as we go on.
10 We have stated [6] that extravagance and stinginess are excesses

[5] The poet Simonides (ca. 556-468 B.C.) had a reputation for greed. In *Rhetoric* II. 16, 1391a8-12, Aristotle tells the story how Simonides, wh⟨e⟩n asked whether it was better to be wise or wealthy, replied, "Wealthy, for we see the wise spending their time at the doors of the wealthy."
[6] See the beginning of this chapter.

and deficiencies in two respects, i.e., in giving and in taking, for we classify spending with giving. Extravagance is an excess in giving without taking, but it falls short in taking. Stinginess, on the other hand, is a deficiency in giving and an excess in taking, but only in small matters.   15

Now, these two aspects of extravagance do not usually go together. For it is not easy for a person to give to all and take from none. Private individuals soon exhaust their property by giving, and it is of private individuals that we think (when we say that a person) is extravagant.[7] Still, a man who is extravagant in both senses is thought to be considerably superior to a stingy man: age and poverty easily cure him, and he can attain   20 the median state. He has the qualities requisite for a generous man: he gives and does not take, though he does neither rightly and well. If he were to acquire this practice by habit or by changing in some other way, he would be generous: he will then give to the right people and will not take from the wrong source. That is why he is not regarded as bad in character,   25 for excess in giving and in not taking marks a man as foolish, but not as wicked or ignoble. A man who is extravagant in this fashion seems to be far superior to a stingy person for the reasons mentioned, and also because he is helpful to many people, while a stingy man helps nobody, not even himself.

However, most extravagant people, as we have pointed out,   30 also take from the wrong sources and are, in this respect, stingy. They tend to take because they want to spend, but they are unable to do so with an open hand, since their own resources are soon exhausted. As a result, they are compelled to provide means from elsewhere. At the same time, their indifference to what is noble makes them take indiscriminately   1121b from any and every source. They have an appetite for giving, no matter how or from what source. For that reason, their gifts are not even generous. Their gifts are not noble, they are not given because it is noble to give, and they are not given in the right way. On the contrary, persons of this sort some-

7 As we have seen above, at 1120b25-27, tyrants cannot be regarded as extravagant.

5 times make wealthy those who ought to be poor; they would give nothing to people of respectable character but much to those who flatter them or provide them with other kinds of pleasure. Hence, most of them are also self-indulgent: they are easy spenders and squander their money to indulge them-

10 selves. They incline toward pleasure, since their lives are not oriented toward what is noble.

This is what an extravagant man will develop into if left unschooled, but if he receives proper care he may attain the median, the right state. But stinginess is incurable and more deeply ingrained in men than extravagance, for we can see that old age and any kind of disability can make men stingy.

15 Most people love to hang on to material goods rather than to give them away. Moreover, stinginess reaches far and takes many forms, for there seem to be many kinds of it.

There are two aspects to stinginess: deficiency in giving and excess in taking. This means that it is not found in its entirety in all men, but is sometimes divided, so that some

20 exceed in taking while others fall short in giving. Names such as "miser," "niggard," "penny-pincher," are all used of people who fall short in giving but do not covet or wish to take what belongs to another. Some are motivated by a sense of honesty and have scruples against acting basely—for there are those

25 who seem (or, at any rate, profess) to keep what they have in order to avoid being compelled to do something base. Here belongs the skinflint and everyone like him who gets his name from his excessive reluctance to give anything. Some do not touch another man's property through fear, in the belief that it is not easy to take what belongs to another while at the

30 same time preventing others from taking what belongs to oneself. Accordingly, they are satisfied neither to take nor to give.

Still others exceed in taking in that they take anything from any source; such, for example, are those who follow occupations not fit for free men, such as pimps and all thei: ilk, and usurers who lend small sums at high interest. All

1122a these people take from the wrong sources and more than they

should. What they have in common is clearly the motive of profiteering, for they all endure notoriety for the sake of profit, and small profit at that. But those who take the wrong things from the wrong source on a large scale, such as tyrants who sack cities and plunder temples, are not called "stingy"   5
or "mean" but "wicked," "impious," and "unjust." However, gamblers and highwaymen [8] are classified as stingy and mean, for they are profiteers in that both ply their trade and endure notoriety for the sake of profit, the one taking the greatest risks to get booty, and the other to make a profit at the expense of his friends to whom he ought to give. Now, since both   10
wish to gain profit from the wrong sources, they are profiteers, and all such ways of taking are stingy and mean.

It is with good reason that stinginess is said to be the opposite of generosity. For not only is it a greater evil than extravagance, but people are more prone to go wrong in fol-   15
lowing it than in following extravagance as we have described it.[9] So much for generosity and the vices opposed to it.

2. *Magnificence, vulgarity, and niggardliness*

It seems logical to discuss magnificence [10] next, for it, too, is evidently a virtue concerned with material goods. However, unlike generosity, which covers all actions involving material   20
goods, magnificence is confined to those that involve spending, but in these it surpasses generosity in scale. For, as the very name suggests, it is a "suitable" expenditure on a "grand" scale. Now, a scale is relative: the expense of equipping a

[8] In view of the "both" in the next sentence, I follow what was apparently Aspasius' reading and omit καὶ ὁ λῃστὴς, 'and the robber,' from the translation.

[9] For these criteria of determining the opposite extremes, see II. 8, 1109a5-17.

[10] 'Magnificence' seems to be the closest English equivalent of *megaloprepeia*. Literally, the term means 'greatness befitting (an occasion).' This virtue involves the kind of public spirit that was exhibited in Athens by the so-called "liturgies," i.e., the financing of dramatic productions, of the equipment of warships, etc.

trireme is not the same as that of heading a sacred embassy.[11]
25 What is suitable is, then, relative to the person, the circumstances, and the object. A man who, like the proverbial "to
many a wanderer did I give," [12] spends appropriate amounts
on insignificant or only moderately important occasions is
not called magnificent. But he is if he does so on important
occasions. A magnificent man is generous, but that does not
mean that a generous man is magnificent. The deficiency of
30 this characteristic is called niggardliness and its excess vulgarity, gaudiness, and the like; it is an excess that does not
consist in too great an amount spent on a proper object, but in
putting on a showy display on the wrong occasions and in the
wrong manner. We shall discuss them later.

A magnificent man is like a skilled artist: he has the ca-
35 pacity to observe what is suitable and to spend large sums
1122b with good taste. For as we said at the outset,[13] a characteristic is defined by its activities and by its objects. Therefore,
the expenses of a magnificent man are great and suitable, and
so are, consequently, the results which he produces. For ⟨only⟩
in this way will the expenditure be great and suited to the
result. Accordingly, a result must be worth the expense and
5 the expense worth the result or even exceed the result. A
magnificent man will spend amounts of this kind because it is
noble to do so; for this motive is common to all the virtues.
Moreover, he will spend with pleasure and with a free hand, for
exact bookkeeping is niggardly. He will try to find out how
to achieve the most noble and suitable result rather than how
much it will cost him and how it can be done most cheaply.
10 Therefore, a magnificent man will necessarily also be generous.
A generous man, too, will spend the right amount in the right
manner, but in spending the right amount in the right man-

11 A sacred embassy (theōria) was customarily sent out by a Greek
city as an official delegation to attend an important festival of another
city, and especially to represent the city at the Panhellenic festivals. The
head of the embassy would have to defray expenses such as transportation,
the cost of the sacrifices to be offered, etc.
12 Said by Odysseus in Homer, Odyssey XVII. 420.
13 See II. 1 (end) and 2.

ner—the sphere of generosity—the "grand" of a *magnificent man*,[14] his greatness, will come to the fore: at the same expense he will achieve a more magnificent result. For the excellence of a possession is not the same as the excellence of a result achieved. The most valued possession is the most costly,   15
such as gold, but the most valued achievement or result is one that is great and noble: to look at it will be to admire it, and what is magnificent is admirable. In other words, the excellence or virtue of a result achieved, i.e., its magnificence, consists in greatness.

Magnificence involves expenditures which we call honorable, e.g., expenditures on the worship of the gods—votive offerings, buildings, and sacrifices—and similarly on the various   20
forms of worshiping the lesser divinities, and on public enterprises which people ambitiously vie with one another to undertake, as, for example, when they think they should equip a chorus or a trireme or give a feast for the city in a brilliant fashion. But in all these cases, as we have said,[15] we must also take account of who the agent is and what his resources are, for the expenditure must be in keeping with   25
that and must be suited not only to the result achieved but also to the spender. That is why a poor man is unlikely to be magnificent; for he does not have the means for a suitable expenditure of large sums. If he tries ⟨to spend large sums⟩, he is a fool; for he spends more than he can afford or ought to spend, whereas virtuous spending is right spending. But such expenditure is suited to persons who have the requisite   30
means either by dint of their own effort or from their ancestors or their connections. It is suited to persons of high birth and reputation, and so forth, since all these qualities carry greatness and prestige. Such a man, above all, is magnificent, and, as we have said, magnificence consists in expenditures of this kind; for they are the greatest and most honorable. In private   35
affairs, magnificence is shown in those expenditures which are made only once—e.g., a wedding and the like, and anything of   1123a

14 See p. 89, note 10 on the etymology of *megaloprepeia*.
15 At the beginning of this chapter.

interest to the whole city or to eminent people—and also in receiving and taking leave of foreign guests and in exchanging
gifts. For a man is magnificent not when he spends on himself, but when he spends for the common good. There is a
5   similarity between gifts and votive offerings. It is also typical
of a magnificent man to furnish his house commensurate with
his wealth—for it, too, is a kind of ornament—and to prefer
spending his money on works that endure, since they are the
noblest; in each particular case he will spend an amount
suited to the occasion. For the same thing is not fit for both
10   gods and men, and what suits a temple does not suit a tomb.
Now, the greatness of expenditure depends on its kind. The
most magnificent absolutely is great expenditure on a great
object, the most magnificent in a particular case is great
expenditure for that particular object; moreover, greatness
in the result achieved is different from greatness in expenditure. The most beautiful ball or oil flask is magnificent as a
15   gift for a child, though its price is small and far from generous. From all this it follows that a magnificent man is characterized by achieving his results, of whatever kind they may
be, magnificently—for such results cannot easily be surpassed
—and in a manner worth the expenditure.

    Such, then, is the magnificent man. His opposite on the
side of excess is the vulgar man who, as we said,[16] exceeds
20   in spending more money than he should. He spends much
where small expenditures are called for and makes an improper show of himself. He gives a dinner to his club on the
scale of a wedding banquet, and when he defrays the expenses
of a comic chorus, he makes them enter the theater in purple,
as they do at Megara.[17] He will do all kinds of similar things,
25   not for a noble motive, but to show off his wealth, and in the

[16] At the beginning of this chapter.
[17] Since comic choruses were considerably less expensive than those
of tragedy, and since purple was very costly and more appropriate to
tragedy, it would be quite vulgar and inappropriate to make a comic
chorus enter in this way.

belief that he will be admired for doing so. Where he ought to spend much money he spends little, and where little he spends much.

A niggardly person, on the other hand, will fall short in every respect. After spending tremendous sums, he will for a trifle spoil the beauty of his achievement. In everything he does he will hestitate and try to find ways of economizing. He 30 will grumble about spending the little that he does, thinking that he is doing everything on a greater scale than he ought. Accordingly, these characteristics are vices, yet they do not bring reproach upon a person because they are neither harmful to one's neighbor nor excessively unseemly.

3. High-mindedness, pettiness, and vanity

High-mindedness, as its very name suggests,[18] seems to be concerned with great and lofty matters. Let us take the nature 35 of these matters as the first point of our discussion. It makes no difference whether we investigate the characteristic or the 1123b man who is characterized by it. A man is regarded as high-minded when he thinks he deserves great things and actually deserves them; one who thinks he deserves them but does not is a fool, and no man, insofar as he is virtuous, is either fool-ish or senseless. This then is the description of a high-minded man. A person who deserves little and thinks he deserves little 5 is not high-minded, but is a man who knows his limitations.[19] For high-mindedness implies greatness, just as beauty implies stature in body: small people may have charm and proportion

18 *Megalopsychia* literally means 'greatness of soul' and was translated into Latin as *magnanimitas*, from which English 'magnanimity' is derived. However, since, as this chapter will show, the connotations of *megalo-psychia* are much wider than the modern meaning of 'magnanimity,' 'high-mindedness' seems better suited to rendering the pride and confident self-respect inherent in the concept.

19 The Greek word here is *sōphrōn*, which this translation usually renders 'self-controlled' (cf. Glossary). However, in this context Aristotle seems to have in mind the lower limit of the term.

but not beauty.[20] A man who thinks he deserves great things
but does not deserve them is vain, though not everybody who
overestimates himself is vain. One who underestimates him-
10   self is small-minded [21] regardless of whether his actual worth
is great or moderate, or whether it is small and he thinks that
it is smaller still. A man of great deserts, it would seem, is
most ⟨liable to be small-minded⟩, for what would he do if his
deserts were not as great as they are? Thus, measured by the
standard of greatness, the high-minded man is an extreme, but
by the standard of what is right he occupies the median; for
15   his claims correspond to his deserts, whereas the others exceed
or fall short.

Accordingly, if a high-minded man thinks he deserves and
actually does deserve great things, especially the greatest, there
is one matter that will be his major concern. "Deserts" is a
relative term that refers to external goods; and as the greatest external good, we may posit that which we pay as a
tribute to the gods, for which eminent people strive most,
and which is the prize for the noblest achievements. Honor
20   fits that description, for it is the greatest of external goods.
Consequently, it is in matters of honor and dishonor that a
high-minded man has the right attitude. It is an obvious fact,
and need not be argued, that the high-minded are concerned
with honor. For they regard themselves as worthy of honor
above all else, but of an honor that they deserve. A small-
minded man falls short both in view of his own deserts and
25   in relation to the claims of a high-minded person, while a vain

20 Aristotle's meaning is clarified by reference to *Poetics* 7, 1450b35-40
as tr. by G. M. A. Grube, *On Poetry and Style*, "Library of Liberal Arts,"
No. 68 (New York, 1958): "However, an animal, or indeed anything
which has parts, must, to be beautiful, not only have these parts in the
right order but must also be of a definite size. Beauty is a matter of
size and order. An extraordinarily small animal would not be beautiful,
nor an extraordinarily large one."

21 *Mikropsychia*, meaning 'smallness of soul,' is of course diametrically
opposed to 'greatness of soul.' The concept also includes a tone of
false humility.

man exceeds his own deserts but does not exceed the high-minded.

This means that the high-minded man, inasmuch as he deserves what is greatest, is the best. For the deserts of the better man are always greater, and those of the best man the greatest. It follows that a truly high-minded man must be good. And what is great in each virtue would seem to be the 30 mark of a high-minded person. It would be quite out of character for him to run away in battle with arms swinging or to do wrong to anyone. For what motive does he have to act basely, he to whom nothing is great? If we were to examine ⟨his qualities⟩ one by one, we should see the utter absurdity of thinking of a high-minded man as being anything but good. If he were base, he would not even deserve honor, for honor is the prize of excellence and virtue, and it is reserved 35 as a tribute to the good. High-mindedness thus is the crown, 1124a as it were, of the virtues: it magnifies them and it cannot exist without them. Therefore, it is hard to be truly high-minded and, in fact, impossible without goodness and nobility.[22]

A high-minded man is, then, primarily concerned with 5 honor and dishonor. From great honors and those that good men confer upon him he will derive a moderate amount of pleasure, convinced that he is only getting what is properly his or even less. For no honor can be worthy of perfect virtue. Yet he will accept it, because they have no greater tribute to pay to him. But he will utterly despise honors conferred by ordinary people and on trivial grounds, for that is not what 10 he deserves. Similarly, he will despise dishonor, for no dishonor can be justified in his case. A high-minded man, as we have stated, is concerned primarily with honors. But he will of course also have a moderate attitude toward wealth, power, and every manner of good or bad luck that may befall him. He will not be overjoyed when his luck is good, nor will bad 15

[22] *Kalokagathia* is similar to the ideal of the 'gentleman,' combining good appearance and manners with moral qualities. See Glossary.

luck be very painful to him. For even toward honor, his attitude is that it is not of the greatest moment. Power and wealth are desirable for the honor they bring; at any rate, those who have them wish to gain honor through them. But a person who attaches little importance even to honor will also attach little importance to power and wealth. As a result, he is regarded as haughty.

20   Gifts of fortune, it is believed, also contribute to high-mindedness. Men of noble birth, of power, or of wealth are regarded as worthy of honor, since they occupy a superior position, and whatever is superior in goodness is held in greater honor. That is why the gifts of fortune make men more high-minded, for they are honored by some people ⟨for having

25   them⟩. But in truth it is the good man alone that ought to be honored, though a man who has both excellence and good fortune is regarded as still more worthy of honor. Whoever possesses the goods of fortune without possessing excellence or virtue is not justified in claiming great deserts for himself, nor is it correct to call him high-minded, for neither is possible without perfect virtue. Their good fortune notwithstanding,

30   such people become haughty and arrogant, for without virtue it is not easy to bear the gifts of fortune gracefully. Unable

1124b   to bear them and considering themselves superior, they look down upon others, while they themselves do whatever they please. They imitate the high-minded man wherever they can, but they are not really like him. Thus, they look down upon others, but they do not act in conformity with excellence. A

5   high-minded person is justified in looking down upon others for he has the right opinion of them, but the common run of people do so without rhyme or reason.

A high-minded man does not take small risks and, since there are only a few things which he honors, he is not even fond of risks. But he will face great risks, and in the midst of them he will not spare his life, aware that life at any cost is not worth having. He is the kind of man who will do good, but who is ashamed to accept a good turn, because the former

10   marks a man as superior, the latter as inferior. Moreover, he

will requite good with a greater good, for in this way he will
not only repay the original benefactor but put him in his
debt at the same time by making him the recipient of an
added benefit. The high-minded also seem to remember the
good turns they have done, but not those they have received.
For the recipient is inferior to the benefactor, whereas a high-
minded man wishes to be superior. They listen with pleasure
to what good they have done, but with displeasure to what
good they have received. That is apparently why Thetis does   15
not mention the good turns she had done to Zeus,[23] and why
the Spartans did not mention theirs to the Athenians,[24] but
only the good they had received. It is, further, typical of a
high-minded man not to ask for any favors, or only reluc-
tantly, but to offer aid readily. He will show his stature in his
relations with men of eminence and fortune, but will be
unassuming toward those of moderate means. For to be supe-
rior to the former is difficult and dignified, but superiority over   20
the latter is easy. Furthermore, there is nothing ignoble in
asserting one's dignity among the great, but to do so among
the lower classes is just as crude as to assert one's strength
against an invalid. He will not go in for pursuits that the common people value, nor for those in which the first place belongs
to others. He is slow to act and procrastinates, except when
some great honor or achievement is at stake. His actions are   25
few, but they are great and distinguished. He must be open
in hate and open in love, for to hide one's feelings and to care
more for the opinion of others than for truth is a sign of
timidity. He speaks and acts openly: since he looks down

[23] The reference is to Thetis' intercession with Zeus to help avenge
the wrong done her son Achilles by Agamemnon; see Homer, *Iliad* I. 504-
510. Actually, Thetis starts by reminding Zeus, "if I have ever helped
you by word or deed among the immortals," but Aristotle is right to
the extent that no specific benefactions are enumerated.

[24] An ancient commentator on this passage, citing the *Greek History*
of Callisthenes (Aristotle's nephew), refers to a Spartan request for
Athenian help against the Thebans in 369 b.c. However, in the account
of the event given in Xenophon, *Hellenica* VI. 5. 33-34, the Spartans do
mention the good turns they have done.

30   upon others his speech is free and truthful, except when he
     deliberately depreciates himself in addressing the common
     run of people. He cannot adjust his life to another, except
1125a a friend, for to do so is slavish. That is, ⟨by the way,⟩ why all
     flatterers are servile and people from the lower classes are
     flatterers. He is not given to admiration, for nothing is great to
     him. He bears no grudges, for it is not typical of a high-
     minded man to have a long memory, especially for wrongs,
5   but rather to overlook them. He is not a gossip, for he will
     talk neither about himself nor about others, since he is not
     interested in hearing himself praised or others run down.
     Nor again is he given to praise; and for the same reason he
     does not speak evil of others, not even of his enemies, except
     to scorn them. When he encounters misfortunes that are un-
     avoidable or insignificant, he will not lament and ask for help.
10   That kind of attitude belongs to someone who takes such
     matters seriously. He is a person who will rather possess
     beautiful and profitless objects than objects which are profit-
     able and useful, for they mark him more as self-sufficient.
         Further, we think of a slow gait as characteristic of a high-
     minded man, a deep voice, and a deliberate way of speaking.
     For a man who takes few things seriously is unlikely to be in
15   a hurry, and a person who regards nothing as great is not
     one to be excitable. But a shrill voice and a swift gait are
     due to hurry and excitement.
         Such, then, is the high-minded man. A man who falls short
     is small-minded, and one who exceeds is vain. Now here, too,[25]
     these people are not considered to be bad—for they are not
     evildoers—but only mistaken. For a small-minded man de-
20   prives himself of the good he deserves. What seems to be bad
     about him is due to the fact that he does not think he deserves
     good things and that he does not know himself; if he did, he
     would desire what he deserves, especially since it is good.
     It is not that such people are regarded as foolish, but rather
     ⟨that they are looked upon⟩ as retiring. However, a reputa-
     tion of this sort seems to make them even worse. For while

     [25] I.e., just as in the case of niggardliness and vulgarity.

any given kind of man strives to get what he deserves, these　25
people keep aloof even from noble actions and pursuits and
from external goods as well, because they consider themselves undeserving.

Vain people, on the other hand, are fools and do not know
themselves, and they show it openly. They take in hand
honorable enterprises of which they are not worthy, and
then they are found out. They deck themselves out with
clothes and showy gear and that sort of thing, and wish to　30
publicize what fortune has given them. They talk about their
good fortune in the belief that that will bring them honor.

Small-mindedness is more opposed to high-mindedness than
vanity is, for it occurs more frequently and is worse. Thus,
as we have said,[26] high-mindedness is concerned with high　35
honors.

4. *Ambition and lack of ambition as the extremes of a nameless virtue*

There seems to be a virtue, also in the sphere of honor,　1125b
which, as we stated when we first broached the subject,[27] is
believed to be as closely related to high-mindedness as generosity is to magnificence. Neither this virtue nor generosity
operates on a grand scale, and both give us the proper disposition in matters of moderate or small importance. Just as　5
there is a mean, an excess, and a deficiency in taking and in
giving material goods, so too can we desire honor more than
we should and less than we should, and from the right source
and in the right manner. We blame an ambitious man for
striving for honor more than he should and for trying to get
it from the wrong sources; and we blame an unambitious man　10
for deliberately desiring not to be honored even for noble
achievements. However, occasionally we praise the ambitious
as manly and as fond of what is noble and the unambitious
as moderate and self-controlled, as we said when we first dis-

---

26 See II. 7, 1107b26, and the beginning of this chapter.
27 See II. 7, 1107b24-1108a1.

cussed the subject.[28] But since "fond" of something is clearly used in more senses than one, we do not always apply the term 15 "fond of honor" or "ambitious" to the same thing. As a term of praise it means "fonder of honor than most people," and as a term of blame "fonder of honor than one ought to be." As there is no name for the mean, the extremes dispute for its possession as for an unclaimed inheritance, as it were. But where there is excess and deficiency there is also a median. Men desire honor both more than they should and less; there- 20 fore, it must also be possible to desire it to the right degree. It is this characteristic which is praised, a nameless character- istic that constitutes the mean in the sphere of honor. In comparison with ambition it appears like lack of ambition, in comparison with lack of ambition like ambition, and in com- parison with both it somehow looks like both at once. The same seems to be true also of the other virtues. But in this case the men at the extremes are seen only in their opposition 25 to one another, because the man who occupies the median position does not have a name.

5. Gentleness, short temper, and apathy

Gentleness is the mean in feelings of anger. Although there is no name for the *person* occupying the median position and hardly even for the extremes, we apply the term "gentleness" to the median, despite the fact that it inclines toward the deficiency, which has no name, either. The excess may be called something like "short temper." For the emotion is a 30 feeling of anger,[29] which is brought about by many different factors.

Now, a man is praised for being angry under the right cir- cumstances and with the right people, and also in the right manner, at the right time, and for the right length of time. He may be ⟨termed⟩ gentle, since gentleness is used as a term

28 *Ibid.*
29 It is hard to reproduce the verbal echo in English between *orgilotēs* ('short temper') and *orgē* ('feeling of anger').

of praise. For being gentle means to be unruffled and not to
be driven by emotion, but to be angry only under such circumstances and for as long a time as reason may bid. But he   35
seems to be more prone to going wrong in the direction of   1126a
deficiency: a gentle person is forgiving rather than vindictive.
The deficiency, whether it is a kind of apathy or whatever
else it may be, receives blame. For those who do not show
anger at things that ought to arouse anger are regarded as
fools; so, too, if they do not show anger in the right way, at   5
the right time, or at the right person. Such people seem to
have no feelings, not even for pain; they do not seem to
rise to their own defense, since they do not show anger; but to
let one's own character be smeared and to put up with insults
to those near and dear to him is slavish.

In all these points, excess is also possible. Anger can be
shown against the wrong persons, under the wrong circumstances, to an improper degree, too quickly, and for an unduly   10
long time. Yet these factors are not all found in the same
person. That would be impossible, for evil destroys even itself,
and when it is present in its entirety it becomes unbearable.
Short-tempered people are quick to be angered at the wrong
people, under the wrong circumstances, and more than is
right, but they get over it quickly, and that is their best   15
quality. What happens to them is that they do not restrain
their feeling of anger, but quick as they are they retaliate in an
open way and then have done with it. Choleric people are excessively quick and short-tempered about everything and on every
occasion, hence their name.[30] Sullen people are hard to appease
and their anger lasts for a long time, since they repress their   20
passion. But once they retaliate, they are relieved; for revenge
puts an end to their anger and engenders pleasure in place of
the pain. If that does not happen, they go on carrying their
burden. Since it does not appear on the surface, no one reasons
them out of it, and to digest one's anger in oneself takes time.
Such men are very troublesome to themselves and to their   25

[30] *Akrocholos* is a compound of *akro-*, 'extreme,' and *cholos*, 'bile.'
The point is of course that the extreme is excessive.

clcsest friends. "Bad-tempered" we call those who show anger under the wrong circumstances, to an improper degree, and for too long a time, and those who cannot be reconciled without exacting their revenge or punishment.

We regard the excess as more opposed to gentleness than the deficiency. In the first place, it is much more common, 30 for it is more human to seek revenge. Secondly, bad-tempered people are worse to live with.

Our present discussion corroborates the point we made earlier: [31] it is not easy to determine in what manner, with what person, on what occasion, and for how long a time one ought to be angry, and at what point right action ends and 35 wrong action begins. We do not blame a man for straying a little either toward the more or toward the less. Sometimes we 1126b praise those who are deficient in anger and call them gentle, and sometimes we praise the angry as manly and regard them as capable of ruling. Therefore, it is not easy to give a formula how far and in what manner a man may stray before he deserves blame, for the decision depends on the particular circumstances and on our (moral) sense. But this much is 5 clear: what deserves praise is the median characteristic that makes us show anger at the right people, on the right occasions, in the right manner, and so forth, while the extremes and deficiencies deserve blame: slight blame for small deviations, more blame for greater deviations, and very severe blame for very great deviations. Thus, it is clear that we must hold fast to the median characteristic. So much for the char-10 acteristics concerned with feelings of anger.

6. Friendliness, obsequiousness, and grouchiness

In social relations, in living together, and in associating with our fellow men in conversation and business, there are people whom we regard as obsequious. They praise you just to give you pleasure, never object to anything, and think that they must avoid giving pain to those they meet. Their oppo-

. [31] See II. 9, 1109b14-26.

sites, who object to everything without caring in the least 15
whether they give pain, are called grouchy and quarrelsome.
That the characteristics just described deserve blame is clear
enough, and so is the fact that the middle position between
them deserves praise, i.e., the position of a man who will put
up with—and likewise refuse to put up with—the right things
in the right manner. No name has been given to this characteristic, but it bears the greatest resemblance to friendship.[32] 20
For a man who conforms to the intermediate characteristic is
the kind of person we mean when we speak of a "good friend,"
though "friend" also involves affection.

This characteristic differs from friendship in that it involves no emotion or affection for those with whom one associates. It is not because of his feelings of friendship or
hatred that such a man takes everything the right way, but
because he is the kind of man he is. His behavior will be the
same toward those he knows and those he does not, toward 25
people with whom he is familiar and people with whom he
is not, except that in each particular case his behavior will be
appropriate to the person. For it is not proper to show the
same consideration to familiar people and to strangers, nor
again to be equally concerned to avoid giving them pain. We
have stated in general terms that his behavior in society will
be as it ought to be. But further, in aiming to avoid giving
pain or to contribute to pleasure, he will act by the standard
of what is noble and beneficial. For his concern seems to be 30
with the pleasures and pains that are found in social relations.
Wherever it is not noble or harmful for him to contribute to
the pleasure of others, he will refuse and will prefer to give
pain ⟨by his refusal⟩; and when an action will bring considerable discredit or harm upon the agent, he will not ac-

---

[32] In II. 7, 1108a27-28, Aristotle actually does call the mean *philia*
('friendship'), which we translate there as 'friendliness.' The difficulty is
that the Greek language uses *philia* for the human relation of 'friendship'
as well as for the characteristic of 'friendliness' and for the emotion underlying it. Although Aristotle uses *philia* for all these meanings, he evidently
felt uncomfortable about using it for the characteristic and the emotion,
as we see here and further along in this chapter. See also Glossary.

35 quiesce in it but refuse, if his own opposition to it will cause
only a small amount of pain. He will behave differently toward eminent men and toward ordinary people, toward those
1127a he knows well and those he knows less well, and he will
observe other similar distinctions in his behavior, paying the
proper tribute to each. Everything else being equal, he will
choose to contribute to the pleasure of others and scrupulously avoid giving pain. But he will guide his behavior by
considering whether the consequences are of greater moment,
5 i.e., by considering what is noble and beneficial. Moreover,
he will inflict small pain in order to gain great pleasure in
the future.

Such is the man in the median position, but there is no
name for him. A man who contributes to the pleasures of
others is obsequious if he has no ulterior motive and simply
aims at being pleasant. But if his purpose is to gain some
material advantage for himself in the form of money or of
what money can buy, he is a flatterer. A man who refuses to
10 put up with anything is, as we said, grouchy and quarrelsome.
The extremes appear to be only opposed to one another, because there is no name for the middle.

7. Truthfulness, boastfulness, and self-depreciation

In almost the same sphere, we find the mean—also nameless—of which boastfulness is an extreme. But it is not a bad
idea to discuss nameless virtues, too, for if we go through
15 them one by one we shall gain a greater knowledge of the
factors involved in character and confirm our belief that the
virtues are means, if our survey shows that this is true in
every instance.[33] Now, we have already discussed [34] those
people who in social life give pleasure and pain to their

[33] This is an excellent example of what Aristotle means by 'induction'
(epagōgē). Cf. Topics I. 12, 105a13-16: "Induction is the procedure which
leads from particulars to universals, e.g., if the best helmsman and the
best charioteer are those who have knowledge, it is true as a general rule
that in each particular field the best is he who has knowledge."
[34] See above, chap. 6.

fellow men. Let us now speak about those who are truthful and those who are false in speech and action as well as in   20 pretense.

A man who is regarded as boastful pretends to qualities that carry high prestige, though he does not possess them, or to greater qualities than he possesses. A self-depreciator,[35] on the contrary, disclaims or belittles the qualities he possesses, while the man in the median position is the kind that calls everything by its proper name. He is truthful in his life and in his speech; he admits to the qualities he possesses and   25 neither exaggerates nor understates them. Now, each of these lines of behavior may be pursued with or without an ulterior motive. When an individual has no ulterior motive, he speaks, acts, and lives his real character. Falsehood is base in its own right and deserves blame, but truthfulness is noble and deserves praise. In the same way, a truthful man, occupying the   30 median position, deserves praise, while untruthful persons of either type, but especially the boastful, deserve blame.

Let us discuss them both, starting with the truthful man. We are not speaking of a man who is truthful in the contracts he makes or in matters relevant to injustice and justice—for that would properly belong to another virtue. But we are speaking of a man who, when no question of this kind is   1127b involved, is truthful in his speech and in his life simply because it is part of his character to be that kind of man. Such a man would seem to be honest.[36] For a man who loves truth and who is truthful when nothing is at stake will be even more truthful when something is at stake. He will scrupulously   5 avoid falsehood as being base, especially since he has always been scrupulous to avoid it when no other considerations

35 'Self-depreciation' is perhaps the least inaccurate rendering of *eirōneia*. The best description of the quality is found here: it is the exact opposite of boastfulness and involves qualities such as understatement, pretending ignorance, mock modesty and the like, but sometimes also has overtones of slyness. Self-depreciation, in the form of feigned ignorance, was frequently attributed to Socrates (e.g., Plato, *Apology* 38a; *Republic* I. 337a; *Symposium* 216e).
36 See Glossary, *epieikēs*.

were involved: such a man deserves praise. He is more inclined to understating the truth. That is clearly in better
taste, since exaggeration is obnoxious.

10   A man who pretends to greater qualities than he possesses
with no ulterior motive is a vile sort of person, else he would
not take delight in falsehood; but he is evidently inept rather
than wicked. But if his pretensions have reputation and honor
as an ulterior motive, he does not deserve too much blame
(considering that he is a boaster). But if his motive is money
or something that will get him money, he shows a greater lack
of propriety. It is not the capacity that makes a boaster, but
15   the moral choice. His characteristic and the kind of person
he is mark him as boastful. Similarly, one man is a liar because he enjoys lying as such, and another because he desires
reputation or profit. Accordingly, people who boast in order to
gain reputation pretend to qualities for which a man is praised
or regarded as happy; while those who boast for profit pretend to qualities which benefit their neighbors or to accomplishments which they do not have but can claim to have without ⟨fear of⟩ being detected, e.g., ⟨proficiency as⟩ a soothsayer,
20   a scholar, or a physician. That is why most people indulge in
this kind of pretense and boast, for they do not have the
qualifications just mentioned.[37]

   Those who depreciate themselves by understatement are
evidently more subtle in character. For, it seems, their speech
is not motivated by profit but by ⟨the concern⟩ to avoid bom-
25   bast. They disclaim especially those qualities which are highly
valued by others, as Socrates used to do. When they disclaim
insignificant and obvious qualities, they are called "humbugs"
and are more contemptible. Sometimes this is obvious boastfulness, as for example Spartan dress.[38] In fact, both excess

   [37] I.e., the person who pretends that he can be beneficial and has
certain accomplishments actually is a qualified soothsayer, scholar, or
physician. But he is a quack, and, therefore, not as proficient and as
good as he claims to be, and that makes him boastful.
   [38] Evidently, Aristotle regards the drab and simple way of dressing,
practiced by the Spartans, as an affectation.

and exaggerated deficiency tend to be boastful. But people who make moderate use of self-depreciation and understate such of their own qualities as are not too noticeable and obvious strike one as cultivated. It is the boastful man who is evidently the opposite of the truthful man, because he is inferior (to the self-depreciator). 30

8. *Wittiness, buffoonery, and boorishness*

Since relaxation is also an essential part of life, and since it includes spending one's time in amusement, it seems possible here, too, to display good taste in our social relations and propriety in what we say and how we say it. The same 1128a is also true of listening. It will make a difference in what kind of company we speak and to what kind of company we listen. Clearly, in this field, too, it is possible to exceed and fall short of the median.

People who exceed in being funny are regarded as buffoons and as crude. They try to be funny at any cost, and their aim 5 is more to raise a laugh than to speak with decorum and without giving pain to the butt of their jokes. Those who cannot say anything funny themselves and take offense when others do are considered to be boorish and dour. Those whose fun remains in good taste are called "witty," implying quick 10 versatility in their wits.[39] For such sallies are believed to be movements of the character, and, like bodies, characters too are judged by the way they move. But since one need not go far afield to find something to laugh about, and since most people enjoy fun and joking more than they should, even buffoons often pass as cultivated and are called witty. But 15 that there is a difference, and a considerable difference at that, is clear from our discussion.

Tact is also a quality that belongs to the median characteristic, and a man is tactful who says and listens to the sort

---

[39] *Eutrapelos*, 'witty,' means literally 'turning well.' The metaphor is here explained by reference to *eutropos*, 'versatile,' a word used apparently to describe bodily nimbleness.

of thing that befits an honest and a free man. For there are some things that are proper for such a man to say and to
20 hear by way of jest. There is a difference between the jesting of a free and that of a slavish man, and between that of an educated and of an uneducated person. This difference can also be seen in old and in modern comedy: for the writers of old comedy the ridiculous element was obscenity, while the moderns tend toward innuendo.[40] The difference in propriety between the two is quite considerable. Can we then
25 define a good jester as a man who says nothing that is improper for a free man, or as a man who will not give pain, or even as one who will give joy, to his listener? Surely that sort of thing is undefinable, for different things are hateful and pleasant to different people. ⟨The kind of jokes he will tell will also be⟩ the kind of jokes he will hear: for what jokes a person can endure to listen to also seem to be the jokes he makes. But he will draw a line somewhere, for a jest at the
30 expense of a person is a kind of slander, and for some things, lawgivers forbid us to slander people. Perhaps they should also forbid us to make fun ⟨of some things⟩.

A cultivated and free man, then, will have this kind of attitude, being, as it were, a law unto himself. Thus he occupies the median position, whether we call him tactful or witty. A buffoon, however, cannot resist any temptation to be funny,
35 and spares neither himself nor others for a laugh. He says
1128b things that no cultivated man would say, and some that he would not even listen to. A boor, on the other hand, is useless in social relations of this kind. He contributes nothing and takes offense at everything, despite the fact that relaxation and amusement are a necessary part of life.

As we have seen, the means we have described are three in
5 number, and all are concerned with human relations in speech and in action. The difference between them is that one mean

[40] The comedy of the fifth century, of which Aristophanes' plays are our only complete representatives, was considerably rougher and less inhibited than the rather tame comedy, e.g., of Menander, of Aristotle's own day.

concerns truthfulness and the other two pleasantness.[41] Of the latter, one is found in amusement and the other in social relations in life in general.

9. Shame and shamelessness

It is incorrect to speak of a sense of shame as being a virtue   10
or excellence, for it resembles an emotion more than a characteristic. At any rate, it is defined as a kind of fear of disrepute, and the effect it produces is very much like that produced by fear of danger: people blush when they feel ashamed and turn pale when they fear death. Both these phenomena are of course in a sense physical, and that is held to be more typical of emotions than of characteristics.   15
The emotion of shame does not befit every stage of life but only youth. For we think that young people ought to be bashful because, living by their emotions as they do, they often go wrong and then shame inhibits them. We praise young people who have a sense of shame, but no one would praise an elderly man for being bashful, for we think he ought   20
not to do anything that will bring him shame. In fact, shame is not the mark of a decent man at all, since it is a consequence of base actions. Now, base actions should not be performed, regardless of whether they really are disgraceful or whether people merely think they are. In either case they ought not to be performed, and as a result, a man ought not to be ashamed. But a base man is even characterized by the   25
fact that he is the kind of person who would perform any disgraceful action. It is absurd for a man to believe himself actually to be decent because he is the kind of person who would be ashamed if he performed some such act. For shame is felt for voluntary actions, and no decent man will ever voluntarily do what is base. So it would appear that shame is conditionally good: a decent man will feel ashamed if he   30
were to act this way; but there is nothing conditional about

[41] The three means are those discussed in chaps. 6-8: truthfulness, friendliness, and wittiness.

the virtues. But if shamelessness, i.e., to act basely and not be ashamed of it, is base, it does not follow that it is decent for a man to act this way and then feel ashamed of it. For even moral strength is not a virtue but a mixed kind of character-
35 istic, as we shall show later on.[42] But let us now discuss justice.

[42] See VII. 1-10.

1. *The different kinds of justice; complete justice*

In studying justice and injustice,[1] we must examine the kind of actions with which they are concerned, what kind of mean justice is, and what the extremes are between which a just act occupies the median position. In this examination, we   5
shall follow the same system of investigation that we used in our preceding discussions.[2]

We see that all men mean by "justice" that characteristic which makes them performers of just actions, which makes them act justly, and which makes them wish what is just. The same applies to "injustice": it makes people act unjustly and   10
wish what is unjust. Let this general outline serve as our first basis of discussion. For what is true of the sciences and capacities is not true of characteristics.[3] As is well known, a given capacity, and also a given science, deals with a pair of opposites,[4] whereas a given characteristic is not related to anything that is opposite to itself. Health, for example, does not pro-   15

1 A few remarks about the meaning of *dikaiosynē* have been made in IV, note 3. Although much of Book V is devoted to a discussion of justice in a narrow, or what Aristotle calls "partial," sense, Aristotle remains ever conscious of the wider connotations of the term: 'justice' is for him the same as 'righteousness,' 'honesty.' It is, in short, the virtue which regulates all proper conduct within society, in the relations of individuals with one another, and to some extent even the proper attitude of an individual toward himself.

2 The system of investigation (*methodos*) in the *Ethics* is that of using opinions commonly held about a subject as the starting point of the discussion. See Introduction, pp. xx-xxi.

3 For these terms, see Glossary, *epistēmē, dynamis,* and *hexis.*

4 E.g., medicine deals with disease as well as health. Aristotle here makes the same point which Plato made, e.g., in *Republic* I. 333e-334b: if justice were a capacity or a science, the just man would actually turn out to be a clever thief.

111

duce effects opposite to health but only what is healthy: we say that a man has a healthy gait when he walks as a healthy man would.

Now, we often gain knowledge of (a) a characteristic by the opposite characteristic, and (b) of characteristics by those things in which they are exhibited. In other words, if (a) we can recognize a sound physical condition, we can also recog-
20 nize an unsound physical condition; and (b) a sound condition can be recognized from things that are in a sound condition and they from it. If, for example, firmness of flesh constitutes a sound physical condition, it necessarily follows (a) that an unsound physical condition consists in flabbiness of the flesh, and (b) that that which produces a sound physical condition causes firmness in the flesh. It follows as a general rule, ⟨to which there are exceptions, however,⟩ that if one term in a pair of opposites is used in more senses than one, the other
25 term, also, will be used in more than one sense. For example, if "just" is used in more senses than one, "unjust" will likewise have several senses.

Now, justice and injustice seem to be used in more than one sense, but because their different meanings are very close to one another, the ambiguity escapes notice and is less obvious than it is when the meanings are far apart, as it is, for example, if there is a great difference in external appearance: thus the word *kleis* is used ambiguously both of the "collar-
30 bone" beneath the neck of an animal and of the "key" with which we lock a door.[5] Let us, then, take the various senses in which we speak of an "unjust" man. We regard as unjust both a lawbreaker and also a man who is unfair and takes more than his share, so that obviously a law-abiding and a fair man will be just. Consequently, "just" is what is lawful and fair,
1129b and "unjust" is what is unlawful and unfair.

Since an unjust man is one who takes more than his share,

[5] If we wanted to give an example of this in English, we might speak of a 'key' that locks a door and a 'key' in which a piece of music is written.

he will be concerned with good things—not all good things, but only those which are involved in good and bad fortune. These are things which are always good in an unqualified sense, but which are not always good for a particular person. These are the things that men pray for and pursue, although they ought not to do so. They should rather pray that the things which are good in an unqualified sense may also be good for them; and they should choose what is good for them.

An unjust man does not always choose the larger share. When the choice is between things which are without qualification bad, he chooses the smaller. However, since the lesser evil seems in a sense to be good, and since taking a larger share means taking a larger share of the good, he seems to be a self-aggrandizer. He is unfair, for "unfair" includes and is common to both (taking more than one's share of the good and taking less than one's share of the bad).

Since a lawbreaker is, as we saw, unjust and a law-abiding man just, it is obvious that everything lawful is in a sense just. For "lawful" is what the art of legislation has defined as such, and we call each particular enactment "just." The laws make pronouncements on every sphere of life, and their aim is to secure either the common good of all or of the best, or the good of those who hold power either because of their excellence [6] or on some other basis of this sort. Accordingly, in one sense we call those things "just" which produce and preserve happiness for the social and political community. The law enjoins us to fulfill our function as brave men (e.g., not to abandon our post, not to flee, and not to throw away our arms), as self-controlled men (e.g., not to commit adultery or outrage), as gentle men (e.g., not to strike or defame anyone), and similarly with the other kinds of virtue and wickedness. It commands some things and forbids others, and it does so correctly when it is framed correctly, and not so well if it was drawn up in haste.

6 I retain the reading of the majority of manuscripts and do not follow Bywater in bracketing κατ' ἀρετήν.

Thus, this kind of justice is complete virtue or excellence, not in an unqualified sense, but in relation to our fellow men. And for that reason justice is regarded as the highest of all virtues, more admirable than morning star and evening star,[7] and, as the proverb has it, "In justice every virtue is summed

30 up."[8] It is complete virtue and excellence in the fullest sense, because it is the practice of complete virtue. It is complete because he who possesses it can make use of his virtue not only by himself but also in his relations with his fellow men; for there are many people who can make use of their virtue in their own affairs, but who are incapable of using it in their relations

1130a with others. Therefore, the saying of Bias[9] seems to be apt that "Ruling will show the man," for being a ruler already implies acting in relation to one's fellow men and within society. For the very same reason, justice alone of all the virtues is thought to be the good of another, because it is a relation to our fellow men in that it does what is of advantage

5 to others, either to a ruler or to a fellow member of society.[10] Now, the worst man is he who practices wickedness toward himself as well as his friends, but the best man is not one who practices virtue toward himself, but who practices it toward others, for that is a hard thing to achieve. Justice in this sense, then, is not a part of virtue but the whole of excellence or

10 virtue, and the injustice opposed to it is not part of vice but the whole of vice. The difference between virtue and justice in this sense is clear from what we have said. They are the same thing, but what they are ⟨in terms of their definition⟩ is

7 According to a scholiast, this is a quotation from Euripides' lost play *Melanippe*.

8 Quoted with a slight variation from Theognis, line 147.

9 Bias of Priene, who lived about the middle of the sixth century B.C., was one of the Seven Wise Men of Greece, a traditional group (some members varying) of statesmen and philosophers renowned for practical wisdom.

10 One of Thrasymachus' contentions in Plato's *Republic* I. 343c is that justice and the just are what is of advantage to another, viz., the ruler, but what brings harm to oneself.

not the same: [11] insofar as it is exhibited in relation to others it is justice, but insofar as it is simply a characteristic of this kind it is virtue.

2. *Partial justice: just action as distribution and as rectification*

What we are investigating, however, is justice as a part of virtue; for, we assert, there is such a thing as justice in this sense, as there is also injustice in this partial sense. 15.

An indication of its existence is this: in every other kind of wickedness, the man who practices it does wrong without getting a larger share, if, for example, he throws away his shield through cowardice or slanders another in a bad temper or refuses to give financial assistance because of his stinginess. But when he does get too large a share, it is frequently not in terms of any of these vices, nor even in terms of all of them, 20 but it certainly is in terms of some sort of baseness—for we blame him—and in terms of injustice. There exists, consequently, some other kind of injustice as a part of the injustice that comprises the whole of vice, and there is a sense in which we speak of "unjust" to express part of the unjust in the wider sense of "contrary to the law." Moreover, if one man commits adultery for profit and makes money on it, while another does it at the prompting of appetite and spends and 25 thus loses money on it, the latter would seem to be self-indulgent rather than grasping for a larger share, while the former is unjust but not self-indulgent, and obviously so because he makes a profit by it. Further, we usually ascribe all other offenses to some particular wickedness, e.g., adultery to self-indulgence, deserting a comrade-in-arms to cowardice, and 30

11 From J. A. Stewart, *Notes on the Nicomachean Ethics* (Oxford, 1892), Vol. I, p. 401: Virtue and universal justice, then, being the same state conceived from different points of view, virtue is the state conceived simply as a state; justice is the state conceived as putting its possessor in a certain relation to society.

assault to anger; but making unjust profit is not ascribed to any wickedness other than injustice.

It is, therefore, apparent that there exists, apart from the injustice that comprises the whole of vice, another partial kind of injustice which shares the name and nature of the first in that its definition falls within the same genus. The capacity of both is revealed in our relations with others, but while the sphere of the former is everything that is the concern of a morally good man, the latter deals with honor, material goods, security, or whatever single term we can find to express all these collectively, and its motive is the pleasure that comes from profit.

It is, accordingly, clear that there is more than one kind of justice, and that there exists a justice distinct from that which comprises the whole of virtue. We must now take up the problem of what it is and what qualities it has.

We drew a distinction between unjust in the sense of "unlawful" and in the sense of "unfair," and between just in the sense of "lawful" and in the sense of "fair." Now, the injustice we discussed above corresponds to the sense of "unlawful." But "unfair" and "unlawful" are not identical but distinct and related to one another as the part is related to the whole; for everything unfair is unlawful, but not everything unlawful is unfair. Therefore, the unjust and injustice in the partial sense, too, are distinct from the unjust and injustice in the complete sense; for the partial kind of injustice is part of complete injustice, and similarly partial justice is part of complete justice. We must, accordingly, discuss partial justice and partial injustice, and also the just and the unjust in the partial sense.

So let us dismiss that justice which is coextensive with the whole of virtue as well as its corresponding injustice, as the one consists in the exercise of the whole of virtue in our relations with our fellow men and the other in the exercise of the whole of vice. Likewise, it is clear how we must determine the terms "just" and "unjust" which correspond to

them. For the great majority of lawful acts are ordinances
which are based on virtue as a whole: the law commands to
live in conformity with every virtue and forbids to live in
conformity with any wickedness. What produces virtue entire
are those lawful measures which are enacted for education in   25
citizenship. We must determine later [12] whether the education
of the individual as such, which makes a person good simply
as a man, is part of politics or of some other science. For being
a good man is perhaps not the same as being a good citizen of
some particular kind of state, whatever it may be.

One form of partial justice and of what is just in this sense   30
is found in the distribution of honors, of material goods, or of
anything else that can be divided among those who have a
share in the political system. For in these matters it is possible
for a man to have a share equal or unequal [13] to that of his
neighbor. A second kind of just action in the partial sense
has a rectifying function in private transactions, and it is   1131a
divided into two parts: (a) voluntary and (b) involuntary
transactions.[14] (a) Voluntary transactions are, for example, sale,
purchase, lending at interest, giving security, lending without
interest, depositing in trust, and letting for hire. They are
called "voluntary" because the initiative in these transactions   5
is voluntary. (b) Some involuntary transactions are clandestine,
e.g., theft, adultery, poisoning, procuring, enticement of slaves,
assassination, and bearing false witness; while others happen
under constraint, e.g., assault, imprisonment, murder, violent
robbery, maiming, defamation, and character-smearing.

12 See X. 9. The problem is also discussed in *Politics* III. 4; 5; 18; VII.
14; and VIII. 1.
13 The terms *isos* and *anisos*, translated by 'equal' and 'unequal' here,
have a much wider sense than their English equivalents. They are, in
fact, the same terms that we translated as 'fair' and 'unfair' above; and
it is for this reason that 'unfair' ('unequal') has as its natural synonym
pleonektēs, 'having more than one's share.'
14 See p. 52, note 1, for the meaning of these terms: a voluntary transaction is one undertaken with the consent of both parties involved; in an
involuntary transaction the consent is only unilateral.

3. *Just action as fairness in distribution*

10   Since an unjust man and an unjust act are unfair or unequal, it is obvious that there exists also a median term between the two extremes of inequality. This is the fair or equal. For any action that admits of a more and a less also admits of an equal. Now if the unjust is unequal, the just must be equal; and that is, in fact, what everyone believes without argument.[15] Since the equal is a median, the just, too, will be a median. Now the
15   equal involves at least two terms.[16] Accordingly, the just is necessarily both median and equal, and it is relative, and ⟨it is just⟩ for certain individuals. Inasmuch as it is median, it must be median between some extremes, i.e., between the more and the less; inasmuch as it is equal, it involves two shares that are equal; and inasmuch as it is just, it must be just for certain parties. Consequently, the just involves at least
20   four terms: there are two persons in whose eyes it is just, and the shares which are just are two.

Also, there will be the same equality between the persons and the shares: the ratio between the shares will be the same as that between the persons.[17] If the persons are not equal, their ⟨just⟩ shares will not be equal; but this is the source of quarrels and recriminations, when equals have and are awarded unequal shares or unequals equal shares. The truth of this is further illustrated by the principle "To each
25   according to his deserts." Everyone agrees that in distributions the just share must be given on the basis of what one deserves,

[15] See p. 117, note 13.

[16] I.e., we can speak of equality only if a thing is equal to something else.

[17] Stewart's note on this passage (*Notes on the Nicomachean Ethics,* Vol. I, p. 421) is illuminating: ". . . if the persons, as comparable [participants] of the same social system, are absolutely equal, their shares will be also absolutely equal: if they are not absolutely equal, but stand in a certain definite ratio of superiority and inferiority, their shares will also stand in the same ratio."

though not everyone would name the same criterion of deserving: democrats say it is free birth, oligarchs that it is wealth or noble birth, and aristocrats that it is excellence.

Consequently, the just is something proportionate, for proportion is not only applicable to abstract number, but also to number in a generalized sense. Proportion is equality of ratios and involves at least four terms. That a "discrete proportion" [18] involves four terms is obvious; but the same is also true of a "continuous proportion," for it uses one term as though it were two and mentions it twice, e.g., line x : line y = line y : line z. Here line y is mentioned twice, so that there will be four proportionate terms if line y is taken twice. The just, too, involves at least four terms, and the ratio ⟨between the terms of one pair⟩ is equal ⟨to that between the terms of the other⟩, for the persons and things are similarly distributed. Therefore, $A : B = c : d$ and, by alternation, $A : c = B : d$.[19] It also follows that one whole, ⟨i.e., person plus share,⟩ will stand in the same ratio to the other ⟨whole, as person stands to person⟩.[20] This is the union of terms that distribution ⟨of honors, wealth, etc.⟩ brings about, and if it is effected in this manner, the union is just. Consequently, the combination of term ⟨person⟩ A with term ⟨share⟩ c and of term ⟨person⟩ B with term ⟨share⟩ d in the distribution is just, and this kind of the just is median while the corresponding unjust violates the proportion.[21] For the proportional is median, and the just is proportional. Mathematicians call this kind of proportion

30

1131b

5

10

---

18 E.g., $a : b = c : d$. "Continuous proportion," in Aristotle's sense of the word, is explained below. In modern mathematics, this kind of proportion is treated merely as a special case of what Aristotle calls a "discrete proportion." One might add that both terms, discrete and continuous, as used in present-day mathematics, have a totally different meaning unrelated to the problems of proportion.

19 For the sake of clarity, I use capital letters for the persons and small letters for the things.

20 I.e., $(A + c) : (B + d) = A : B$.

21 In other words, just distribution matches the right person with the right share.

"geometrical," since in geometrical proportion one whole is to the other as either part is to its corresponding part.[22] But 15 ⟨the just⟩ is not a continuous proportion, for in fact the person and his share cannot coincide in one single term.

The just, then, in this sense is the proportional, and the unjust is what violates the proportion. Consequently, the unjust admits of a more and a less, and this is what takes place in actual fact: a man who acts unjustly has more than his share of good, and a man who is treated unjustly has less. The 20 reverse is true in the case of evil: for in relation to a greater evil the lesser evil counts as a good, since the lesser evil is more desirable than the greater, and since what is desirable is good and what is more desirable is a greater good. This, then, is one kind of what is just.

4. *Just action as rectification*

25   The one remaining form of what is just is the rectifying kind, which we find in transactions both voluntary and involuntary. The just in this sense is different in kind from the former. What is just in the distribution of common goods ⟨such as honor and wealth⟩ always follows the proportion we have described.[23] If it is a distribution of common funds, it will 30 follow the same ratio in which the contributions of the various members stand to one another; and the unjust opposed to just in this sense is that which violates the proportion. Now the just in transactions is also something equal (and the unjust something unequal), but ⟨it is something equal⟩ which 1132a corresponds not to a geometrical but to an arithmetical proportion.[24] It makes no difference whether a decent man has

[22] Modern mathematicians do not use the term "geometrical proportion" in this sense.

[23] I.e., the "geometrical proportion" described in the preceding chapter.

[24] What Aristotle calls "arithmetical proportion" is best explained by Burnet. An "arithmetical proportion" is for us not a proportion at all but a series in an arithmetical progression. In it the first term is larger

defrauded a bad man or vice versa, or whether it was a decent
or a bad man who committed adultery. The only difference
the law considers is that brought about by the damage: it
treats the parties as equals and asks only whether one has done 5
and the other has suffered wrong, and whether one has done
and the other has suffered damage. As the unjust in this
sense is inequality, the judge tries to restore the equilibrium.
When one man has inflicted and another received a wound,
or when one man has killed and the other has been killed, the
doing and suffering are unequally divided; by inflicting a loss
on the offender, the judge tries to take away his gain and restore
the equilibrium. For in involuntary transactions we use the 10
term "gain" without any qualification, even though it is not
the proper term in some instances (e.g., when a person has
inflicted a wound), and we use the term "loss" in a similar
way when he is the sufferer. But, at any rate, we do speak of
"loss" and "gain" whenever the damage sustained can be
measured. Thus, the equal occupies the middle position between the more and the less. But gain and loss are a more 15
and a less, respectively, in opposite ways: more good or less
evil are gain, and the reverse is loss. The median between
them, as we saw, is the equal or fair which, we assert, is just.
The just as a corrective is, therefore, a median between loss
and gain. That is the reason why people have recourse to a

---

than the second by the same amount by which the third term is larger
than the fourth: $a - b = c - d$. It is "something equal" because in such proportions the sum of the means is equal to the sum of the extremes: $a + d =$
$b + c$. Its application here is well stated by Ross, *Ethica Nicomachea* (Oxford, 1925), in his note on this passage:

> The problem of "rectificatory justice" has nothing to do with punish-
> ment proper but is only that of rectifying a wrong that has been done,
> by awarding damages; i.e., rectificatory justice is that of the civil, not
> that of the criminal courts. The parties are treated as equal (since a law
> court is not a court of morals), and the wrongful act is reckoned as
> having brought equal gain to the wrongdoer and loss to his victim; it
> brings A to the position $A + C$, and B to the position $B - C$. The judge's
> task is to find the arithmetical mean between these, and this he does
> by transferring C from A to B. . . .

20 judge when they are engaged in a dispute. To go to a judge
means to go to the just, for to be a judge means, as it were, to
be the embodiment of what is just. They seek out a judge
who will be midway between them—some ⟨states⟩, in fact, call
judges "mediators"—in the belief that they will get what is
just if they get what is median. This is another indication that
the just is a kind of median, since a judge, too, may be described as mediating.

25 The judge restores equality. As though there were a line
divided into two unequal parts, he takes away the amount
by which the larger part is greater than half the line and
adds it to the smaller. Only when the whole has been divided
into two equal parts can a man say that he has what is properly his, i.e., when he has taken an equal part. The equal
is median between the greater and the smaller according to
30 arithmetical proportion.[25] That is the reason why the just has
its name, dikaion: it is a division into two equal parts (dicha),
as if we were to call it dichaion and the judge dichastēs, ⟨i.e.,
he who divides in two,⟩ instead of dikastēs.[26] For when x amount
is subtracted from one of two equals and added to the other, the
other will be larger by 2 x; if x had been subtracted from the
one but had not been added to the other, the other would
1132b have been larger only by x. Consequently, it is x larger
than the median, and the median is x larger than the unit
from which the subtraction was made. Accordingly, we can
use this procedure to ascertain both what we must subtract
from the party that has too much, and what we must add to
the party that has too little: we must add to the party that
5 has too little that amount by which the median is larger and
subtract from the greatest [27] the amount by which the median
is smaller. Let lines AA', BB', and CC' be equal to one an-

[25] See the preceding note.
[26] According to Alexander of Aphrodisias (ca. A.D. 200), an ancient
commentator on Aristotle, this rather fanciful and incorrect etymology
goes back to the Pythagoreans.
[27] The superlative is used because three terms are involved: the lesser,
the greater, and the median.

other; [28] subtract AE from AA' and add it to CC' as DC, so that the whole line DCC' is larger than EA' by $DC + CF$. DCC' is, therefore, larger than BB' by DC.[29]

The terms "loss" and "gain" we have been using come from voluntary exchange. To possess more than what was one's own ⟨previously⟩ is called "making a gain," and to have less than one started out with is called "incurring a loss," e.g., in buying, selling, and all other transactions in which the law per- 15 mits to the agent freedom of action. But when neither party has more or less but exactly what they had contributed to the transaction, they say that they have their own without loss and without gain. In the same way, the just in involuntary transactions occupies the median between a gain and a loss: it is to have an equal amount both before and after the transaction. 20

5. Just action as reciprocity in the economic life of the state

Some people believe with the Pythagoreans that the just in the unqualified sense is reciprocity,[30] for the Pythagoreans used to define the just without any qualification as "suffering that which one has done to another." Now, reciprocity corre-

28

EA' represents the lesser, DCC' the greater, and BB' the median, i.e., the just amount.

29 After this, all the manuscripts carry a sentence which is identical with chap. 5, 1133a14-16: "This is true of the other arts as well: they would disappear, if there were not a relationship between an active and a passive element such that the one performs and the other undergoes 10 precisely the same thing, of the same quantity and the same quality." Although the sentence is difficult in either context, it is more out of place here and probably entered the manuscript tradition by mistake.

30 The term translated 'reciprocity' (antipeponthos) means literally 'suffering in return for one's action' and comes close to the concepts of "an eye for an eye" and "let the punishment fit the crime."

sponds neither to just action as distribution nor to just action
25   as rectification; [31] and yet people interpret even Rhadamanthys' rule of the just in this sense: "If he suffers what he committed, then justice will be straight." [32] For there are many
cases in which reciprocity and the just are not identical, e.g.,
if a magistrate, while in office, strikes a man, he should not be
struck in return, and if someone strikes a magistrate, he should
not only be struck in return but should, in addition, be pun-
30   ished. Moreover, there is a great difference between voluntary
and involuntary action.

But in associations that are based on mutual exchange, the
just in this sense constitutes the bond that holds the association together, that is, reciprocity in terms of a proportion and
not in terms of exact equality in the return. For it is the reciprocal return of what is proportional ⟨to what one has re-
ceived⟩ that holds the state together. People seek either to
requite evil with evil—for otherwise their relation is regarded
1133a   as that of slaves—or good with good, for otherwise there is no
mutual contribution. And it is by their mutual contribution
that men are held together. That is the reason why ⟨the state⟩
erects a sanctuary of the Graces in a prominent place, in order
to promote reciprocal exchange. For that is the proper province of gratitude: we should return our services to one who
5   has done us a favor, and at another time take the initiative in
doing him a favor.[33]

Reciprocal exchange in the right proportion is determined

---

[31] This becomes clear if we remember that distribution is "geometri-
cally" proportionate and depends on the merit of the parties concerned,
while the loss and gain in rectification have to be measured by the
judge in every instance.

[32] Rhadamanthys, the son of Zeus and Europa, did not die but went
to Elysium, where he continues to administer the justice for which he
was famous on earth. An ancient commentator attributes the verse quoted
here to Hesiod (frg. 174 Rzach).

[33] The Greek word for 'grace,' *charis*, also embodies the notions of
'gratitude' and 'favor.' According to the famous traveller Pausanias (*fl.*
A.D. 150), many Greek cities, including Sparta, Orchomenus, and Olympia,
had prominent sanctuaries to the Graces (*Charites*).

by diagonal combination of terms. Let A be a builder, B a shoemaker, c a house, and d a shoe. Now, the builder must take the shoemaker's product from the shoemaker and give him part of his own product.[34] Thus, if (1) proportional equality is established between the goods, and (2) reciprocity effected, the fair exchange we spoke of will be realized. But if there is no proportionality, the exchange is not equal and fair, and ⟨the association of the two will⟩ not hold together. For there is nothing to prevent the product of the one from being greater than that of the other, and they must, therefore, be equalized. This is true of the other arts as well: they would disappear if there were not a relationship between an active and a passive element such that the one performs and the other undergoes precisely the same thing of the same quantity and the same quality. For a community is not formed by two physicians, but by a physician and a farmer, and, in general, by people who are different and unequal. But they must be equalized; and hence everything that enters into an exchange must somehow be comparable.

It is for this purpose that money has been introduced: it becomes, as it were, a middle term. For it measures all things, ⟨not only their equality but⟩ also the amount by which they exceed or fall short ⟨of one another⟩. Thus it tells us how many shoes are equal to a house or to a given quantity of food. The relation between builder and shoemaker must, therefore, correspond to the relation between a given amount of shoes and a house or a quantity of food. For if it does not, there will

[34] The following diagram will explain what Aristotle means by diagonal combination of terms:

The product (c) of the builder (A) goes to the shoemaker (B), and the product (d) of the shoemaker (B) goes to the builder (A) in this reciprocal exchange.

be no exchange and no community. And the relation will not
25   be the same unless the goods are somehow equal. Consequently, all goods must be measured by some single standard,
as stated earlier, and that standard is, in fact, need, which
holds everything together (in a community). For if men were
to require nothing, or were not to require things equally, there
would be no exchange or not the same kind of exchange. Now,
money has by general agreement come to represent need. That
30   is why it has the name of "currency": it exists by current convention [35] and not by nature, and it is in our power to change
and invalidate it.

Thus, reciprocity will be attained when the terms have been
equalized, and when, as a result, the product of the shoemaker
is to the product of the farmer as the farmer is to the shoemaker.
1133b   But the figure of the proportion must not be drawn up after
the exchange has taken place (else one extreme will have both
excesses), but when each side still has possession of its own
product.[36] In this way, they are equal and members of the
community, since this kind of equality can be established in

[35] The Greek word for 'money,' 'coin,' 'currency' (*nomisma*) comes
from the same root as *nomos*, 'law,' 'convention.'

[36] The meaning of this rather awkward sentence seems to be the following. Aristotle has stated above (see p. 125, note 34) that reciprocal
exchange is determined by diagonal combination of terms. This is the
figure of proportion that must be established before (not after) the
exchange takes place. If a builder (A) and a shoemaker (B) are to exchange their products, a house (c) and shoes (d), the just amount of
reciprocity can only be ascertained by finding an equivalent (in terms
of need = money) between shoes and house, so that $c = xd$, for only in
that way can A and B be regarded as equal parties to the exchange. Thus
the figure of proportion is $A:B = xd:c$, and the value of x must be established before the exchange, while A still has the house and B still has
the shoes. For if no previous equation is established between c and d, B
will get one house for one pair of shoes, so that he, being one extreme
in the exchange, will have both excesses: he will not only have the house,
which is worth more than the pair of shoes he has given for it, but he
will also have all those shoes (minus the one pair he has given) which
would be the true equivalent of the house. Unfortunately, Aristotle gives
us no hint about the way in which such equivalences are to be established.

their case. Let A be a farmer, c food, B a shoemaker, and d his
product equalized to c. If it were impossible to establish reci- 5
procity between them in this manner, a community or association between them would be impossible. That it is need which
holds the parties together as if they were one single unit is
shown by the fact that there is no exchange when one or both
parties do not stand in need of the other. For example, ⟨no
exchange takes place⟩ when someone needs what we do not
have, e.g., wine, and we can only offer him the privilege of ex-
porting grain.[37] Consequently, in a case like this, equality ⟨of 10
need⟩ must be established.

Now it is money which gives us a guarantee of future exchange. If we need nothing at the moment, it guarantees that
exchange will take place when the need arises. For when we
bring money, it must be possible to get what we need. ⟨But it
is true that⟩ what happens to goods also happens to money,
i.e., it does not always have equal value. Still, it tends to be
constant. Therefore, the price of all goods should be fixed, for
in that way there will always be exchange, and if there is ex- 15
change there is a community. Thus, money acts like a measure: it makes goods commensurable and equalizes them. For
just as there is no community without exchange, there is no
exchange without equality and no equality without commen-
surability.

Now, of course it is impossible that things differing so
greatly from one another should in reality become commensurable. But it can be done adequately by relating them to 20
need. Accordingly, there must be some unit, and it must be
established by arbitrary usage—hence the name "currency."[38]
This unit makes everything commensurable, for everything is
measured by money. Let a be a house, b ten minae, and c a

---

37 The meaning of this passage is obscure, and a fully satisfactory
explanation seems impossible. The easiest way out of the difficulties is to
follow Münscher, Burnet, and Gauthier-Jolif in inserting οὐκ before ἔχει.
But this creates a new problem in that it compels us to treat αὐτός and
τις as referring to different parties.

38 Cf. p. 126, note 35.

bed. If the house is worth five minae, or equal to five minae,
25 $a = b/2$; the bed c, ⟨if its value is one mina,⟩ is $b/10$. It is, therefore, obvious how many beds are equal to one house, namely
five. Clearly, this is the way in which exchange took place before the existence of money, for it makes no difference whether
five beds or the money value of five beds is the equivalent of a
house.

We have discussed what the unjust is and what the just is.
Now that they have been differentiated from one another, it
30 is clear that just action is median between acting unjustly and
suffering unjustly: the one is having too much and the other
is having too little. Justice is a sort of mean, not in the same
way as the other virtues are, but in that it is realized in a me-
1134a dian amount, while injustice belongs to the extremes. Moreover, justice is that quality in terms of which we can say of a
just man that he practices by choice what is just, and that, in
making distribution between himself and another, or between
two others, he will not give himself the larger and his neighbor
the smaller share of what is desirable (and vice versa in dis-
5 tributing what is harmful), but he will give an equal share as
determined by proportion, and he will act in the same way in
distributing between two others. Injustice, on the other hand,
is the quality similarly related to what is unjust,[39] and the unjust is an excess and a deficiency of what is helpful and harmful, and it violates proportion. Injustice is, therefore, excess
and deficiency, because it tends toward excess and deficiency:
10 in one's own case toward an excess of what is in itself helpful
and toward a deficiency of what is harmful; in the case of distribution among others, although the result is by and large the
same, the violation of proportion may take place in either direction. Of the offenses the lesser is to suffer unjustly and the
greater to act unjustly. So much for our discussion of the na-
15 ture of justice and injustice, and also of the just and the unjust in their general sense.

[39] In other words, injustice is the characteristic which makes us say
that an unjust man acts through choice of what is unjust.

6. *What is just in the political sense*

Since a man who acts unjustly is not *ipso facto* unjust, what
kind of offenses must a man commit to be marked as unjust,
in each of the various senses of injustice, for instance, to be
marked as a thief, an adulterer, or a robber? Certainly, the
fact that the offense has been committed does not make any
difference: a man might have sexual intercourse with a woman
knowing who she is, but the motive that initiated the act   20
might be emotion and not choice. He acts unjustly, but he is
not unjust. In other words, a man may have stolen but not be
a thief, and he may have committed adultery but not be an
⟨habitual⟩ adulterer, and so forth.[40]

We stated earlier the relation between reciprocity and the
just.[41] But we must not forget that we are looking both for
what is just in an unqualified sense and for what is just in   25
social and political matters. The just in political matters is
found among men who share a common life in order that their
association bring them self-sufficiency, and who are free and
equal, either proportionately or arithmetically.[42] Hence, in a
society where this is not the case, there is nothing just in the
political sense in the relations of the various members to one
another, but there is only something which bears a resemblance to what is just. For the just exists only among men
whose mutual relationship is regulated by law, and law exists   30
where injustice may occur. For legal judgment decides and

[40] The subject matter of this paragraph is more germane to the
problems discussed below in chaps. 8-9 than to the problems of chaps. 6-7.
Why it is inserted here is hard to determine. Perhaps it is merely intended as a general reminder—which might be inserted almost anywhere
—that justice, like all the other virtues, depends on choice.

[41] See the beginning of chap. 5 above.

[42] The citizens of an aristocracy are proportionately equal in that
the honor and civic rights of each depend on his merit, while those of
a democracy are arithmetically equal because every freeborn citizen has
one and the same vote, and, in the Athenian democracy, equal access to
public office.

distinguishes between what is just and what is unjust. Where there is injustice there is also unjust action—although unjust action does not always imply that there is injustice—and unjust action means to assign to oneself too much of things intrinsically good and too little of things intrinsically evil.

35 That is why we do not allow the rule of a man but the rule of reason, because a man takes too large a share for himself and

1134b becomes a tyrant. A ⟨true⟩ ruler, however, is the guardian of what is just, and as such he is also the guardian of equality and fairness. We think of a just ruler as one who does not get more than his share. He does not assign to himself a larger share of what is intrinsically good, unless such a share is proportionate to his deserts. His labor is, therefore, for the bene-

5 fit of others, and for this reason justice is called "another's good," as we stated above.[43] Consequently, he must be given some recompense, and this consists in honor and privilege. Those for whom this is not adequate recompense become tyrants.

What is just for the master of a slave and just for a father is similar to, but not identical with, the politically just. There can be no unqualified injustice in one's relation to what is his

10 own: a piece of property, ⟨i.e., a slave,⟩ and a child are part of one's person, as it were, until ⟨the latter⟩ reaches a certain age and becomes independent, and no one would deliberately desire to harm himself. For the same reason, there is no such thing as injustice toward oneself, and it follows that what is politically unjust and just does not apply here. For the politically just, as we saw, depends upon law and applies to people who have a natural capacity for law, that is people who have

15 the requisite equality in ruling and being ruled. Hence, just action is sooner possible toward one's wife than to one's children and property. For what is just toward one's wife is what is just in household management ⟨where husband and wife share as equals⟩. But even this is different from what is just in social and political matters.

43 Cf. chap. 1, 1130a3-5, with note 10.

7. *Just by nature and just by convention*

What is just in the political sense can be subdivided into what is just by nature and what is just by convention. What is by nature just has the same force everywhere and does not depend on what we regard or do not regard as just. In what is just by convention, on the other hand, it makes originally no   20
difference whether it is fixed one way or another, but it does make a difference once it is fixed, for example, that a prisoner's ransom shall be one mina, or that a sacrifice shall consist of a goat but not of two sheep, and all the other measures enacted for particular occasions (such as the sacrifice offered to Brasidas) [44] and everything enacted by decree. Now, some people [45] think that everything just exists only by convention, since whatever is by nature is unchangeable and has the same   25
force everywhere—as, for example, fire burns both here and in Persia—whereas they see that notions of what is just change. But this is not the correct view, although it has an element of truth. Among the gods, to be sure, it is probably not true at all, but among us there are things which, though naturally just, are nevertheless changeable, as are all things human. Yet in spite of that, there are some things that are just by nature   30
and others not by nature. It is not hard to see among the things which admit of being other than they are, which ones are by nature and which ones not by nature but by convention or agreement, although both kinds are equally subject to change. The same distinction will fit other matters as well: by nature, the right hand is the stronger, and yet it is possible for any man to become ambidextrous. What is just as determined   35

---

[44] After the brilliant Spartan general Brasidas had been killed while liberating Amphipolis from Athenian control in 422 B.C., the people of Amphipolis worshipped him as a hero with annual games and sacrifices in his honor; cf. Thucydides V. 11.

[45] Aristotle no doubt has some of the Sophists in mind; see in particular the fragment of the Sophist Antiphon (frg. 44A DK[6]) and the speech of Callicles in Plato's *Gorgias* 482c-486d.

1135a   by agreement and advantage is like measures: measures for
wine and for grain are not equal everywhere; they are larger
where people buy and smaller where they sell.[46] In the same
way, what is just not by nature but by human enactment is
no more the same everywhere than constitutions are. Yet there
5 is only one constitution that is by nature the best everywhere.
Each notion of what is just and lawful stands in the same
relation ⟨to a just and lawful act⟩ as the universal to the particular. For there are many specific acts, but only one thing in
each case that is just, viz., the universal. There is a difference
between an act of injustice and what is unjust and between an
act of justice and what is just. The unjust exists by nature or
10 by enactment. When it is performed, it is an act of injustice;
before being performed it was not an act of injustice but simply unjust. The same is true for an act of justice, although
strictly speaking the general term is "just act," and "act of
justice" is reserved for the rectification of an act of injustice.[47]

---

[46] The interpretation of this passage given by all modern commentators—most recently by R. A. Gauthier and J. Y. Jolif, *L'Éthique à
Nicomaque*, Vol. II, Part 1, pp. 395-96—is that Aristotle is thinking of
something like wholesale and retail trade: a wholesaler, it is argued,
would buy wine by the gallon and a retailer would sell it by the pint.
However, since the πανταχοῦ ('everywhere'), as it is used twice in the next
sentence, makes it clear that Aristotle is not thinking of transactions in the
same city but in different cities, this interpretation becomes untenable.
What Aristotle seems to mean is that in states where the citizens are
buyers rather than sellers of a given commodity, e.g., grain, the official
measures tend to be on the large side, since evidently buyers in Greece
wanted to make their units of purchase as large as possible; while in
states where grain was sold rather than bought, the measures would
tend to be smaller. In Athens, for example, where the citizens would
usually buy rather than sell grain, a *medimnos* would be larger than
what would be called *medimnos* in Sicily, where the citizens would be
more likely to sell than to buy grain.

[47] This discussion of proper Greek usage—*dikaiōma* ('act of justice'),
which is used of a judicial act in which a wrong is rectified, in place of
dikaiopragēma ('just act')—cannot be successfully imitated in English. The
point is that, in order to find a verbal counterpoint to *adikēma* ('act of
injustice,' 'unjust act'), Aristotle uses *dikaiōma* in a sense which is not
sanctioned by good Greek usage.

But we must postpone until later an examination of the various kinds of acts of justice and of injustice, and also of their number and the sphere in which they operate.[48]

8. The various degrees of responsibility for just and unjust action

Now that we have described what is just and unjust, we can say that a man acts unjustly and justly when he performs such acts voluntarily. When he performs them involuntarily, he acts neither unjustly nor justly except in an incidental way, inasmuch as he performs acts which happen to be just or unjust. The unjust and the just act are defined by the voluntary and the involuntary.[49] For when a deed is voluntary it is blamed, and it is then at the same time an unjust act. Thus it will be possible for a deed to be unjust without yet being an "unjust act" [50] if the element of voluntariness is absent. By a voluntary act, as has been stated earlier,[51] I mean an act which lies in the agent's power to perform, performed by the agent in full knowledge and without ignorance either of the person acted on, the instrument used, or the result intended by his action. He must know, for example, whom he is striking, with what instrument, and what result he intends to achieve. Moreover, no voluntary act is performed incidentally or under constraint. For example, if A takes B's hand and strikes C, B does not act voluntarily, since the act was not in his power. A man may possibly strike his father, realizing that he is striking a man or a bystander, but without knowing that it is his father whom he is striking. A similar distinction can be drawn as re-

15

20

25

30

48 This promise is not fulfilled in any of the extant writings of Aristotle.

49 Aristotle does not mean that just action is voluntary and unjust involuntary, or vice versa, but that actions which are essentially just and unjust must be voluntary, while involuntary acts can be just or unjust only incidentally.

50 Throughout this context, *adikēma* or 'unjust act' is used for an action whose injustice is not incidental but essential.

51 See III. 1, 1111a3-b3.

gards the result intended and the action as a whole. Thus, acts
which are performed in ignorance or which, though not in
ignorance, are not in the agent's power or are performed under constraint are involuntary. For in fact there are many
1135b   natural processes that we perform or undergo in full knowledge, none of which is either voluntary or involuntary, for example, growing old or dying.

The incidental sense may likewise apply to unjust and just
action. A man might return a deposit involuntarily and
5   through fear, so that we cannot say that he does what is just
or acts justly, except incidentally. Similarly, we can say that a
man acts unjustly and does what is unjust only incidentally
when he fails to return a deposit under compulsion and involuntarily. We perform some voluntary acts by choice and
others not by choice. We perform them by choice when we
10   deliberate in advance, but actions which have not been previously deliberated upon are not performed by choice.[52]

Thus there are three types of injury that occur in communities and associations: (1) injuries committed in ignorance are
mistakes, when the person affected, the act, the instrument, or
result are not what the agent supposed they were. He thought
he was not hitting anyone, or not with that particular missile,
or not that particular person, or not for this purpose, but a
15   result was obtained which he had not intended (for example,
if ⟨a dueller⟩ did not intend to wound but merely to prick) or
the person or the missile were not what he thought they were.
(2) When the injury inflicted happens contrary to reasonable
expectation, it is a mishap; when it happens not contrary to
reasonable expectation, but without malice, it is a mistake. In
the case of a mistake, the source of responsibility lies within
the agent; in a mishap the initiative lies outside him. (3)
When the injury is inflicted in full knowledge but without
20   previous deliberation, it is an unjust act, for example, any act
due to anger or to any other unavoidable or natural emotion
to which human beings are subject. For when people inflict

52 See III. 1, 1112a14-17.

these injuries and commit these mistakes, they act unjustly, to
be sure, and what they perform are unjust acts. Still, they are
not *ipso facto* unjust or wicked for committing these acts, since
the injury inflicted is not due to wickedness. But when a man
acts from choice, he is unjust and wicked.[53] 25

That is why acts due to anger are rightly judged not to be
committed with malice aforethought. The initiative rests not
with the man who acts in anger but with him who provokes
it. Moreover, the issue is not whether the act took place or not
but whether it was just; for feelings of anger are aroused by
an apparent injustice. ⟨In such a case, people⟩ do not dispute
facts as they do in private transcations, where one of the 30
parties must necessarily be a scoundrel, unless they disagree
because they have forgotten the facts;[54] but they agree about
the facts and dispute which side has acted justly (a man who
has deliberately inflicted an injury is well aware that he has
done so), so that one party thinks he has been wronged, while
the other denies it.

However, if a man harms another by choice, he acts un- 1136a
justly, and it is this kind of unjust act which makes the agent
an unjust man if he acts against proportion or equality. Similarly, a man is just if he performs just acts by choice, but his
action is just if only it is voluntary.[55]

Some involuntary acts are pardonable and others are not. 5
Wrongs which are not only performed in ignorance but actually
due to ignorance are pardonable; but they are not pardonable

---

[53] This would seem to constitute a fourth kind of injury, but in fact
it does not. Like (3) it is an unjust act, but while (3) was unjust incidentally, this kind of act is essentially unjust.

[54] If *A* claims and *B* denies that a certain transaction took place or
that certain promises were made, one of them must necessarily be a liar,
unless he has forgotten the facts.

[55] Thus Aristotle returns once more to the distinction drawn at the
beginning of chap. 6 between a just act, which implies only knowledge
and intent of the agent, and justice as a characteristic of agents, which
requires not only knowledge and intent, but also deliberation followed by
conscious choice.

if, although done in ignorance, they are due not to ignorance but to some emotion which is neither natural nor typical of men.[56]

9. Voluntariness and involuntariness in just and unjust action and suffering

10   But the problem remains whether we have drawn our distinctions in the matter of acting and suffering unjustly with sufficient stringency. In the first place, we may ask whether there is any truth in what Euripides has expressed in the strange words:

A: I killed my mother, brief is my report.
B: Were you both willing, or neither she nor you?[57]

15   Is it really possible that a person voluntarily submits to unjust treatment, or is, on the contrary, all unjust treatment suffered involuntarily, just as every unjust act is performed voluntarily? Is all unjust treatment undergone voluntarily or is it all undergone involuntarily? Or do we suffer it sometimes voluntarily and sometimes involuntarily? The same applies to undergoing just treatment: all just action is performed voluntarily, so that it makes sense that acting and being treated
20   (justly or unjustly) should be similarly opposed to one another, and that we should either voluntarily or involuntarily undergo both unjust and just treatment. Yet it would seem strange if we were to receive all just treatment voluntarily, for some people are treated justly without being willing.

[56] Throughout this discussion of involuntary injustice or wrongdoing, one should bear in mind Aristotle's description of Oedipus in *Poetics* 13, 1453a7-17, as a man whose wrongdoing was not due to wickedness but to a "great error" (*hamartia*, cf. the *hamartēma* or 'mistake' enumerated as the first type of injury at 1135b12, above). It seems very likely that Aristotle has Oedipus in mind when he speaks of a man who strikes his father "without knowing that it is his father whom he is striking" (1135a28). This chapter thus sheds some light on what Aristotle says about the character of the tragic hero in the *Poetics*—and inversely.

[57] The quotation probably comes from Euripides' lost *Alcmaeon*, which Aristotle also cites in III. 1, 1110a28-29 with note 2.

Secondly, we might also raise the question whether every person who has suffered something unjust is receiving unjust treatment, or whether the situation is the same in suffering as it is in doing. For it is possible to participate in a just act incidentally, whether as doer or recipient, and the same is obviously also true of an unjust act. Doing unjust things is not the same as acting unjustly, and suffering something unjust is not the same as receiving unjust treatment; and the same applies to acting justly and receiving just treatment.[58] It is impossible to receive unjust treatment unless someone acts unjustly, or to receive just treatment unless someone acts justly.

But if acting unjustly in its widest sense means to harm a person voluntarily, whereas "voluntarily" means knowing the person affected, the instrument, and the manner of acting; and if a morally weak man voluntarily harms himself, it would follow that he suffers unjust treatment voluntarily, and that it is possible for a man to act unjustly toward himself. (Here we have one more problem, namely whether it is possible to act unjustly toward oneself.)[59] Moreover, moral weakness might make a man voluntarily submit to harm inflicted by another person acting voluntarily, with the result that it would be possible to receive unjust treatment voluntarily.

Surely, our definition of acting unjustly is not correct: to "harming a person knowing the person affected, the instrument, and the manner of acting" we must add "against that person's wish." Then we can conclude that, though a person can voluntarily be harmed and suffer something unjust, no one voluntarily receives unjust treatment;[60] for no one, not even a morally weak person, wishes to be harmed. A morally weak man acts contrary to his wish, for no one wishes some-

25

30

1136b

5

---

58 Cf. the beginning of chap. 6 above.
59 This problem is discussed in chap. 11 below.
60 We have here again the same kind of distinction as drawn at the beginning of chap. 6 above. The meaning is that an unjust act as such is never desired by the patient. He may be willing to submit to treatment which is incidentally unjust, but he does so for some other reason, not *because* it is unjust.

thing that he does not believe to be morally good, yet a
morally weak man does what he believes he ought not to do.
But when a man gives away what is his—as Homer says
10   Glaucus gave to Diomedes "armour of gold for bronze, for
nine oxen's worth the worth of a hundred" [61]—he does not
receive unjust treatment. For while it is in his power to give,
it is not in his power to receive unjust treatment: for that
there must be someone to treat him unjustly. Thus it is clear
that one cannot receive unjust treatment voluntarily.
15   There still remain two points that we intended to discuss.
(1) Can it ever happen that, when an unduly large share
is distributed, the unjust act is committed by the person who
distributes, or is it always the person who acquires it? And (2)
is it possible to act unjustly toward oneself?
If it is possible to answer the first of these questions in the
affirmative, that is to say, if the man who distributes and not
the man who acquires too large a share acts unjustly, it follows that a person who knowingly and voluntarily assigns to
someone else a larger share than to himself acts unjustly to-
20   ward himself. Moderate people are thought to act this way,
for a decent [62] man takes less than his share. (But even this
statement needs some qualification, for such a man may obtain
more than his share of some other good thing, for example, of
glory or of something intrinsically noble, ⟨i.e., goodness⟩.)
Moreover, this problem is solved by reference to our definition of acting unjustly: a man who takes less than his share
suffers nothing against his wish, so that he receives no unjust
treatment, at least not because he takes the smaller share, but,
25   if at all, only because he suffers harm.
It is evident also that the man who distributes, and not always
he who acquires, too large a share acts unjustly. It is not the
person who has the unjust share in his possession who acts
unjustly, but one who performs such an act voluntarily, and
that is the person with whom rests the initiative of the action.
Now the initiative rests with the distributor and not with the

61 Homer, *Iliad* VI. 236, tr. Richmond Lattimore.
62 See Glossary, *epieikēs*, and p. 141, note 69.

recipient. Furthermore, the word "do" is used in many senses:
it is possible to speak of an inanimate object as committing   30
murder, or of a hand, or of a servant who does his master's
bidding. In such a case, no one acts unjustly ⟨by choice⟩,
though an unjust act is "done."

Again, if a judge passes judgment in ignorance of a material
detail, he does not act unjustly as defined by the law and his
decision is not unjust ⟨in this sense⟩, although it is in another
sense. For what is just in the sight of the law is not the same
as what is just in the primary sense.[63] But if he passed unjust
judgment knowingly, he too [64] takes more than his share,   1137a
either of favor ⟨for one party⟩ or of revenge ⟨against the other⟩.
Thus, a man who has passed unjust judgment for reasons of
favoritism or revenge gets too large a share, just as much
as if he were to share in the proceeds of unjust action. And
that is in fact the case if, in awarding land unjustly, his own
share is not land but money.   5

Men believe that it is in their power to act unjustly and
that it is, therefore, easy to be just. But that is not so. To
have intercourse with a neighbor's wife, to strike a bystander,
or to slip money into someone's hand is easy and in our
power; but to do so as a result of a basic attitude or characteristic is neither easy nor in our power. Similarly, people
think it does not take much wisdom to know what is just and   10
what is unjust, because it is not hard to understand the matters with which the laws deal. But these things are not just
except incidentally.[65] No, to know how an act must be per-

63 What Aristotle apparently means by this elliptical statement is to
differentiate questions of *fact* from questions of law. If a judge is misin-
formed but judges according to the law, his decision is "just in the sight
of the law." But it is obviously not "just in the primary sense," i.e., in
the true sense, since if he had been properly informed he would have
judged otherwise.

64 I.e., as well as the party favored by the unjust decision.

65 As he does at greater length in X. 9, 1181a12-19, Aristotle seems here
to be answering Isocrates, who in his *Antidosis* 80-83 identified the art
of legislation with collecting many laws. Aristotle's suggestion that what
is defined by the law is not *ipso facto* just but may be so incidentally,

formed and how a distribution must be made in order to be just is a harder task than to know what makes men healthy. For in this field also it is easy to know what honey, wine,

15 hellebore, cautery, and surgery are, but to know how to administer them to whom and when, in order to make the patient healthy, is as great a task as to be a physician. For that very reason [66] people believe that a just man can also act unjustly, no less than an unjust man, because a just man should be not less but more capable of committing either just or unjust acts.[67] For he might have intercourse with a

20 woman or strike another person, and a brave man might throw away his shield, turn around, and run in any direction. However, being a coward and acting unjustly does not consist in doing these things, except incidentally, but in doing them as a result of a basic attitude, or characteristic, just as being a physician and curing one's patients does not consist in performing or not performing an operation, or in administer-

25 ing or not administering drugs, but in doing so in a certain way, ⟨i.e., in the way a physician does in virtue of his knowledge of medicine⟩.

Just action is possible between people who share in things intrinsically good, and who can have an excess and a deficiency of them. For there are some beings—including, no doubt, the gods—who cannot have too much of these goods. There are others, the incurably bad, to whom not even the slightest share of good things would be beneficial but whom any of these would harm. And there are others for whom things

30 intrinsically good are beneficial up to a certain point. And this is the case of mankind.[68]

---

makes clear that even what is just by convention (cf. chap. 7 above) is not reducible to positive law. Aristotle thus recognizes the possibility of unjust laws.

[66] I.e., because of their belief that it is in our power to act unjustly.
[67] This argument was used by Socrates against Polemarchus in Plato, *Republic* I. 333e-334b.
[68] I follow Stewart and Burnet in bracketing the δià of the manuscripts.

10. *Equity and the equitable*

The next subject we have to discuss is equity and the equitable,[69] and the relation of equity to justice and of the equitable to what is just. For on examination they appear to be neither absolutely identical nor generically different. Sometimes we go so far in praising a thing or a man as "equitable" that we use the word in an extended sense as a general term of praise for things in place of "good," and really mean "better" when we say "more equitable." But at other times, when we follow the logical consequences, it appears odd that the equitable should be distinct from the just and yet deserve praise. If the two terms are different, then either the just is not of great moral value,[70] or the equitable is not just. If both are of great moral value, they are the same.

These, then, are roughly the reasons why a problem about the equitable has arisen. All our points are in a sense correct and there is no inconsistency. For the equitable is just despite the fact that it is better than the just in one sense. But it is not better than the just in the sense of being generically different from it. This means that just and equitable are in fact identical (in genus), and, although both are morally good, the equitable is the better of the two. What causes the problem is that the equitable is not just in the legal sense of "just" but as a corrective of what is legally just. The reason is that all law is universal, but there are some things about which it is not possible to speak correctly in universal terms. Now, in situations where it is necessary to speak in universal terms but impossible to do so correctly, the law takes the majority of cases, fully realizing in what respect it misses the mark. The law itself is none the less correct. For the mistake lies neither in the law nor in the lawgiver, but in the nature of the case.

35
1137b

5

10

15

---

69 See Glossary, *epieikēs*. The meaning of *epieikēs* and its cognate noun *epieikeia* is considerably wider than 'equitable' and 'equity' and includes any notion of decency, fair play, etc.

70 Because, as stated above, 'equitable' is often used interchangeably with 'good.'

For such is the material of which actions are made. So in a situation in which the law speaks universally, but the case at issue happens to fall outside the universal formula, it is correct to rectify the shortcoming, in other words, the omission and mistake of the lawgiver due to the generality of his statement. Such a rectification corresponds to what the lawgiver himself would have said if he were present, and what he would have enacted if he had known ⟨of this particular case⟩.[71] That is why the equitable is both just and also better than the just in one sense. It is not better than the just in general, but better than the mistake due to the generality ⟨of the law⟩. And this is the very nature of the equitable, a rectification of law where law falls short by reason of its universality. This is also the reason why not all things are determined by law. There are some things about which it is impossible to enact a law, so that a special decree is required. For where a thing is indefinite, the rule by which it is measured is also indefinite, as is, for example, the leaden rule used in Lesbian construction work.[72] Just as this rule is not rigid but shifts with the contour of the stone, so a decree is adapted to a given situation.

Thus it is clear what the equitable is, that it is just, and better than just in one sense of the term. We see from this, too, what an equitable man is. A man is equitable who chooses and performs acts of this sort, who is no stickler for justice in a bad sense, but is satisfied with less than his share even though he has the law on his side. Such a characteristic is equity; it is a kind of justice and not a characteristic different from justice.

[71] Aristotle here follows Plato's analysis of the shortcoming of written laws in the *Statesman* 294a-295c.

[72] The reference is to the Lesbian moulding which had an undulating curve. The leaden rule, as explained by Stewart in *Notes on the Nicomachean Ethics* (Vol. I., p. 531), was "a flexible piece of lead which was first accommodated to the irregular surface of a stone already laid in position, and then applied to other stones with the view of selecting one of them with irregularities which would fit most closely into those of the stone already laid."

11. *Is it possible to be unjust toward oneself?*

The preceding discussion [73] has clarified the problem whether or not it is possible to act unjustly toward oneself. (1) One class of just acts is that which is ordained by the law in conformity with virtue as a whole.[74] For example, the law does not enjoin suicide, and what it does not enjoin it forbids.[75] Moreover, when a man voluntarily—that is to say, in full knowledge of the person affected and the instrument used—harms another, not in retaliation, in violation of the law, he acts unjustly. Now when a person kills himself in a fit of anger, he acts voluntarily in violation of right reason; and that the law does not permit. Consequently, he acts unjustly. But toward whom? Surely toward the state, not toward himself. For he suffers voluntarily, but no one voluntarily accepts unjust treatment. That is also the reason why the state exacts a penalty, and some dishonor [76] is imposed upon a man who has taken his own life, on the grounds that he has acted unjustly toward the state.

(2) Furthermore, in those unjust acts which only [77] make the offender unjust and not completely wicked, it is impossible to act unjustly toward oneself. (This case is different from the former: in one sense an unjust man is wicked almost in the same way in which a coward is wicked, that is, not in the sense of being completely wicked. Hence he is not unjust in the sense of complete wickedness.) For if it were possible to be unjust to oneself, (*a*) that would imply that the same thing

5

10

15

73 The reference is to the whole of Book V, not merely to chap. 10.

74 This is the general sense of justice as defined in chap. 1 above.

75 This is a literal translation of the text. But it seems hardly likely that Aristotle meant to say that every action not explicitly ordered by the law is implicitly forbidden. Perhaps we should follow Stewart in interpreting *nomos* not as 'law' in a narrow and positive sense, but as 'law and custom.'

76 According to Aeschines, *Against Ctesiphon* 244, the hand with which a suicide was committed was buried apart from the body.

77 Aristotle now turns to those acts which are unjust in the partial sense discussed in chap. 2 above, i.e., self-aggrandizement, unfairness, etc.

can be added to and taken away from the same person at the same time. But that is impossible: the just and the unjust
20 always necessarily imply more than one person. Moreover, (b) an unjust act is performed voluntarily, by choice, and prior to the injury suffered. We do not regard as acting unjustly a man who requites the injury he has suffered. But when a man injures himself, he acts and suffers at the same time. Again, (c) if a man could act unjustly toward himself, it would be possible to be treated unjustly voluntarily. In addition, (d) no one acts unjustly without committing some unjust act in the
25 partial sense; but no one can commit adultery with his own wife, or commit burglary in his own home, or steal his own property. Finally, (e) the problem of being unjust to oneself also receives a general solution from our definition dealing with the possibility of suffering unjust treatment voluntarily.[78]

It is further evident that both acting and being treated unjustly are evils. The one is to have less and the other to have
30 more than the median share, which corresponds to what is healthy in medicine and what brings well-being in physical training. And yet, to act unjustly is the greater evil, since acting unjustly involves vice and deserves blame—vice in the most complete and general sense, or nearly so, for not every ⟨unjust act⟩ voluntarily committed involves injustice. Suffering unjust treatment, on the other hand, does not imply vice or
35 injustice. Thus, taken by itself, suffering unjust treatment is
1138b less bad, but that does not mean that it may not incidentally be a greater evil. But that is of no concern to the practical art ⟨of politics⟩; [79] ⟨the art of medicine⟩ calls pleurisy a more serious disorder than tripping, and yet the reverse may be true incidentally, if it happens that when you trip, you fall and
5 as a result are killed or taken prisoner by the enemy.

⟨Although a man cannot be unjust toward himself,⟩ there

[78] See above, chap. 9, and in particular 1136b1-9, where the definition specifies that the unjust treatment is *against the wish* of the victim.

[79] This distinction permits Aristotle to adhere to the Socratic maxim that it is better to suffer than to act unjustly (see Plato, *Gorgias* 469b-c), while at the same time accounting for the apparent paradox.

is an extended sense of the word "just," based upon similarity, which applies not to a man's relation to himself but to that between different parts of himself. This does not involve the just in every sense of the word, but only in the sense in which it regulates the relation between master and slave and between the head of a household and its members. For in these discussions [80] a distinction is drawn between the rational and the irrational parts of the soul, and it is in view of this distinction that they regard injustice toward oneself as possible, because one part can frustrate the desires of the other. So they think that there is something just in the mutual relation between these parts in the same sense in which there is in the mutual relation of ruler and ruled. So much for our description of justice and the other moral virtues.

10

[80] The reference is to Plato and his followers; see, for instance, *Republic* III-IV. Aristotle thus concludes his discussion of justice by showing that it accounts for the doctrine of Plato.

BOOK VI

1. Moral and intellectual excellence; the psychological foundations of intellectual excellence

We stated earlier [1] that we must choose the median, and not
20   excess or deficiency, and that the median is what right reason
dictates. Let us now analyze this second point.

In all the characteristics we have discussed, as in all others,
there is some target on which a rational man keeps his eye
as he bends and relaxes his efforts to attain it. There is also a
standard that determines the several means which, as we claim,
lie between excess and deficiency, and which are fixed by right
25   reason. But this statement, true though it is, lacks clarity.
In all other fields of endeavor in which scientific knowledge
is possible, it is indeed true to say that we must exert ourselves or relax neither too much nor too little, but to an intermediate extent and as right reason demands. But if this is the
only thing a person knows, he will be none the wiser: he will,
30   for example, not know what kind of medicines to apply to his
body, if he is merely told to apply whatever medical science
prescribes and in a manner in which a medical expert applies
them. Accordingly, in discussing the characteristics of the soul,
too, it is not enough that the statement we have made be
true. We must also have a definition of what right reason is
and what standard determines it.

35   In analyzing the virtues of the soul we said that some are
1139a   virtues of character and others excellence of thought or understanding.[2] We have now discussed the moral virtues, ⟨i.e., the
virtues of character⟩. In what follows, we will deal with the
others, ⟨i.e., the intellectual virtues,⟩ beginning with some pre-

[1] See II. 2 and 6.
[2] See I. 13, 1103a4-10. The word which we translate here by 'thought'
or 'understanding' (*dianoia*) denotes the discursive thinking which is involved in any act of reasoning or understanding.

fatory remarks about the soul. We said in our earlier discussion that the soul consists of two parts, one rational and one
irrational.[3] We must now make a similar distinction in regard 5
to the rational part. Let it be assumed that there are two
rational elements: with one of these we apprehend the realities
whose fundamental principles do not admit of being other
than they are, and with the other we apprehend things which
do admit of being other. For if we grant that knowledge pre-
supposes a certain likeness and kinship of subject and object,[4] 10
there will be a generically different part of the soul naturally
corresponding to each of two different kinds of object. Let
us call one the scientific and the other the calculative element.
Deliberating and calculating are the same thing, and no one
deliberates about objects that cannot be other than they are.
This means that the calculative constitutes one element of the
rational part of the soul. Accordingly, we must now take up 15
the question which is the best characteristic of each element,
since that constitutes the excellence or virtue of each. But
the virtue of a thing is relative to its proper function.

2. The two kinds of intellectual excellence and their objects

Now, there are three elements in the soul which control
action and truth: sense perception, intelligence,[5] and desire.
Of these sense perception does not initiate any action. We can
see this from the fact that animals have sense perception but 20
have no share in action.[6] What affirmation and negation are

---

3 See I. 13, 1102a26-28 with note 47.

4 The fact that this assumption, which we find enunciated for the
first time, but in a rather primitive form, by Empedocles (frg. B 109
DK6) and afterwards by Plato (e.g., *Republic* VI. 490b, 509d-511e; cf. also
Timaeus 45b-46a), is not argued here at all, whereas it is subjected to a
close scrutiny in *De Anima* I. 5, 409b26-410a13; *De An.* II. 5, 417a1-418a6,
suggests again that the *Nic. Eth.* does not contain Aristotle's last word on
psychology.

5 Intelligence (*nous*) will be discussed in chap. 6.

6 Throughout the *Nic. Eth.*, Aristotle uses *praxis* ('action') as equivalent
to 'moral action,' 'conduct'; and animals are not capable of this.

in the realm of thought, pursuit and avoidance are in the realm of desire. Therefore, since moral virtue is a characteristic involving choice, and since choice is a deliberate desire,[7] it follows that, if the choice is to be good, the reasoning must
25 be true and the desire correct; that is, reasoning must affirm what desire pursues. This then is the kind of thought and the kind of truth that is practical and concerned with action. On the other hand, in the kind of thought involved in theoretical knowledge and not in action or production, the good and the bad state are, respectively, truth and falsehood; in fact, the attainment of truth is the function of the intellectual faculty as a whole. But in intellectual activity concerned with action,
30 the good state is truth in harmony with correct desire.

Choice is the starting point of action: it is the source of motion but not the end for the sake of which we act, ⟨i.e., the final cause⟩.[8] The starting point of choice, however, is desire and reasoning directed toward some end. That is why there cannot be choice either without intelligence and thought or without some moral characteristic; for good and bad ac-

----

[7] See, II. 6 and III. 3.

[8] Aristotle's doctrine of the four causes is involved here. It is most concisely stated in *Metaphyhics* Δ. 2, 1013a24-35:

We speak of "cause" in one sense (a) ⟨i.e., material cause,⟩ as that whose presence makes it possible for a thing to come into being, e.g., bronze is in this sense the cause of a statue, silver of a cup, and so with other kinds of material. In another sense, (b) the form and pattern is a cause, i.e., the definition of the essential nature of the thing and the classes in which this definition is found, e.g., the ratio 2:1 and number in general is the cause of the octave, and also the parts of which the essential definition consists. Furthermore, (c) there is the cause which is the first starting point of change or of rest, e.g., a man who deliberates is a cause, a father is a cause of his child, and, in general, the producing agent of the produced thing and the agent introducing change of the thing changed. Again, (d) cause is the same as "end," i.e., the final cause, e.g., health is the cause of taking a walk. Why does a man take a walk? We answer, "In order to be healthy," and, in saying that, we think we have explained the cause.

This is not the place to discuss Aristotle's doctrine of causation in detail;

tion[9] in human conduct are not possible without thought and   35
character. Now thought alone moves nothing; only thought
which is directed to some end and concerned with action can
do so. And it is this kind of thought also which initiates pro-   1139b
duction. For whoever produces something produces it for
an end. The product he makes is not an end in an unqualified
sense, but an end only in a particular relation and of a particular operation. Only the goal of action is an end in the unqualified sense: for the good life is an end, and desire is directed toward this. Therefore, choice is either intelligence
motivated by desire or desire operating through thought, and
it is as a combination of these two that man is a starting point   5
of action.

(No object of choice belongs to the past: no one chooses to
have sacked Troy. For deliberation does not refer to the past
but only to the future and to what is possible; and it is not
possible that what is past should not have happened. Therefore, Agathon is right when he says: 10

> One thing alone is denied even to god:
> to make undone the deeds which have been done.[10])

As we have seen, truth is the function of both intellectual
parts ⟨of the soul⟩. Therefore, those characteristics which permit each part to be as truthful as possible will be the virtues
of the two parts.

---

for an excellent summary of its bearing on the *Nic. Eth.*, see H. H.
Joachim, *Aristotle: The Nicomachean Ethics*, pp. 176-87.

9 It is impossible to capture in English all the connotations of *eupraxia*,
which is one of the key concepts in Aristotle's ethical theory. It is a
noun formation of an adverb-verb combination that means not only
'to act well,' but also 'to fare well,' 'to be successful,' 'to be happy.' In
other words, as the principal ingredient in the 'good life' the noun is
practically equivalent to 'happiness.'

10 Agathon, frg. 5 (Nauck[2]). Agathon was a tragic poet who flourished in
the last quarter of the fifth century B.C. The scene of Plato's *Symposium*
is laid in his house.

3. The qualities by which truth is attained: (a) pure science or knowledge

So let us make a fresh beginning and discuss these characteristics once again. Let us take for granted that the faculties by which the soul expresses truth by way of affirmation or denial are five in number: art, science, practical wisdom, theoretical wisdom, and intelligence.[11] Conviction and opinion do not belong here, for they may be false.

What pure science or scientific knowledge is—in the precise sense of the word and not in any of its wider uses based on mere similarity—will become clear in the following. We are all convinced that what we *know* scientifically cannot be otherwise than it is; but of facts which can possibly be other than they are we do not know whether or not they continue to be true when removed from our observation. Therefore, an object of scientific knowledge exists of necessity, and is, consequently, eternal. For everything that exists of necessity in an unqualified sense is eternal, and what is eternal is ungenerated and imperishable ⟨and hence cannot be otherwise⟩.

Moreover, all scientific knowledge is held to be teachable, and what is scientifically knowable is capable of being learned. All teaching is based on what is already known, as we have stated in the *Analytics;*[12] some teaching proceeds by induction and some by syllogism. Now, induction is the starting point ⟨for knowledge⟩, of the universal as well ⟨as the particular⟩, while syllogism proceeds *from* universals.[13] Consequently,

11 For the meaning of these terms, see Glossary, *technē, epistēmē,* and *phronēsis.* The peculiarly Aristotelian notions of these terms and also of "intelligence" are explained in the following chapters.

12 *Posterior Analytics* I. 1, 71a1.

13 We cannot here give a full explanation of syllogism and induction, the discovery of the former of which is Aristotle's greatest contribution to logic. For our purposes it suffices to state that a syllogism is defined as "an argument in which, certain assumptions having been made, something other than these assumptions necessarily follows from the fact that they are true" (*Prior Analytics* I. 1, 24b18-20), and that it involves, in

there are starting points or principles from which a syllogism   30
proceeds and which are themselves not arrived at by a syllogism. It is, therefore, induction that attains them. Accordingly,
scientific knowledge is a capacity [14] for demonstration and has,
in addition, all the other qualities which we have specified in
the *Analytics*.[15] When a man believes something in the way
there specified, and when the starting points or principles on
which his beliefs rest are known to him, then he has scientific
knowledge; unless he knows the starting points or principles
better than the conclusion, he will have scientific knowledge
only incidentally. So much for our definition of scientific   35
knowledge or pure science.

4. *(b) Art or applied science*

Things which admit of being other than they are include   1140a
both things made and things done. Production is different
from action—for that point we can rely even on our less
technical discussions.[16] Hence, the characteristic of acting
rationally is different from the characteristic of producing
rationally. It also follows that one does not include the other,   5
for action is not production nor production action. Now,
building is an art or applied science, and it is essentially a
characteristic or trained ability of rationally producing. In
fact, there is no art that is not a characteristic or trained
ability of rationally producing, nor is there a characteristic of
rationally producing that is not an art. It follows that art
is identical with the characteristic of producing under the   10

---

its most fundamental form, two premises, at least one of which is a
universal proposition, and a conclusion. E.g., all men are mortal, Greeks
are men, therefore Greeks are mortal. For induction, see *Posterior
Analytics* II. 19.

14 The Greek word here is *hexis;* see Glossary. Here as elsewhere the
term describes an acquired possession now firmly established in the mind.
But since our usual translation 'characteristic' is hardly appropriate in
this context, 'capacity' has been substituted.

15 See *Posterior Analytics* I, 71b9-72b4 and 73a21-74a3.

16 See p. 9, note 17.

guidance of true reason. All art is concerned with the realm of coming-to-be, i.e., with contriving and studying how something which is capable both of being and of not being may come into existence, a thing whose starting point or source is in the producer and not in the thing produced. For art is concerned neither with things which exist or come into being 15 by necessity, nor with things produced by nature: these have their source of motion within themselves.

Since production and action are different, it follows that art deals with production and not with action. In a certain sense, fortune and art are concerned with the same things, as Agathon says: "Fortune loves art and art fortune." So, as 20 we have said, art is a characteristic of producing under the guidance of true reason, and lack of art, on the contrary, is a characteristic of producing under the guidance of false reason; and both of them deal with what admits of being other than it is.

5. (c) Practical wisdom

We may approach the subject of practical wisdom by study-
25 ing the persons to whom we attribute it. Now, the capacity of deliberating well about what is good and advantageous for oneself is regarded as typical of a man of practical wisdom— not deliberating well about what is good and advantageous in a partial sense, for example, what contributes to health or strength, but what sort of thing contributes to the good life in general. This is shown by the fact that we speak of men as having practical wisdom in a particular respect, (i.e., not in an unqualified sense,) when they calculate well with respect to 30 some worthwhile end, one that cannot be attained by an applied science or art. It follows that, in general, a man of practical wisdom is he who has the ability to deliberate.

Now no one deliberates about things that cannot be other than they are or about actions that he cannot possibly perform. Since, as we saw, pure science involves demonstration, while things whose starting points or first causes can be other

than they are do not admit of demonstration—for such things too ⟨and not merely their first causes⟩ can all be other than 35
they are—and since it is impossible to deliberate about what exists by necessity, we may conclude that practical wisdom 1140b
is neither a pure science nor an art. It is not a pure science, because matters of action admit of being other than they are, and it is not an applied science or art, because action and production are generically different.

What remains, then, is that it is a truthful characteristic of acting rationally in matters good and bad for man. For pro- 5
duction has an end other than itself, but action does not: good action [17] is itself an end. That is why we think that Pericles and men like him have practical wisdom.[18] They have the capacity of seeing what is good for themselves and for mankind, and these are, we believe, the qualities of men 10
capable of managing households and states.

This also explains why we call "self-control" sōphrosynē: it "preserves" our "practical wisdom." [19] What it preserves is the kind of conviction we have described. For the pleasant and the painful do not destroy and pervert every conviction we hold—not, for example, our conviction that a triangle has or does not have the sum of its angles equal to two right 15
angles—but only the convictions we hold concerning how we should act. In matters of action, the principles or initiating motives are the ends at which our actions are aimed. But as soon as a man becomes corrupted by pleasure or pain, the goal no longer appears to him as a motivating principle: he no longer sees that he should choose and act in every case for the sake of and because of this end. For vice tends to destroy the principle or initiating motive of action.

[17] For the term eupraxia, 'good action,' see p. 149, note 9.

[18] The name of Pericles (ca. 495-429 b.c.) is almost synonymous with the Athenian democracy. For an estimate of his character and the practical wisdom of his policies, see Thucydides II. 65.

[19] A few remarks on the etymology of sōphrosynē have been made on p. 77, note 29. Aristotle here derives the noun from the verb sōizein, 'to save,' 'preserve,' and the abstract noun phronēsis, 'practical wisdom' (following Plato, Cratylus 411e).

20   Necessarily, then, practical wisdom is a truthful rational
characteristic of acting in matters involving what is good for
man. Furthermore, whereas there exists such a thing as excellence in art, it does not exist in practical wisdom.[20] Also, in
art a man who makes a mistake voluntarily is preferable to
one who makes it involuntarily; but in practical wisdom, as in
every virtue or excellence, such a man is less desirable. Thus
it is clear that practical wisdom is an excellence or virtue and
25   not an art. Since there are two parts of the soul that contain
a rational element, it must be the virtue of one of them,
namely of the part that forms opinions.[21] For opinion as well
as practical wisdom deals with things that can be other than
they are. However, it is not merely a rational characteristic
or trained ability. An indication (that it is something more
may be seen) in the fact that a trained ability of that kind
30   can be forgotten, whereas practical wisdom cannot.

6. (d) Intelligence

Since pure science or scientific knowledge is a basic conviction concerning universal and necessary truths, and since
everything demonstrable and all pure science begins from
fundamental principles (for science proceeds rationally), the
fundamental principle or starting point for scientific knowledge cannot itself be the object either of science, of art, or
35   of practical wisdom. For what is known scientifically is demonstrable, whereas art and practical wisdom are concerned with
1141a   things that can be other than they are. Nor are these fundamental principles the objects of theoretical wisdom: for it is
the task of a man of theoretical wisdom to have a demonstra-

20 Because practical wisdom is itself a complete virtue or excellence,
while the excellence of art depends on the goodness or badness of its
product.
21 "Opinion" here corresponds to the "calculative element" in chap.
1: both are defined by reference to contingent facts, those which may be
otherwise than they are.

tion for certain truths.[22] Now, if scientific knowledge, practical
wisdom, theoretical wisdom, and intelligence are the faculties
by which we attain truth and by which we are never deceived
both in matters which can and in those matters which cannot be   5
other than they are; and if three of these—I am referring to
practical wisdom, scientific knowledge, and theoretical wisdom
—cannot be the faculty in question, we are left with the conclusion that it is intelligence that apprehends fundamental
principles.[23]

7. (c) Theoretical wisdom [24]

We attribute "wisdom" in the arts to the most precise and
perfect masters of their skills: we attribute it to Phidias as a   10
sculptor in marble and to Polycletus as a sculptor in bronze.

[22] In other words, the undemonstrable first or fundamental principles
cannot be the proper and complete object of theoretical wisdom: as the
next chapter shows, they are included within its sphere.

[23] This brief statement becomes clearer in the light of *Posterior
Analytics* II. 19, 100b5-14:

> Some of the intellectual characteristics by which we attain truth are
> always truthful, while others, such as opinion and calculation, admit
> of falsehood. Now, since (a) scientific knowledge and intelligence are
> always truthful, and no other kind (of intellectual characteristic) is
> more precise than scientific knowledge—except for intelligence: (b)
> fundamental principles are more knowable than demonstrations; and (c)
> all scientific knowledge involves reasoning; (it follows that) scientific
> knowledge does not apprehend fundamental principles, and since only
> intelligence can be more truthful than scientific knowledge, it is
> intelligence which apprehends the fundamental principles. This result
> also follows from the fact that there cannot be demonstration of the
> fundamental principle of demonstration, nor, consequently, scientific
> knowledge of scientific knowledge.

[24] As we shall see as this chapter progresses, Aristotle understands
by *sophia* the highest intellectual, and especially philosophical, excellence of which the human mind is capable. However, before he reaches
this definition of *sophia*, he discusses some current uses of the term. In
popular usage, *sophia* first appears in Greek to describe the skill of a
clever craftsman, and also of poets and artists, a concept which was then
extended to other fields of endeavor, e.g., to the itinerant teachers of

In this sense we signify by "wisdom" nothing but excellence of art or craftsmanship. However, we regard some men as being wise in general, not in any partial sense or in some other particular respect, as Homer says in the *Margites:*

15   The gods let him not be a digger or a ploughman
        nor wise at anything.[25]

It is, therefore, clear, that wisdom must be the most precise and perfect form of knowledge. Consequently, a wise man must not only know what follows from fundamental principles, but he must also have true knowledge of the fundamental principles themselves. Accordingly, theoretical wisdom must comprise both intelligence and scientific knowledge. It

20 is science in its consummation, as it were, the science of the things that are valued most highly.

For it would be strange to regard politics or practical wisdom as the highest kind of knowledge, when in fact man is not the best thing in the universe. Surely, if "healthy" and "good" mean one thing for men and another for fishes, whereas "white" and "straight" always mean the same, "wise" must mean the same for everyone, but "practically wise" will be different. For each particular being ascribes practical wisdom

25 in matters relating to itself to that thing which observes its interests well, and it will entrust itself to that thing. That is the reason why people attribute practical wisdom even to some animals—to all those which display a capacity of forethought in matters relating to their own life.

It is also evident that theoretical wisdom is not the same as politics. If we are to call "theoretical wisdom" the knowl-

---

rhetoric, the 'Sophists,' whose skill enabled them to sway—and thus gain power over—their audience, and finally to the 'wisdom' of the scientist and philosopher. For the sake of clarity, we translate the general use of the term as 'wisdom' and the special sense which Aristotle gives it as 'theoretical wisdom.'

[25] The *Margites* was a mock-heroic poem, ascribed by the ancients to Homer.

edge of what is helpful to us, there will be many kinds of 30
wisdom. There is no single science that deals with what is
good for all living things any more than there is a single art
of medicine dealing with everything that is, but a different
science deals with each particular good. The argument that
man is the best of living things makes no difference. There
are other things whose nature is much more divine than man's: 1141b
to take the most visible example only, the constituent parts of
the universe.[26]

Our discussion has shown that theoretical wisdom comprises
both scientific knowledge and ⟨apprehension by the⟩ intelligence of things which by their nature are valued most highly.
That is why it is said that men like Anaxagoras and Thales
have theoretical but not practical wisdom: when we see that 5
they do not know what is advantageous to them, we admit
that they know extraordinary, wonderful, difficult, and superhuman things, but call their knowledge useless because the
good they are seeking is not human.

Practical wisdom, on the other hand, is concerned with
human affairs and with matters about which deliberation is
possible. As we have said, the most characteristic function of
a man of practical wisdom is to deliberate well: no one de- 10
liberates about things that cannot be other than they are, nor
about things that are not directed to some end, an end that
is a good attainable by action. In an unqualified sense, that
man is good at deliberating who, by reasoning, can aim at
and hit the best thing attainable to man by action.

Nor does practical wisdom deal only with universals. It
must also be familiar with particulars, since it is concerned 15
with action and action has to do with particulars. This explains why some men who have no scientific knowledge are
more adept in practical matters, especially if they have experience, than those who do have scientific knowledge. For if

[26] That the sun and stars are meant is clear from *Metaphysics* E. 1,
1026a18 and *Physics* II. 4, 196a33, where the visible divine nature of
the stars is stressed.

a person were to know that light meat is easily digested, and hence wholesome, but did not know what sort of meat is light, he will not produce health, whereas someone who knows that
20 poultry is light and [27] wholesome is more likely to produce health.[28]

Now, practical wisdom is concerned with action. That means that a person should have both ⟨knowledge of universals and knowledge of particulars⟩, or knowledge of particulars rather ⟨than knowledge of universals⟩. But here, too, it seems, there is a supreme and comprehensive science involved, ⟨i.e., politics⟩.

8. *Practical wisdom and politics* [29]

Political wisdom [30] and practical wisdom are both the same characteristic, but their essential aspect is not the same. There are two kinds of wisdom concerning the state: the one, which
25 acts as practical wisdom supreme and comprehensive, is the art of legislation; the other, which is practical wisdom as dealing with particular facts, bears the name which, ⟨in everyday speech,⟩ is common to both kinds, politics, and it is concerned with action and deliberation. For a decree, ⟨unlike a law, which lays down general principles,⟩ is a matter for action, inasmuch as it is the last step ⟨in the deliberative process⟩.[31]

[27] I follow Burnet in rejecting Bywater's and Trendelenburg's brackets around κοῦφα καὶ·

[28] The point here is that, in practical matters, a man who knows by experience that poultry is wholesome is likely to be more successful than a man who only has the scientific knowledge that light meat is digestible and therefore wholesome, without knowing the particular fact that poultry is light meat.

[29] In the following chapters, 8-11, Aristotle apparently digresses to a discussion of other virtues, but in fact he develops and clarifies the notion of practical wisdom by contrasting it with similar or related characteristics.

[30] The Greek term here is *politikē*, which we usually render as 'politics' in this translation; cf. Glossary. But since its juxtaposition with practical wisdom here stresses that politics is for Aristotle (as for Plato) a branch of knowledge, the variant 'political wisdom' seems more appropriate here.

[31] Cf. the discussion of deliberation in III. 3, especially 1112b11-24.

That is why only those who make decrees are said to engage in politics, for they alone, like workmen, "do" things.[32]

It is also commonly held that practical wisdom is primarily concerned with one's own person, i.e., with the individual, and it is this kind that bears the name "practical wisdom," which properly belongs to others as well. The other kinds are called household management, legislation, and politics, the last of which is subdivided into deliberative and judicial.[33]

Now, knowing what is good for oneself is, to be sure, one kind of knowledge; but it is very different from the other kinds. A man who knows and concerns himself with his own interests is regarded as a man of practical wisdom, while men whose concern is politics are looked upon as busybodies. Euripides' words are in this vein:

> How can I be called "wise," who might have filled
> a common soldier's place, free from all care,
> sharing an equal lot . . . ?
> For those who reach too high and are too active. . . .[34]

For people seek their own good and think that this is what they should do. This opinion has given rise to the view that it is such men who have practical wisdom. And yet, surely one's own good cannot exist without household management nor without a political system. Moreover, the problem of how

[32] I.e., lawgivers and other men who are concerned with political wisdom in the supreme and comprehensive sense are not generally regarded as being engaged in politics. The analogy to workmen represents of course not Aristotle's view, which vigorously distinguishes action from production, but rather reflects a widespread attitude toward politics.

[33] In Athens, "deliberative" politics referred to matters debated in the Council and the Popular Assembly, and "judicial" politics to matters argued in the lawcourts.

[34] These lines come from the prologue of Euripides' lost *Philoctetes* (frgg. 787 and 782 Nauck²) and were spoken by Odysseus. The third line quoted here runs in its entirety: "sharing an equal lot with the most wise." Then, after some missing lines, there comes a passage of which the last line quoted here is the second:

> Ah, what is more vainglorious than man?
> For those who reach too high and are too active
> we honor as the leaders in the state.

30

1142a

5

10

to manage one's own affairs properly needs clarification and remains to be examined.

An indication that what we have said is correct is the following common observation. While young men do indeed become good geometricians and mathematicians and attain theoretical wisdom in such matters, they apparently do not attain practical wisdom. The reason is that practical wisdom is concerned with particulars as well (as with universals), and knowledge of particulars comes from experience. But a young 15 man has no experience, for experience is the product of a long time. In fact, one might also raise the question why it is that a boy may become a mathematician but not a philosopher or a natural scientist. The answer may be that the objects of mathematics are the result of abstraction, whereas the fundamental principles of philosophy and natural science come from experience. Young men can assert philosophical and scientific principles but can have no genuine convictions about them, whereas 20 there is no obscurity about the essential definitions in mathematics.

Moreover, in our deliberations error is possible as regards either the universal principle or the particular fact: we may be unaware either that all heavy water is bad, or that the particular water we are faced with is heavy.

That practical wisdom is not scientific knowledge is (therefore) evident. As we stated,[35] it is concerned with ultimate particulars, since the actions to be performed are ultimate 25 particulars. This means that it is at the opposite pole from intelligence. For the intelligence grasps limiting terms and definitions that cannot be attained by reasoning, while practical wisdom has as its object the ultimate particular fact, of which there is perception but no scientific knowledge. This perception is not the kind with which (each of our five senses apprehends) its proper object,[36] but the kind with which we

[35] See the end of chap. 7, 1141b14-22.
[36] Aristotle's distinction between the various kinds of perception is most concisely stated in De Anima II. 6, 418a7-20:

In discussing the various kinds of sense perception, we must first deal with the objects of the senses. The term "object of sense perception"

perceive that in mathematics the triangle is the ultimate figure.[37] For in this direction, too, we shall have to reach a stop.[38] But this ⟨type of mathematical cognition⟩ is more truly perception than practical wisdom, and it is different in kind from the other ⟨type of perception which deals with the objects proper to the various senses⟩.   30

9. Practical wisdom and excellence in deliberation

There is a difference between investigating and deliberating: to deliberate is to investigate a particular kind of object. We must also try to grasp what excellence in deliberation is: whether it is some sort of scientific knowledge, opinion, shrewd guessing, or something generically different from any of these.

Now, scientific knowledge it is certainly not:[39] people do not investigate matters they already know. But good delibera-   1142b

---

is used of three kinds of object. Two of these, we say, we perceive directly and one indirectly. The first of the two ⟨kinds of object which we perceive directly⟩ is the object proper to each given sense, while the second kind of object is common to all the senses. By "proper object" I mean an object which cannot possibly be perceived by any other sense and about which a person cannot possibly be mistaken. For example, sight has color as its proper object, hearing has sound, and taste has flavor. Touch, it is true, has a number of different objects. At any rate, each sense draws distinctions in its own sphere and makes no mistake about the fact that it is a color or that it is a sound, though it may go wrong in identifying what or where the colored object is, or what object is making the sound or where it is located. These are called objects proper to a particular sense. The objects common to all senses, on the other hand, are motion, rest, number, shape, and size, since these are not proper to any one sense but common to them all: a motion, for example, is perceived by both touch and sight.

[37] I do not follow Bywater in bracketing ἐν τοῖς μαθηματικοῖς ('in mathematics'), since Aristotle's point here seems to be that every polygonal figure in geometry can be resolved into a number of triangles, but that the triangle in turn cannot be resolved into a simpler figure.

[38] Cf. the statement about deliberation above, III. 3, 1112b20-24 and note 12.

[39] Here, as in most of the following paragraph, Aristotle seems to be taking issue with Plato, who had identified the two, e.g., in Republic IV. 428b.

tion is a kind of deliberation, and when a person deliberates he is engaged in investigating and calculating ⟨things not yet decided⟩. Nor yet is it shrewd guessing. For shrewd guessing involves no reasoning and proceeds quickly, whereas deliberation takes a long time. As the saying goes, the action which follows deliberation should be quick, but deliberation itself
5   should be slow. Furthermore, quickness of mind is not the same as excellence in deliberation: quickness of mind is a kind of shrewd guessing. Nor again is excellence in deliberation any form of opinion at all. But since a person who deliberates badly makes mistakes, while he who deliberates well deliberates correctly, it clearly follows that excellence in deliberation is some kind of correctness. But it is correctness neither of scientific knowledge nor of opinion. There cannot be correctness
10   of scientific knowledge any more than there can be error of scientific knowledge; and correctness of opinion is truth. Moreover, anything that is an object of opinion is already fixed and determined, ⟨while deliberation deals with objects which remain to be determined⟩. Still, excellence in deliberation does involve reasoning, and we are, consequently, left with the alternative that it is correctness of ⟨a process of⟩ thought; for thinking is not yet an affirmation. For while opinion is no longer a process of investigation but has reached the point of affirmation, a person who deliberates, whether he does so
15   well or badly, is still engaged in investigating and calculating something ⟨not yet determined⟩.

Good deliberation is a kind of correctness of deliberation. We must, therefore, first investigate what deliberation is and with what objects it is concerned.[40] Since the term "correctness" is used in several different senses, it is clear that not every kind of correctness in deliberation ⟨is excellence in deliberation⟩. For (1) a morally weak or a bad man will, as a result of calculation, attain the goal which he has proposed to himself as the right goal [41] to attain. He will, therefore,

---

[40] As Aristotle proceeds to discuss correctness and not deliberation, many editors bracket this sentence. Actually, deliberation has already been discussed in III. 3 and above, chap. 5, 1140a31-b4.

[41] Instead of ἰδεῖν preserved by the majority of manuscripts, I read

have deliberated correctly, but what he will get out of it will be a very bad thing. But the result of good deliberation is 20 generally regarded as a good thing. It is this kind of correctness of deliberation which is good deliberation, a correctness that attains what is good.

But (2) it is also possible to attain something good by a false syllogism, i.e., to arrive at the right action, but to arrive at it by the wrong means when the middle term is false.[42] Accordingly, this process, which makes us attain the right goal but not by the right means, is still not good deliberation. 25

Moreover, (3) it is possible that one man attains his goal by deliberating for a long time, while another does so quickly. Now, long deliberation, too, is not as such good deliberation: excellence in deliberation is correctness in assessing what is beneficial, i.e., correctness in assessing the goal, the manner, and the time.

Again, (4) it is possible for a person to have deliberated well either in general, in an unqualified sense, or in relation to some particular end. Good deliberation in the unqualified sense of course brings success in relation to what is, in an 30 unqualified sense, the end, ⟨i.e., in relation to the good life⟩. Excellence in deliberation as directed toward some particular end, however, brings success in the attainment of some particular end.

Thus we may conclude that, since it is a mark of men of practical wisdom to have deliberated well,[43] excellence in deliberation will be correctness in assessing what is conducive to the end, concerning which practical wisdom gives a true conviction.

---

with Burnet, Rackham, and Dirlmeier δεῖν, which is preserved in two fifteenth-century manuscripts and which seems to underlie the medieval Latin translation of the *Nic. Eth.* by Robert Grosseteste.

[42] Aristotle's terminology is a little loose here. Strictly speaking, the middle *term* of a syllogism can be neither true nor false. What he means is that even when the middle term does not provide a true link between the premises, the conclusion may still be true. Cf. *Prior Analytics* II. 2, 53b4-10, and 4, 57a40-b17.

[43] See above, chap. 5, 1140a25-28, and chap. 7, 1141b8-12.

10. *Practical wisdom and understanding* [44]

Understanding, i.e., excellence in understanding, the quality which makes us call certain people "men of understanding" and "men of good understanding," is in general not identical with scientific knowledge or with opinion. For ⟨if it were opinion,⟩ everyone would be a man of understanding, ⟨since everyone forms opinions⟩. Nor is it one of the particular branches of science, in the sense in which medicine, for example, is the science of matters pertaining to health, or geometry the science which deals with magnitudes. For understanding is concerned neither with eternal and unchangeable truth nor with anything and everything that comes into being ⟨and passes away again⟩. It deals with matters concerning which doubt and deliberation are possible. Accordingly, though its sphere is the same as that of practical wisdom, understanding and practical wisdom are not the same. Practical wisdom issues commands: its end is to tell us what we ought to do and what we ought not to do. Understanding, on the other hand, only passes judgment.[45] ⟨There is no difference between understanding and excellence in understanding:⟩ for excellence in understanding is the same as understanding, and men of understanding are men of good understanding.

Thus understanding is neither possession nor acquisition of practical wisdom. Just as learning is called "understanding" when a man makes use of his faculty of knowledge,[46] so ⟨we speak of "understanding"⟩ when it implies the use of one's faculty of opinion in judging statements made by another

1143a

5

10

44 The Greek term *synesis*, 'understanding,' denotes primarily the comprehension of what someone else has said, but it also contains the notion of understanding practical problems.

45 This distinction between imperative and critical faculties is taken from Plato, *Statesman* 260b, and corresponds in part to Aristotle's distinction between practical and theoretical cognition.

46 The Greek *manthanein* means both 'to learn' and 'to understand.' Cf. the two meanings of 'learn' in English: (*a*) "I learn a new language" and (*b*) "I learn that you have been ill."

person about matters which belong to the realm of practical
wisdom—and in judging such statements rightly, for *good*   15
understanding means that the judgment is right. It is from this
act of learning or understanding ⟨what someone else says⟩
that the term "understanding" as predicated of "men of good
understanding" is derived. For we frequently use the words
"learning" and "understanding" synonymously.

11. *Practical wisdom and good sense*

As for what is called "good sense," [47] the quality which
makes us say of a person that he has the sense to forgive
others, ⟨i.e., sympathetic understanding,⟩ and that he has good
sense, this is a correct judgment of what is fair or equitable.   20
This is indicated by the fact that we attribute to an equitable
man especially sympathetic understanding and that we say
that it is fair, in certain cases, to have the sense to forgive.
Sympathetic understanding is a correct critical sense or judgment of what is fair; and a correct judgment is a true one.

All these characteristics, as one would expect, tend toward   25
the same goal. We attribute good sense, understanding, practical wisdom, and intelligence to the same persons, and in saying that they have good sense, ⟨we imply⟩ at the same time that
they have a mature intelligence and that they are men of practical wisdom and understanding. For what these capacities ⟨have
in common is that they are⟩ all concerned with ultimate particular facts. To say that a person has good judgment in mat-

---

[47] English has no single equivalent to express the whole range of *gnōmē*.
The most common use of the term describes a particular 'insight' or
'judgment,' especially as it is related to matters affecting the conduct of
one's life. But the term may denote both a particular judgment and a
man's ability to pass good judgments, i.e., his 'judgment' in general or
what we might call 'sound understanding.' In addition, a *gnōmē* is the
equivalent of 'maxim,' 'adage.' What makes a translation here especially
difficult is the fact that Aristotle relates *gnōmē* to several cognates, such
as *syngnōmē*, 'forgiveness,' 'pardon,' 'sympathetic understanding' (literally, 'judgment with' or 'on the side of' another person) and *eugnōmōn*,
'well-judging' in the sense of 'kindly,' 'well disposed.'

30 ters of practical wisdom implies that he is understanding and has good sense or that he has sympathetic understanding; for equitable acts are common to all good men in their relation with someone else. Now, all matters of action are in the sphere of the particulars and ultimates. Not only must a man of practical wisdom take cognizance of particulars, but understanding and good sense, too, deal with matters of action, and
35 matters of action are ultimates. As for intelligence, it deals with ultimates at both ends of the scale. It is intelligence, not reasoning, that has as its objects primary terms and defini-
1143b tions [48] as well as ultimate particulars. Intelligence grasps, on the one hand, the unchangeable, primary terms and concepts for demonstrations; on the other hand, in questions of action, it grasps the ultimate, contingent fact and the minor premise.[49] For it is particular facts that form the starting points or principles for ⟨our knowledge of⟩ the goal of action: universals arise out of particulars. Hence one must have percep-
5 tion of particular facts, and this perception is intelligence.[50]

That is why these characteristics are regarded as natural endowments and, although no one is provided with theoretical wisdom by nature, we do think that men have good sense, understanding, and intelligence by nature. An indication of this is that we think of these characteristics as depending on different stages of life, and that at a given stage of life a person acquires intelligence and good sense: the implication is that

[48] Cf. above, chap. 8, 1142a25-26, where we also find a contrast between *nous* or 'intelligence,' the faculty of immediate intellectual insight, and *logos*, literally 'speech,' i.e., the process of discursive reasoning.

[49] For intelligence as the faculty which grasps first principles ("terms and concepts for demonstration"), see above, chap. 6. In a practical syllogism, the minor premise will be an immediate fact of experience, also perceived by the intelligence.

[50] I.e., we can attain the end—happiness—only by discovering the general rules of moral conduct, and these, in turn, rest on the immediate apprehension by intelligence of particular moral facts. For the general epistemological doctrine of universals arising out of particulars, see *Posterior Analytics* II. 19.

⟨human⟩ nature is the cause.[51] Therefore, we ought to pay as much attention to the sayings and opinions, undemonstrated though they are, of wise and experienced older men as we do to demonstrated truths. For experience has given such men an eye with which they can see correctly.[52]

We have now completed our discussion of what practical and theoretical wisdom are; we have described the sphere in which   15 each operates, and we have shown that each is the excellence of a different part of the soul.[53]

12. *The use of theoretical and practical wisdom*

One might raise some questions about the usefulness of these two virtues. Theoretical wisdom, ⟨as we have described it,⟩ will study none of the things that make a man happy, for it is not at all concerned with the sphere of coming-to-be   20 ⟨but only with unchanging realities⟩. Practical wisdom, on the other hand, *is* concerned with this sphere, but for what purpose do we need it? (1) It is true that practical wisdom deals with what is just, noble, and good for man; and it is doing such things that characterizes a man as good. But our ability to perform such actions is in no way enhanced by knowing them, since the virtues are characteristics, ⟨that is to say, fixed capacities for action, acquired by habit⟩. The same also applies, after all, to matters of health and well-being (not in the   25 sense of "producing health and well-being" but in the sense

51 In the manuscripts there follows the sentence: "Intelligence is, therefore, both starting point and end; for demonstrations start with ultimate   10 terms and have ultimate facts as their objects." As was first pointed out by Rassow, the sentence is out of place here, and, if it is to be retained at all, it should follow ". . . and this perception is intelligence" at the end of the preceding paragraph.

52 The "eye given by experience" is of course *nous*, 'intelligence.'

53 This brings us back to the distinction of the two rational parts of the soul in chap. 1 above: theoretical wisdom is the perfection of the faculty which has necessary truths as its object, while the faculty of practical wisdom (like that of art) is concerned with contingent objects.

of "being healthy and well" as the manifestation of a physical condition or a characteristic): our ability to perform actions ⟨which show that we are healthy and well⟩ is in no way enhanced by a mastery of the science of medicine or of physical training.

(2) But if we are to say that the purpose of practical wisdom is not to *know* what is just, noble, and good, but to *become* just, noble, and good, it would be of no use at all to a man who is already good. Moreover, it is of no use to those who do
30 not have virtue, for it makes no difference whether they have practical wisdom themselves or listen to others who have it. It is quite sufficient to take the same attitude as we take toward health: we want to be healthy, yet we do not study medicine.

(3) In addition, it would seem strange if practical wisdom, though ⟨intrinsically⟩ inferior to theoretical wisdom, should surpass it in authority, because that which produces a thing
35 rules and directs it.

These, then, are the questions we must discuss: so far we have only stated them as problems.

1144a   First of all, then, we should insist that both theoretical and practical wisdom are necessarily desirable in themselves, even if neither of them produces anything. For each one of them is the virtue of a different part of the soul.[54]

Secondly, they do in fact produce something: theoretical wisdom produces happiness, not as medicine produces health, but as health itself makes a person healthy.[55] For since theo-
5 retical wisdom is one portion of virtue in its entirety, possessing and actualizing it makes a man happy. ⟨For happiness, as we have seen (I. 7) consists in the activity of virtue.⟩

---

[54] I.e., of the scientific and of the calculative part of the soul respectively; cf. above, chap. 1, 1139a3-17, and the end of chap. 11.

[55] Literally: "as health produces health." The point is that theoretical wisdom is the formal but not the efficient cause of happiness (see p. 148, note 8): it produces happiness not as something different from itself (as the knowledge of a physician is the efficient cause of health in the patient), but as the formal principle or cause which makes a thing what it is (as "health" makes a man healthy).

In the third place, a man fulfills his proper function only by way of practical wisdom and moral excellence or virtue: virtue makes us aim at the right target, and practical wisdom makes us use the right means. The fourth part of the soul, the nutritive,[56] does not have a virtue (which makes man fulfill his proper function), since it does not play any role in the   10 decision to act or not to act.

Finally, the argument has to be met that our ability to perform noble and just acts is in no way enhanced by practical wisdom. We have to begin a little further back and take the following as our starting point. It is our contention [57] that people may perform just acts without actually being just men, as in the case of people who do what has been laid down by the laws but do so either involuntarily or through ignorance   15 or for an ulterior motive, and not for the sake of performing just acts. (Such persons are not just men) despite the fact that they act the way they should, and perform all the actions which a morally good man ought to perform. On the other hand, it seems that it is possible for a man to be of such a character that he performs each particular act in such a way as to make him a good man—I mean that his acts are due to choice and are performed for the sake of the acts themselves. Now, it is virtue which makes our choice right. It is not virtue,   20 however, but a different capacity, which determines the steps which, in the nature of the case, must be taken to implement this choice.

We must stop for a moment to make this point clearer. There exists a capacity [58] called "cleverness," which is the power to perform those steps which are conducive to a goal we   25 have set for ourselves and to attain that goal. If the goal is

---

56 Of the other three parts of the soul, two have been mentioned in note 54 above. The third part is the seat of desire; cf. I. 13, 1102b13-31. The virtue of the scientific part is intellectual wisdom, of the calculative part practical wisdom, and of desire the moral virtues. For the statement that the nutritive part has no virtue, see also I. 7, 1097b34-1098a1, and 13, 1102b12.

57 See V. 6, 1134a17-23.

58 For the meaning of *dynamis* ('capacity'), see Glossary.

noble, cleverness deserves praise; if the goal is base, cleverness is knavery. That is why men of practical wisdom are often described as "clever" and "knavish." But in fact this capacity ⟨alone⟩ is not practical wisdom, although practical wisdom does not exist without it. Without virtue or excellence, this
30 eye of the soul, ⟨intelligence,⟩ does not acquire the characteristic ⟨of practical wisdom⟩: that is what we have just stated and it is obvious. For the syllogisms which express the principles initiating action [59] run: "Since the end, or the highest good, is such-and-such . . ."—whatever it may be; what it really is does not matter for our present argument. But whatever the true end may be, only a good man can judge it correctly.
35 For wickedness distorts and causes us to be completely mistaken about the fundamental principles of action. Hence it is clear that a man cannot have practical wisdom unless he is good.

13. *Practical wisdom and moral virtue*

1144b   Accordingly, we must also re-examine virtue or excellence. Virtue offers a close analogy to the relation that exists between practical wisdom and cleverness. Just as these two qualities are not identical but similar, so we find the same relation between natural virtue and virtue in the full sense. It seems that the various kinds of character inhere in all of
5 us, somehow or other, by nature. We tend to be just, capable of self-control, and to show all our other character traits from the time of our birth. Yet we still seek something more, the good in a fuller sense, and the possession of these traits in another way. For it is true that children and beasts are endowed with natural qualities or characteristics, but it is evident that without intelligence these are harmful. This much, to be sure,
10 we do seem to notice: as in the case of a mighty body which, when it moves without vision, comes down with a mighty fall because it cannot see, so it is in the matter under discussion.

[59] For the practical syllogism, see p. 55, note 3; see also pp. 150-51, note 13.

⟨If a man acts blindly, i.e., using his natural virtue alone, he will fail;⟩ but once he acquires intelligence, it makes a great difference in his action. At that point, the natural characteristic will become that virtue in the full sense which it previously resembled.

Consequently, just as there exist two kinds of quality, cleverness and practical wisdom, in that part of us which forms opinions, ⟨i.e., in the calculative element,⟩ so also there are two kinds of quality in the moral part of us, natural virtue and virtue in the full sense. Now virtue in the full sense cannot be attained without practical wisdom. That is why some people maintain that all the virtues are forms of practical wisdom, and why Socrates' approach to the subject was partly right and partly wrong. He was wrong in believing that all the virtues are forms of wisdom, but right in saying that there is no virtue without wisdom.[60] This is indicated by the fact that all the current definitions of virtue,[61] after naming the characteristic and its objects, add that it is a characteristic "guided by right reason." Now right reason is that which is determined by practical wisdom. So we see that these thinkers all have some inkling that virtue is a characteristic of this kind, namely, a characteristic guided by practical wisdom.

But we must go a little beyond that. Virtue or excellence is not only a characteristic which is guided by right reason,

15

20

25

[60] Socrates' habitual identification of virtue and knowledge is too well known and too frequent in the works of both Plato and Xenophon to require references here. However, it is interesting to observe that, while different words for 'knowledge' or 'wisdom' are attributed by Plato to Socrates in different contexts, Socrates is made to identify virtue with *phronēsis* in Plato, *Meno* 88a-89a, while later in the *Phaedo* 69a-b he states only that true virtue needs *phronēsis*. For Aristotle, it is the first formula which is most characteristic of Socrates. Plato's statement in the *Phaedo* comes very close to Aristotle's own position.

[61] The reference is to the doctrines of Plato's successors in the Academy. It is interesting to observe how close Aristotle's own doctrine is to that which he ascribes to the Platonists. In discussing moral virtue, he and his rivals are united by their loyalty to the Socratic tradition as represented in Plato's dialogues.

but also a characteristic which is united with right reason; and right reason in moral matters is practical wisdom.[62] In other words, while Socrates believed that the virtues *are* rational principles—he said that all of them are forms of knowledge— we, on the other hand, think that they are *united with* a
30 rational principle.

Our discussion, then, has made it clear that it is impossible to be good in the full sense of the word without practical wisdom or to be a man of practical wisdom without moral excellence or virtue. Moreover, in this way we can also refute the dialectical argument which might be used to prove that the virtues exist independently of one another. The same individual, it might be argued, is not equally well-endowed by nature for all the virtues, with the result that at a given
35 point he will have acquired one virtue but not yet another. In the case of the natural virtues this may be true, but it cannot happen in the case of those virtues which entitle a man to
1145a be called good in an unqualified sense. For in the latter case, as soon as he possesses this single virtue of practical wisdom, he will also possess all the rest.

It is now clear [63] that we should still need practical wisdom, even if it had no bearing on action, because it is the virtue of a part of our soul. But it is also clear that ⟨it does have an important bearing on action, since⟩ no choice will be
5 right without practical wisdom and virtue. For virtue determines the end, and practical wisdom makes us do what is conducive to the end.

Still, practical wisdom has no authority over theoretical wisdom or the better part of our soul [64] any more than the art of medicine has authority over health. ⟨Just as medicine

[62] I.e., right reason is not only an external standard of action, but it also lives in us and makes us virtuous.

[63] Here begins a summary of the conclusions reached in chaps. 12 and 13.

[64] That is, the scientific or cognitive part in the soul, the rational element which grasps necessary and permanent truths; see above, chap. 1. The use of this important distinction, made at the opening of this book, at its close here illustrates the unity of Book VI.

does not use health but makes the provisions to secure it, so) practical wisdom does not use theoretical wisdom but makes the provisions to secure it. It issues commands to attain it, but it does not issue them to wisdom itself. To say the contrary would be like asserting that politics governs the gods, because it issues commands about everything in the state, ⟨including public worship⟩.

BOOK VII

1. Moral strength and moral weakness: their relation to virtue and vice and current beliefs about them

15   We have to make a fresh start now by pointing out that the qualities of character to be avoided are three in kind: vice, moral weakness, and brutishness. The opposites of two of these are obvious: one is called virtue or excellence and the other moral strength. The most fitting description of the opposite of brutishness would be to say that it is superhuman virtue, 20 a kind of heroic and divine excellence; just as Homer has Priam say about Hector that he was of surpassing excellence:

> for he did not seem like
> one who was child of a mortal man, but of god.[1]

Therefore, if, as is said, an excess of virtue can change a man into a god, the characteristic opposed to brutishness must 25 evidently be something of this sort. For just as vice and virtue do not exist in brute beasts, no more can they exist in a god. The quality of gods is something more worthy of honor than ⟨human⟩ virtue or excellence, and the quality of a brute is generically different from ⟨human⟩ vice.

If it is rare to find a man who is divine—as the Spartans, for example, customarily use the attribute "divine man" to express an exceptionally high degree of admiration for a per-30 son—it is just as rare that a brute is found among men. It does happen, particularly among barbarians, but in some cases disease and physical disability can make a man brutish. "Brutishness" is also used as a term of opprobrium for those who exceed all other men in vice.

But we must defer until later [2] some mention of this kind of disposition, and vice has already been discussed.[3] We must

[1] Homer, *Iliad* XXIV. 258-259, tr. Richmond Lattimore.
[2] See below, chap. 5.
[3] In the discussion of the moral virtues in Books II-V.

174

now discuss moral weakness, softness, and effeminacy, and   35
also moral strength and tenacity. We will do so on the assumption that each of these two sets of characteristics is neither
identical with virtue or with wickedness nor generically differ-   1145b
ent from it, but different species respectively of the covering
genera, ⟨namely, qualities to be sought and qualities to be
avoided⟩.

The proper procedure will be the one we have followed in
our treatment of other subjects: we must present phenomena,
⟨that is, the observed facts of moral life and the current beliefs about them,⟩ and, after first stating the problems inherent in these, we must, if possible, demonstrate the validity
of all the beliefs about these matters,[4] and, if not, the validity   5
of most of them or of the most authoritative. For if the difficulties are resolved and current beliefs are left intact, we shall
have proved their validity sufficiently.

Now the current beliefs are as follows: (1) Moral strength
and tenacity are qualities of great moral value and deserve
praise, while moral weakness and softness are base and deserve blame. (2) A man who is morally strong tends to abide   10
by the results of his calculation, and a morally weak man
tends to abandon them. (3) A morally weak man does, on the
basis of emotion, what he knows to be base, whereas a morally
strong man, knowing that certain appetites are base, refuses
to follow them and accepts the guidance of reason. (4) Though a
self-controlled man is called morally strong and tenacious, some
people affirm and others deny ⟨the converse, namely,⟩ that   15
a morally strong person is self-controlled in every respect; likewise, some people call a self-indulgent person "morally weak"
and a morally weak person "self-indulgent" without discriminating between the two, while others say that they are differ-

4 'Matters' here translates the Greek word *pathos*, which we usually
render as 'emotion' or 'affect.' Here, however, it is used in a loose and
general sense to include the whole class of moral phenomena. In other
words, Aristotle does not mean to deny here that the qualities enumerated above are lasting characteristics (*hexeis*). For the methodological importance of this section for Aristotle's ethical doctrine, see Introduction,
pp. xx-xxi.

ent. (5) Sometimes it is said that a man of practical wisdom cannot possibly be morally weak, and sometimes people who have practical wisdom and who are clever are said to be morally weak. (6) Finally, it is said that moral weakness is shown even in anger and in the pursuit of honor and profit.
20 These, then, are the opinions commonly heard.

2. Problems in the current beliefs about moral strength and moral weakness

The problems we might raise are these. ⟨As to (3):⟩ how can a man be morally weak in his actions, when his basic assumption is correct ⟨as to what he should do⟩? Some people claim that it is impossible for him to be morally weak if he has knowledge ⟨of what he ought to do⟩. Socrates, for example, believed that it would be strange if, when a man possesses knowledge, something else should overpower it and drag it
25 about like a slave.[5] In fact, Socrates was completely opposed to the view ⟨that a man may know what is right but do what is wrong⟩, and did not believe that moral weakness exists. He claimed that no one acts contrary to what is best in the conviction ⟨that what he is doing is bad⟩, but through ignorance ⟨of the fact that it is bad⟩.[6]

Now this theory is plainly at variance with the observed facts, and one ought to investigate the emotion ⟨involved in the acts of a morally weak man⟩: if it comes about through ignorance, what manner of ignorance is it? For evidently a man who is morally weak in his actions does not think ⟨that
30 he ought to act the way he does⟩ before he is in the grip of emotion.

There are some people [7] who accept only certain points ⟨of Socrates' theory⟩, but reject others. They agree that nothing is better or more powerful than *knowledge*, but they do not

[5] Plato, *Protagoras* 352b-c.
[6] Cf., for example, Xenophon, *Memorabilia* III. 9. 4-5.
[7] Plato's followers in the Academy are meant.

agree that no one acts contrary to what he *thought* was the better thing to do. Therefore, they say, a morally weak person does not have knowledge but opinion when he is overpowered   35
by pleasures.

However, if it really is opinion and not knowledge, if, in other words, the basic conviction which resists ⟨the emotion⟩ is not strong but weak, as it is when people are in doubt, we   1146a
can forgive a man for not sticking to his opinions in the face of strong appetites. But we do not forgive wickedness or any-thing else that deserves blame ⟨as moral weakness does. Hence it must be something stronger than opinion which is over-powered⟩. But does that mean that it is practical wisdom [8] which resists ⟨the appetite⟩? This, after all, is the strongest ⟨kind of conviction⟩. But that would be absurd: for it would mean   5
that the same man will have practical wisdom and be morally weak at the same time, and there is no one who would assert that it is the mark of a man of practical wisdom to perform voluntarily the basest actions. In addition, it has been shown before that a man of practical wisdom is a man of action [9]—for he is concerned with ultimate particulars [10]—and that he possesses the other virtues.[11]

Furthermore, ⟨as regards (4)⟩: if being a morally strong per-son involves having strong and base appetites, a self-controlled   10
man will not be morally strong nor a morally strong man self-controlled. It is out of character for a self-controlled per-son to have excessive or base appetites. Yet a morally strong man certainly must have such appetites: for if the appetites are good, the characteristic which prevents him from following them is bad, and that would mean that moral strength is not

---

[8] The point is this: if the kind of conviction a morally weak man has is neither knowledge nor a weak conviction, it must be a strong convic-tion, and practical wisdom is such a conviction, cf. VI. 9, 1142b33. Cf. also *De Anima* III. 3, 427b24-26, where knowledge, opinion, practical wisdom, and their opposites are described as *hypolēpseis* ('convictions').

[9] See VI. 5, 1140b4-6.

[10] See VI. 7, 1141b14-22; 8, 1142a23-30.

[11] See VI. 13, 1144b30-1145a2.

always morally good. If, on the other hand, our appetites are
15 weak and not base, there is nothing extraordinary in resisting
them, nor is it a great achievement if they are base and weak.[12]

Again, ⟨to take (1) and (2),⟩ if moral strength makes a person abide by any and every opinion, it is a bad thing; for
example, if it makes him persist in a false opinion. And if
moral weakness makes a man abandon any and every opinion,
moral weakness will occasionally be morally good, as, for
example, in the case of Neoptolemus in Sophocles' *Philoctetes.*
20 Neoptolemus deserves praise when he does not abide by the
resolution which Odysseus had persuaded him to adopt, because it gives him pain to tell a lie.[13]

Further, ⟨concerning (1) and (3),⟩ the sophistic argument
presents a problem. The Sophists want to refute their opponents by leading them to conclusions which contradict
generally accepted facts. Their purpose is to have success
bring them the reputation of being clever, and the syllogism
which results only becomes a problem or quandary ⟨for their
opponents⟩. For the mind is in chains when, because it is

[12] The problem here is difficult to render in English, but quite clear
in the Greek. The point is that *sōphrōn* ('self-controlled') and *enkratēs*
('morally strong') refer not only to different virtues but to essentially different types of personality. A *sōphrōn* is well-balanced through-and-
through; he gives the impression of 'self-control' without effort or strain.
The *enkratēs*, on the other hand, has an intense and passionate nature
which he is, indeed, strong enough to control, but not without a struggle.
His 'moral strength' resides in his victory; the *sōphrōn's* 'self-control'
makes a struggle unnecessary.

[13] For Odysseus' persuasion, see Sophocles, *Philoctetes* 54-122, and for
Neoptolemus' refusal to lie, lines 895-916. Burnet quotes L. Campbell's
excellent summary of the points relevant here:

But Odysseus knew that Philoctetes would not listen to him, and would
be too proud to return after such treatment. Therefore he had recourse
to guile, and persuaded Neoptolemus to second him by false pretences.
The interest of the drama lies in the gradual effect produced upon the
heart of the boy by the sufferings of Philoctetes, by his frank belief in
the fictitious tale, by his open-hearted friendship, and by his unbounded
trust in one who is deceiving him; until at length, in spite of the
strongest motives, it becomes a moral impossibility for Neoptolemus to
persevere in his attempt.

dissatisfied with the conclusion it has reached, it wishes not 25
to stand still, while on the other hand its inability to resolve
the argument makes forward movement impossible. Now, they
have one argument which leads to the conclusion that folly
combined with moral weakness is virtue. This is the way it
runs: ⟨if a man is both foolish and morally weak,⟩ he acts
contrary to his conviction because of his moral weakness; but
⟨because of his folly,⟩ his conviction is that good things are
bad and that he ought not to do them. Therefore, ⟨acting 30
contrary to his conviction,⟩ he will do what is good and not
what is bad.

A further problem ⟨arises from (2) and (4)⟩. A person who,
in his actions, pursues, and prefers what is pleasant, convinced
or persuaded ⟨that it is good⟩,[14] would seem to be better than
one who acts the same way not on the basis of calculation, but
because of moral weakness. For since he may be persuaded to
change his mind, he can be cured more easily. To a morally
weak man, on the other hand, applies the proverb, "When
water chokes you, what can you wash it down with?" For if 35
he had been persuaded to act the way he does, he would have
stopped acting that way when persuaded to change his mind. 1146b
But as it is, though persuaded that he ought to do one thing,
he nevertheless does another.[15]

Finally, if everything is the province of moral weakness and
moral strength, who would be morally weak in the unqualified
sense of the word? No one has every form of moral weakness,
but we do say of some people that they are morally weak in
an unqualified sense. 5

These are the sort of problems that arise. Some of the con-
flicting opinions must be removed and others must be left
intact. For the solution of a problem is the discovery ⟨of
truth⟩.

14 I.e., a self-indulgent man.

15 I follow Ramsauer in reading, νῦν δὲ ἄλλα πεπεισμένος οὐδὲν ἧττον
ἄλλα πράττει, and reject Bywater's bracket around the second ἄλλα.

3. Some problems solved: moral weakness and knowledge

Our first step is, then, to examine (1) whether morally weak people act knowingly or not, and, if knowingly, in what sense. Secondly, (2) we must establish the kind of questions with which a morally weak and a morally strong man are 10 concerned. I mean, are they concerned with all pleasure and pain or only with certain distinct kinds of them? Is a morally strong person the same as a tenacious person or are they different? Similar questions must also be asked about all other matters germane to this study.

The starting point of our investigation is the question (a) whether the morally strong man and the morally weak man 15 have their distinguishing features in the situations with which they are concerned or in their manner ⟨of reacting to the situation⟩. What I mean is this: does a morally weak person owe his character to certain situations ⟨to which he reacts⟩, or to the manner ⟨in which he reacts⟩, or to both? Our second question (b) is whether or not moral weakness and moral strength are concerned with all ⟨situations and feelings. The answer to both these questions is that⟩ a man who is morally weak in the unqualified sense is not ⟨so described because of his re- 20 action⟩ to every situation, but only to those situations in which also a self-indulgent man may get involved. Nor is he morally weak because of the mere fact of his relationship to these situations, ⟨namely, that he yields to temptation⟩. In that case moral weakness would be the same as self-indulgence. Instead, his moral weakness is defined by the manner ⟨in which he yields⟩. For a self-indulgent person is led on by his own choice, since he believes that he should always pursue the pleasure of the moment. A morally weak man, on the other hand, does not think he should, but pursues it, nonetheless.

(1) The contention that it is true opinion rather than 25 knowledge which a morally weak man violates in his actions has no bearing on our argument. For some people have no doubts when they hold an opinion, and think they have exact

knowledge. Accordingly, if we are going to say that the weakness of their belief is the reason why those who hold opinion will be more liable to act against their conviction than those who have knowledge, we shall find that there is no difference between knowledge and opinion. For some people are no less firmly convinced of what they believe than others are of what they know: Heraclitus is a case in point.[16] (a) But the verb "to know" has two meanings: a man is said to "know" both when he does not use the knowledge he has and when he does use it. Accordingly, when a man does wrong it will make a difference whether he is not exercising [17] the knowledge he has, ⟨viz., that it is wrong to do what he is doing⟩, or whether he is exercising it. In the latter case, we would be baffled, but not if he acted without exercising his knowledge.

Moreover, (b) since there are two kinds of premise,[18]

[16] The reference is not to any specific utterance of Heraclitus, but to the tone of intense conviction with which he asserted all his doctrines, some of which Aristotle finds patently false, and hence examples of opinion rather than knowledge.

[17] The verb *theōrein* describes the activity of the mind, most frequently in the sense of 'to contemplate,' 'study.' However, as Burnet points out, *theōrein* is also commonly used to describe the activity or actualization (*energeia*) of knowledge, and that must be its meaning here. The literal sense is 'to inspect' or 'to keep one's gaze fixed on' the knowledge which one possesses.

[18] What is involved in this paragraph is the practical syllogism which was briefly explained on p. 55, note 3. However, a refinement is added here, which requires further explanation. A major premise, Aristotle says, may contain two kinds of universal, e.g., the premise that "dry food is good for all men" makes a universal statement about (*i*) men and (*ii*) about dry food. Accordingly, two kinds of syllogism can be developed from this major premise. The first: "dry food is good for all men"; "I am a man"; therefore, "dry food is good for me" is here neglected by Aristotle, because the agent is obviously always aware that he is a man (see *De Motu Animalium* 7, 701a25 for a fuller statement). But the second possible syllogism: "dry food is good for all men"; "this kind of food is dry"; therefore, "this kind of food is good for me," leaves the agent only with the general knowledge that, for example. cereals are good for him: he will not yet know whether the barley he is faced with is a cereal. "Knowledge" of this sort will obviously not serve to check a healthy appetite faced with an attractive bowl of porridge.

1147a ⟨namely, universal and particular,⟩ it may well happen that a man knows both ⟨major and minor premise of a practical syllogism⟩ and yet acts against his knowledge, because the ⟨minor⟩ premise which he uses is universal rather than particular. ⟨In that case, he cannot apply his knowledge to his action,⟩ for the actions to be performed are particulars. Also, there are two kinds of universal term to be distinguished: one

5 applies to (i) the agent, and the other (ii) to the thing. For example, when a person knows that dry food is good for all men, ⟨he may also know⟩ (i) that he is a man, or (ii) that this kind of food is dry. But whether the particular food before him is of this kind is something of which ⟨a morally weak man⟩ either does not have the knowledge or does not exercise it. So we see that there will be a tremendous difference between these two ways of knowing. We do not regard it as at all strange that ⟨a morally weak person⟩ "knows" in the latter sense ⟨with one term nonspecific⟩, but it would be surprising if he "knew" in the other sense, ⟨namely with both terms apprehended as concrete particulars⟩.

10 There is (c) another way besides those we have so far described, in which it is possible for men to have knowledge. When a person has knowledge but does not use it, we see that "having" a characteristic [19] has different meanings. There is a sense in which a person both has and does not have knowledge, for example, when he is asleep, mad, or drunk. But this is precisely the condition of people who are in the grip of the

15 emotions. Fits of passion, sexual appetites, and some other such passions actually cause palpable changes in the body, and in some cases even produce madness. Now it is clear that we must attribute to the morally weak a condition similar to that of men who are asleep, mad, or drunk. That the words they utter spring from knowledge ⟨as to what is good⟩ is no evidence to the contrary. People can repeat geometrical dem-

20 onstrations and verses of Empedocles even when affected by

[19] The Greek word here is *hexis*, which we usually render as 'characteristic': but its special point here is that it is the noun form of *echein*, 'to have.' See Glossary.

sleep, madness, and drink; and beginning students can reel
off the words they have heard, but they do not yet know the
subject. The subject must grow to be part of them, and that
takes time. We must, therefore, assume that a man who displays moral weakness repeats the formulae ⟨of moral knowl-
edge⟩ in the same way as an actor speaks his lines.

Further, (d) we may also look at the cause ⟨of moral weak-
ness⟩ from the viewpoint of the science of human nature,[20] in
the following way. ⟨In the practical syllogism,⟩ one of the
premises, the universal, is a current belief, while the other in-   25
volves particular facts which fall within the domain of sense
perception. When two premises are combined into one, ⟨i.e.,
when the universal rule is realized in a particular case,⟩ the
soul is thereupon bound to affirm the conclusion, and if the
premises involve action, the soul is bound to perform this act
at once. For example, if ⟨the premises are⟩: "Everything sweet
ought to be tasted" and "This thing before me is sweet"
("this thing" perceived as an individual particular object),   30
a man who is able ⟨to taste⟩ and is not prevented is bound to
act accordingly at once.[21]

Now, suppose that there is within us one universal opinion
forbidding us to taste ⟨things of this kind⟩, and another
⟨universal⟩ opinion which tells us that everything sweet is

20 *Physikōs* literally means 'in a manner proper to nature' or, in
Aristotle, 'from the viewpoint of natural philosophy.' The frequent use
of the term as the opposite of *logikōs* ('logically,' 'dialectically'), e.g., in
Physics III. 5, 204b4-10 and in *De Generatione et Corruptione* I. 2,
316a10-11, indicates that Aristotle considered the preceding three arguments (a)-(c) as more logical or dialectical, based upon the way men talk
about moral questions, whereas he is now going to consider the phenomenon of moral weakness from the point of view of moral psychology
or the study of human nature.

21 This is a description of the case in which moral knowledge is fully
realized and therefore fully effective. It prepares the way for the "natural"
or psychological explanation of moral weakness in the next paragraph,
which is the central analysis of Book VII and one of the most important
texts in the *Nic. Eth.* for an understanding of Aristotle's approach to
the problem of choice and for his conception of the role which knowledge plays in determining voluntary action.

pleasant, and also ⟨a concrete perception⟩, determining our activity, that the particular thing before us is sweet; and suppose further that the appetite ⟨for pleasure⟩ happens to be present. ⟨The result is that⟩ one opinion tells us to avoid that thing,

35 while appetite, capable as it is of setting in motion each part of our body, drives us to it. ⟨This is the case we have been looking for, the defeat of reason in moral weakness.⟩ Thus it turns out that a morally weak man acts under the influence of

1147b some kind of reasoning and opinion, an opinion which is not intrinsically but only incidentally opposed to right reason; for it is not opinion but appetite that is opposed to right reason.²²
And this explains why animals cannot be morally weak: they do not have conceptions of universals, but have only the power

5 to form mental images²³ and memory of particulars.

How is the ⟨temporary⟩ ignorance of a morally weak person dispelled and how does he regain his ⟨active⟩ knowledge ⟨of what is good⟩? The explanation is the same as it is for drunkenness and sleep, and it is not peculiar to the affect of moral weakness. To get it we have to go to the students of natural science.²⁴

The final premise, consisting as it does in an opinion about

²² The point is this: there is a kind of reasoning involved in the actions of a morally weak person: he starts out with the opinion that everything sweet is pleasant, he finds a particular sweet thing, and knows that the thing is pleasant. But he also has right reason, which tells him that he should not taste everything sweet. However, the appetite for pleasure, taking hold of his opinion that everything sweet is pleasant, transforms this opinion into the action of tasting. What is contrary to right reason (i.e., contrary to the knowledge that not everything sweet should be tasted) is not his opinion (that sweet things are pleasant) but his appetite for pleasure.

²³ See Glossary, *phantasia*.

²⁴ Aristotle's term here for the 'student of natural science' is *physiologos*, and in fact 'physiology' is precisely what he has in mind: the temporary disturbance of rational control under the influence of pleasure, passion, drunkenness or sleep is to be explained in biological terms—for Aristotle in terms of the blood supply around the heart; for modern biology in terms of blood supply to the brain, glandular secretions, etc. See his account of sleep in *De Somno*.

an object perceived by the senses, determines our action.   10
When in the grip of emotion, a morally weak man either does
not have this premise, or he has it not in the sense of knowing
it, but in the sense of uttering it as a drunken man may utter
verses of Empedocles. ⟨Because he is not in active possession of
this premise,⟩ and because the final ⟨concrete⟩ term of his
reasoning is not a universal and does not seem to be an object
of scientific knowledge in the same way that a universal is,
⟨for both these reasons⟩ we seem to be led to the conclusion
which Socrates sought to establish. Moral weakness does not   15
occur in the presence of knowledge in the strict sense, and it
is sensory knowledge, not science, which is dragged about by
emotion.²⁵

This completes our discussion of the question whether a
morally weak person acts with knowledge or without knowledge, and in what sense it is possible for him to act knowingly.

4. More problems solved: the sphere in which moral weakness operates

(2) The next point we have to discuss is whether it is pos-   20
sible for a man to be morally weak in the unqualified sense,
or whether the moral weakness of all who have it is concerned
with particular situations. If the former is the case, we shall
have to see with what kind of situations he is concerned.

Now, it is clearly in their attitude to pleasures and pains
that men are morally strong and tenacious and morally weak

²⁵ Socrates' conclusion is referred to above, at the beginning of chap. 2,
1145b22-24: "It would be strange if, when a man possesses knowledge,
something else should overpower it and drag it about like a slave."
Aristotle here agrees with Socrates: in the case of a morally weak person,
it is not knowledge in the true sense, which is always a universal, that
is being vanquished, but another kind of knowledge. This "sensory knowledge" is the concrete perception of "this sweet thing" as an application of
the rule of right reason that "not all sweet things are to be tasted." It
is not the general or "scientific" universal that is overpowered by appetite,
but the application of this rule to the particular case: and the apprehension of the particular is the work of sense perception. I accept
Ramsauer's conjecture and insert a δὲ after ταύτην at 1147b10.

and soft. There are two sources of pleasure: some are necessary, and others are desirable in themselves but admit of
25 excess. The necessary kind are those concerned with the body:
I mean sources of pleasure such as food and drink and sexual
intercourse, in short, the kind of bodily pleasures which we
assigned to the sphere of self-indulgence and self-control.[26]
By sources of pleasure which are not necessary but desirable in
30 themselves, I mean, for example, victory, honor, wealth, and
similar good and pleasant things. Now, (a) those who violate
the right reason that they possess by excessive indulgence in
the second type of pleasures, are not called morally weak in
the unqualified sense, but only with a qualification: we call
them "morally weak in regard to material goods," or profit,
or honor, or anger, but not "morally weak" pure and simple.
They are different from the morally weak in the unqualified
sense and share the same name only by analogy, as in our
35 example of the man called Man, who won an Olympic victory.[27] In his case there is not much difference between the
1148a general definition of man and the definition proper to him
alone, and yet there was a difference. ⟨That there is similarly
a difference between the two senses of morally weak⟩ is shown
by the fact that we blame moral weakness—regardless of
whether it is moral weakness in the unqualified sense or moral
weakness concerning some particular bodily pleasure—not only
as an error, but also as a kind of vice. But we do not blame as
5 vicious those ⟨who are morally weak in matters of material
goods, profit, ambition, anger, and so forth⟩.

(b) We now come to those bodily enjoyments which, we
say,[28] are the sphere of the self-controlled and the self-indulgent. Here a man who pursues the excesses of things pleasant
and avoids excesses of things painful (of hunger, thirst, heat,

26 I.e., the sensual pleasures of taste and touch. See III. 10, 1118a23-26.
27 Thanks to a papyrus we now know that the ancient commentators
were right in attributing an Olympic victory to a certain Anthropos
('Man'). He won the boxing contest in 456 B.C. In view of that fact, it is
preferable to retain νενικηκώς of the majority of manuscripts rather than
read νικῶν on the authority of Kᵇ.
28 See III. 10 and 11.

cold, and of anything we feel by touch or taste), and does so
not by choice but against his choice and thinking, is called
"morally weak" without the addition of "in regard to such-   10
and-such," e.g., "in regard to feelings of anger," but simply
morally weak without qualification. The truth of this is
proved by the fact that persons who indulge in bodily pleasures are called "soft," but not persons who indulge in feelings
of anger and so forth. For this reason, we class the morally
weak man with the self-indulgent, and the morally strong with
the self-controlled. But we do not include ⟨in the same cate-
gory⟩ those who indulge in feelings of anger, because moral
weakness and self-indulgence are, in a way, concerned with
the same pleasures and pains. That is, they are concerned   15
with the same pleasures and pains but not in the same way.
Self-indulgent men pursue the excess by choice, but the
morally weak do not exercise choice.

That is why we are probably more justified in calling a
person self-indulgent who shows little or no appetite in
pursuing an excess of pleasures and in avoiding moderate
pains, than a person who is driven by strong appetite ⟨to   20
pursue pleasure and to avoid pain⟩. For what would the
former do, if, in addition, he had the vigorous appetite of
youth and felt strong pain at lacking the objects necessary for
his pleasure?

Some appetites and desires are generically noble and worth
while—⟨let us remember⟩ our earlier [29] distinction of pleasant
things into those which are by nature desirable, the opposite
of these, and those which are intermediate between the two—   25
for example, material goods, profit, victory, and honor. Now,
people are not blamed for being affected by all these and
similar objects of pleasure and by those of the intermediate
kind, nor are they blamed for having an appetite or a liking

---

[29] See the beginning of this chapter, 1147b23-31, where, however, no
mention is made of the opposite class. Thus, what we get here is actually
a new classification to complement the earlier one by the addition of
"things not desirable by nature." The intermediate group, as we shall
see, is identical with the necessary objects of pleasure.

for them; they are blamed only for the manner in which they do so, if they do so to excess. This, by the way, is why ⟨we do not regard as wicked⟩ all those who, contrary to right reason, are overpowered by something that is noble and good by nature, or who pursue it—those, for example, who devote
30 themselves to the pursuit of honor or to their children and parents more than they should. All these things are good, and those who devote themselves to them are praised. And yet even here there is an element of excess, if, like Niobe, one were to fight against the gods ⟨for the sake of one's children⟩, or if
1148b one showed the same excessively foolish devotion to his father as did Satyros, nicknamed "the filial." [30] So we see that there cannot be any wickedness in this area, because, as we stated, each of these things is in itself naturally desirable. But excess in one's attachment to them is base and must be avoided.

Similarly, there cannot be moral weakness in this area ⟨of
5 things naturally desirable⟩. Moral weakness is not only something to be avoided, but it is also something that deserves blame. Still, because there is a similarity in the affect, people do call it "moral weakness," but they add "in regard to ⟨such-and-such⟩," in the same way as they speak of a "bad" doctor or a "bad" actor without meaning to imply that the person is bad in the unqualified sense. So just as in the case of the doctor and the actor ⟨we do not speak of "badness" in the unqualified sense⟩, because their badness is not vice but only
10 something similar to vice by analogy, so it is clear that, in the other case, we must understand by "moral weakness" and

[30] Niobe boasted that, with her six (or in some versions, seven) sons and an equal number of daughters, she was at least equal to the goddess Leto, who only had two children, the twins Apollo and Artemis. Apollo and Artemis thereupon killed all her children, and Niobe was turned into stone. Who exactly Satyros was, we do not know. Ancient commentators tell us that he committed suicide when his father died, or that he called his father a god. Burnet, in his note on this passage, remarks that the kings of Bosporus in the fourth century B.C. were called Satyros, and that "Satyros the Filial" ". . . looks very like a royal title, and if the reference were to the deification of a dead king by his son, the parallel to the case of Niobe would be striking."

"moral strength" only that which operates in the same sphere as self-control and self-indulgence. When we use these terms of anger, we do so only in an analogous sense. Therefore, we add a qualification and say "morally weak in regard to anger," just as we say "morally weak in regard to honor or profit."

5. Moral weakness and brutishness

(1) Some things are pleasant by nature, partly (a) without   15
qualification, and partly (b) pleasant for different classes of animals and humans. Then (2) there are things which are not pleasant by nature, but which come to be pleasant (a) through physical disability, (b) through habit, or (c) through an ⟨innate⟩ depravity of nature. We can observe characteristics corresponding to each of the latter group (2), just as ⟨we did in discussing (1), things pleasant by nature⟩. I mean (2c) characteristics of brutishness, for instance, the female who is said to rip open pregnant women and devour the infants; or what   20
is related about some of the savage tribes near the Black Sea, that they delight in eating raw meat or human flesh, and that some of them lend each other their children for a feast; or the story told about Phalaris.[31]

These are characteristics of brutishness. Another set of characteristics (2a) develops through disease and occasionally through insanity, as, for example, in the case of the man who   25
offered his mother as a sacrifice to the gods and ate of her, or the case of the slave who ate the liver of his fellow slave. Other characteristics are the result of disease or (2b) of habit, e.g., plucking out one's hair, gnawing one's fingernails, or even chewing coal or earth, and also sexual relations between males. These practices are, in some cases, due to nature, but in other cases they are the result of habit, when, for example,   30
someone has been sexually abused from childhood.

31 Phalaris, tyrant of Acragas in the second quarter of the sixth century B.C., was said to have built a hollow brazen bull, in which he roasted his victims alive, presumably to eat them afterwards. There were several other stories current in antiquity about his brutality.

When nature is responsible, no one would call the persons affected morally weak any more than one would call women morally weak, because they are passive and not active in sexual intercourse. Nor would we apply the term to persons in a morbid condition as a result of habit. To have one of these characteristics means to be outside the limits of vice, just as brutishness, too, lies outside the limits of vice. To have such characteristics and to master them or be mastered by them does not constitute moral ⟨strength or⟩ weakness in an unqualified sense but only by analogy, just as a person is not to be called morally weak without qualification when he cannot master his anger, but only morally weak in regard to the emotion involved.

1149a

5 For all excessive folly, cowardice, self-indulgence, and ill-temper is either brutish or morbid. When someone is by nature the kind of person who fears everything, even the rustling of a mouse, his cowardice is brutish, while the man's fear of the weasel was due to disease.[32] In the case of folly, those who are irrational by nature and live only by their senses, as do some distant barbarian tribes, are brutish, whereas those whose irrationality is due to a disease, such as epilepsy, or to insanity, are morbid.

10

Sometimes it happens that a person merely possesses one of these characteristics without being mastered by it—I mean, for example, if a Phalaris had restrained his appetite so as not to eat the flesh of a child or so as not to indulge in some perverse form of sexual pleasure. But it also happens that a man not only has the characteristic but is mastered by it. Thus, just as the term "wickedness" refers in its unqualified sense to man alone, while in another sense it is qualified by the addition of "brutish" or "morbid," in precisely the same way it is plain that there is a brutish and a morbid kind of moral weakness ⟨i.e., being mastered by brutishness or disease⟩, but in its un-

15

[32] The imperfect here seems to indicate a reference to a well-known story. The point of this sentence is that excessive fear of noise is no longer human but brutish, while a more specific phobia, such as fear of a weasel, is a symptom of mental disease.

qualified sense the term "moral weakness" refers only to
human self-indulgence.   20

It is, accordingly, clear that moral weakness and moral
strength operate only in the same sphere as do self-indulgence
and self-control, and that the moral weakness which operates
in any other sphere is different in kind, and is called "moral
weakness" only by extension, not in an unqualified sense.

6. Moral weakness in anger

At this point we may observe that moral weakness in anger
is less base than moral weakness in regard to the appetites.   25
For (1) in a way, anger seems to listen to reason, but to hear
wrong, like hasty servants, who run off before they have heard
everything their master tells them, and fail to do what they
were ordered, or like dogs, which bark as soon as there is a
knock without waiting to see if the visitor is a friend. In the
same way, the heat and swiftness of its nature make anger   30
hear but not listen to an order, before rushing off to take revenge. For reason and imagination indicate that an insult or
a slight has been received, and anger, drawing the conclusion,
as it were, that it must fight against this sort of thing, simply
flares up at once. Appetite, on the other hand, is no sooner
told by reason and perception that something is pleasant than 35
it rushes off to enjoy it. Consequently, while anger somehow   1149b
follows reason, appetite does not. Hence appetite is baser (than
anger). For when a person is morally weak in anger, he is in a
sense overcome by reason, but the other is not overcome by
reason but by appetite.

Further, (2) it is more excusable to follow one's natural
desires, inasmuch as we are also more inclined to pardon such
appetites as are common to all men and to the extent that   5
they are common to all. Now anger and ill temper are more
natural than are the appetites which make us strive for excess
and for what is not necessary. Take the example of the man
who was defending himself against the charge of beating his
father with the words: "Yes, I did it: my father, too, used to

beat his father, and he beat his, and"—pointing to his little boy
10 —"he will beat me when he grows up to be a man. It runs in
the family." And the story goes that the man who was being
dragged out of the house by his son asked him to stop at the
door, on the grounds that he himself had not dragged his
father any further than that.

Moreover, (3) the more underhanded a person is, the more
unjust he is. Now, a hot-tempered man is not underhanded;
15 nor is anger: it is open. But appetite has the same attribute
as Aphrodite, who is called "weaver of guile on Cyprus
born," [33] and as her "pattern-pierced zone," of which Homer
says: "endearment that steals the heart away even from the
thoughtful." [34] Therefore, since moral weakness of this type
⟨which involves the appetite⟩ is more unjust and baser than
moral weakness concerning anger, it is this type which constitutes moral weakness in the unqualified sense and is even a
kind of vice.[35]

20 Again, (4) no one feels pain when insulting another without provocation, whereas everyone who acts in a fit of anger
acts with pain. On the contrary, whoever unprovoked insults
another, feels pleasure. If, then, acts which justify outbursts of
anger are more unjust than others, it follows that moral weakness caused by appetite ⟨is more unjust than moral weakness
caused by anger⟩, for anger does not involve unprovoked
insult.

It is now clear that moral weakness in regard to the appetites is more disgraceful than moral weakness displayed
25 in anger, and also that moral strength and weakness operate
in the sphere of the bodily appetites and pleasures. But we
must still grasp the distinctions to be made within bodily ap-

[33] The author of this phrase is unknown, but the same adjective
'weaver of guile' (doloploke) is also applied to Aphrodite in a famous
poem by Sappho (frg. 1, line 2 L-P).

[34] Homer, Iliad XIV. 214 and 217, tr. Richmond Lattimore.

[35] But it is not vice in the unqualified sense, for that would involve
choice.

petites and pleasures. For, as we stated at the beginning,[36] some pleasures are human, i.e., natural in kind as well as in degree, while others are brutish, and others again are due to physical disability and disease. It is only with the first group of these, ⟨i.e., the human pleasures,⟩ that self-control 30 and self-indulgence are concerned. For that reason, we do not call beasts either self-controlled or self-indulgent; if we do so, we do it only metaphorically, in cases where a [37] general distinction can be drawn between one class of animals and another on the basis of wantonness, destructiveness, and indiscriminate voracity. ⟨This use is only metaphorical⟩ because beasts are incapable of choice and calculation, but ⟨animals of this type⟩ stand outside the pale of their nature, just as 35 madmen do among humans.

Brutishness is a lesser evil than vice, but it is more horrify- 1150a ing. For ⟨in a beast⟩ the better element cannot be perverted, as it can be in man, since it is lacking. ⟨To compare a brute beast and a brutish man⟩ is like comparing an inanimate with an animate being to see which is more evil. For the depravity of a being which does not possess the source that initiates its own motion is always less destructive ⟨than the depravity of a being that possesses this source⟩, and intelligence is such a 5 source. A similar comparison can be made between injustice ⟨as such⟩ and an unjust man: each is in some sense worse than the other, for a bad man can do ten thousand times as much harm as a beast.[38]

36 The "beginning" is less likely to be chap. 1, 1145a27-35, where the following distinctions are hinted at, than chap. 5, 1148b15-31, where they are discussed in greater detail.

37 I accept Bywater's suggested emendation of τινι to τι.

38 The chief point of this paragraph is clear enough: vice is worse and more destructive than brutishness, because it means a perversion of reason and intelligence, which initiate human motions, but not the motions of a beast. The meaning of the last sentence seems to be that "injustice as such" is worse than an unjust man because it is pure vice; similarly, a beast is worse than a brutish man, since it is a pure embodiment of "brutishness." But in fact it is not injustice but an unjust man

7. *Moral strength and moral weakness: tenacity and softness*

As regards the pleasures, pains, appetites, and aversions that come to us through touch and taste, and which we defined
10 earlier [39] as the sphere of self-indulgence and self-control, it is possible to be the kind of person who is overcome even by those which most people master; but it is also possible to master those by which most people are overcome. Those who are overcome by pleasure or master it are, respectively, morally weak and morally strong; and in the case of pain, they are, respectively, soft and tenacious. The disposition which char-
15 acterizes the majority of men lies between these two, although they tend more to the inferior characteristics.

Some pleasures are necessary, up to a certain point, and others are not, whereas neither excesses nor deficiencies of pleasure are necessary. The same is also true of appetites and pains. From all this it follows that a man is self-indulgent when he pursues excesses of pleasant things, or when he ⟨pur-
20 sues necessary pleasures⟩ to excess, by choice,[40] for their own sakes, and not for an ulterior result. A man of this kind inevitably feels no regret, and is as a result incorrigible. For a person who feels no regret is incorrigible.[41] A person deficient ⟨in his pursuit of the necessary pleasures⟩ is the opposite ⟨of self-indulgent⟩, and the man who occupies the middle position is self-controlled. In the same way, a man who avoids bodily pain ⟨is self-indulgent⟩, provided he does so by choice and not because he is overcome by them.
25 A choice is not exercised either by a person who is driven

who causes harm; and similarly, the brutish man can do a great deal more harm than any animal.

39 See III. 10.

40 I follow Susemihl, Burnet, and Rackham in preferring the καὶ διὰ προαίρεσιν of Mᵇ to the ἢ διὰ προαίρεσιν of the other manuscripts.

41 The purpose of this sentence is evidently to explain the etymology of *akolasia* ('self-indulgence'), which literally means 'lack of chastisement,' 'lack of corrective punishment'; cf. p. 82, note 34.

by pleasure, or by a person who is avoiding the pain of ⟨unsatisfied⟩ appetite. There is, accordingly, a difference between indulging by choice and not by choice. Everyone would think worse of a man who would perform some disgraceful act actuated only slightly or not at all by appetite, than of a person who was actuated by a strong appetite. And we would regard as worse a man who feels no anger as he beats another man, than someone who does so in anger. For what would he do, if he were in the grip of emotion when acting? Hence a self-indulgent man is worse than one who is morally weak.

So we see that one of the characteristics described, ⟨viz., the deliberate avoidance of pain,⟩ constitutes rather a kind of softness, while a person possessing the other, ⟨viz., the deliberate pursuit of excessive pleasures,⟩ is self-indulgent.

A morally strong is opposed to a morally weak man, and a tenacious to a soft man. For being tenacious consists in offering resistance, while moral strength consists in mastering. Resistance and mastery are two different things, just as not being defeated differs from winning a victory. Hence, moral strength is more desirable than tenacity. A man who is deficient ⟨in his resistance to pains⟩ which most people withstand successfully is soft and effeminate. For effeminacy is a form of softness. A man of this kind lets his cloak trail, in order to save himself the pain of lifting it up, and plays the invalid without believing himself to be involved in the misery which a true invalid suffers.

The situation is similar in the case of moral strength and moral weakness. If a person is overcome by powerful and excessive pleasures or pains, we are not surprised. In fact, we find it pardonable if he is overcome while offering resistance, as, for example, Theodectes' Philoctetes [42] does when bitten by

---

[42] Theodectes (*ca.* 375-334 B.C.) spent most of his life at Athens. He studied under Plato, Isocrates, and Aristotle, and in addition to writing tragedies, won a considerable reputation as an orator. A scholion on this passage tells us that, in Theodectes' tragedy, Philoctetes, after repressing his pain for a long time, finally bursts out: "Cut off my hand!"

0 the snake, or as Cercyon in Carcinus' *Alope*,[43] or as people who try to restrain their laughter burst out in one great guffaw, as actually happened to Xenophantus.[44] But we are surprised if a man is overcome by and unable to withstand those ⟨pleasures and pains⟩ which most people resist successfully, unless his disposition is congenital or caused by disease, as among the kings of Scythia, for example, in whom softness
5 is congenital,[45] and as softness distinguishes the female from the male.

A man who loves amusement is also commonly regarded as being self-indulgent, but he is actually soft. For amusement is relaxation, inasmuch as it is respite from work, and a lover of amusement is a person who goes in for relaxation to excess.

One kind of moral weakness is impetuosity and another is a lack of strength. People of the latter kind deliberate but do
20 not abide by the results of their deliberation, because they are overcome by emotion, while the impetuous are driven on by emotion, because they do not deliberate. ⟨If they deliberated, they would not be driven on so easily,⟩ for as those who have just been tickled are immune to being tickled again,[46] so some people are not overcome by emotion, whether

---

[43] Carcinus was a fourth-century Athenian tragic poet. According to a scholiast, "Cercyon had a daughter Alope. Upon learning that his daughter Alope had committed adultery, he asked her who had perpetrated the deed, and said: 'If you tell me, I will not be grieved at all.' When Alope told him who the adulterer was, Cercyon was so overcome with grief that he could no longer stand life and renounced living."

[44] The occasion is not known. Xenophantus is said to have been a musician at the court of Alexander the Great (356-323 B.C.). Seneca (*De Ira* II. 2) tells us that when Xenophantus sang, Alexander was so stirred that he seized his weapons in his hands.

[45] According to the Hippocratic treatise *On Airs, Waters, and Places* 22, horseback riding caused softness among the Scythian aristocracy. Herodotus I. 105 attributes this "female disease" to the fact that some Scythians robbed the temple of Heavenly Aphrodite at Ascalon.

[46] The reading προγαργαλισθέντες seems to give a better sense than the active προγαργαλίσαντες. Most commentators explain this passage by reference to *Problemata* XXXV. 6, 965a11-14: "Why can no one tickle himself? It is no doubt for the same reason that you feel another's tick-

pleasant or painful, when they feel and see it coming and have roused themselves and their power of reasoning in good time. Keen and excitable persons are the most prone to the impetu-   25 ous kind of moral weakness. Swiftness prevents the keen and vehemence the excitable from waiting for reason to guide them, since they tend to be led by their imagination.

8. *Moral weakness and self-indulgence*

A self-indulgent man, as we stated,[47] is one who feels no regret, since he abides by the choice he has made. A morally   30 weak person, on the other hand, always feels regret. Therefore, the formulation of the problem, as we posed it above,[48] does not correspond to the facts: it is a self-indulgent man who cannot be cured, but a morally weak man is curable. For wickedness is like a disease such as dropsy or consumption, while moral weakness resembles epilepsy: the former is chronic, the latter intermittent. All in all, moral weakness and vice are generically different from each other. A vicious man   35 is not aware of his vice, but a morally weak man knows his weakness.

Among the morally weak, those who lose themselves ⟨in   1151a emotion, i.e., the impetuous,⟩ are better than those who have a rational principle but do not abide by it, ⟨i.e., those who lack strength⟩. For they are overcome by a lesser emotion and do not yield without previous deliberation, as the impetuous do. A man who has this kind of moral weakness resembles those who get drunk quickly and on little wine, or on less wine than most people do.

That moral weakness is not a vice ⟨in the strict sense⟩ is now   5 evident, though in a certain sense it is perhaps one.[49] For

---

ling less, if you feel it coming, and more, if you do not see it coming. Therefore, a person will be tickled least effectively, if he is aware of what is happening."

47 See above, chap. 7, 1150a21-22.
48 See above, chap. 2, 1146a31-b2.
49 Cf. above, chap. 6, especially 1149b18-20.

moral weakness violates choice, whereas vice is in accordance with choice. Nevertheless, they are similar in the actions to which they lead, just as Demodocus said of the Milesians:

> The Milesians are no stupid crew,
> except that they do what the stupid do.[50]

10   Similarly, the morally weak are not unjust, but they will act like unjust men.

A morally weak man is the kind of person who pursues bodily pleasures to excess and contrary to right reason, though he is not persuaded ⟨that he ought to do so⟩; the self-indulgent, on the other hand, is persuaded to pursue them because he is the kind of man who does so. This means that it is the former who is easily persuaded to change his mind, but the latter is

15   not. For virtue or excellence preserves and wickedness destroys the initiating motive or first cause ⟨of action⟩, and in actions the initiating motive or first cause is the end at which we aim, as the hypotheses are in mathematics. For neither in mathematics nor in moral matters does reasoning teach us the principles or starting points; it is virtue, whether natural or habitual, that inculcates right opinion about the principle or first premise. A man who has this right opinion is self-controlled,

20   and his opposite is self-indulgent.

But there exists a kind of person who loses himself under the impact of emotion and violates right reason, a person whom emotion so overpowers that he does not act according to the dictates of right reason, but not sufficiently to make him the kind of man who is persuaded that he must abandon himself completely to the pursuit of such pleasures. This is the morally weak man: he is better than the self-indulgent, and

25   he is not bad in the unqualified sense of the word. For the best thing in him is saved: the principle or premise ⟨as to how he should act⟩. Opposed to him is another kind of man, who remains steadfast and does not lose himself, at least not under

[50] Demodocus wrote lampooning epigrams in the sixth century B.C. The quotation here is frg. 1 (Diehl³).

the impact of emotion. These considerations make it clear
that moral strength is a characteristic of great moral worth,
while moral weakness is bad.

9. *Steadfastness in moral strength and moral weakness*

Is a man morally strong when he abides by any and every
dictate of reason and choice, or only when he abides by the
right choice? And is a man morally weak when he does not   30
abide by every choice and dictate of reason, or only when he
fails to abide by the rational dictate which is not false and the
choice which is right? This is the problem we stated earlier.[51]
Or is it true reason and right choice as such, but any other
kind of choice incidentally, to which the one remains steadfast
and the other does not? (This seems to be the correct answer,)   35
for if a person chooses and pursues the attainment of *a* by
means of *b*, his pursuit and choice are for *a* as such but for *b*   1151b
incidentally. And by "as such" we mean "in the unqualified
sense." Therefore, there is a sense in which the one abides by
and the other abandons any and every kind of opinion, but in
the unqualified sense, only true opinion.

There are those who remain steadfast to their opinion and
are called "obstinate." They are hard to convince and are not   5
easily persuaded to change their mind. They bear a certain
resemblance to a morally strong person, just as an extravagant
man resembles one who is generous, and a reckless man resembles one who is confident. But they are, in fact, different in
many respects. The one, the morally strong, will be a person
who does not change under the influence of emotion and appetite, but on occasion he will be persuaded (by argument).   10
Obstinate men, on the other hand, are not easily persuaded
by rational argument; but to appetites they are amenable, and
in many cases are driven on by pleasures. The various kinds of
obstinate people are the opinionated, the ignorant, and the
boorish. The opinionated let themselves be influenced by pleas-

[51] See above, chap. 2, 1146a16-31.

ure and pain: they feel the joy of victory, when someone fails
15 to persuade them to change their mind, and they feel pain
when their views are overruled, like decrees that are declared
null and void. As a result, they bear a greater resemblance to
the morally weak than to the morally strong.

Then there are those who do not abide by their decisions
for reasons other than moral weakness, as, for example, Neoptolemus in Sophocles' *Philoctetes*.[52] Granted it was under the
influence of pleasure that he did not remain steadfast, but it
was a noble pleasure: it was noble in his eyes to be truthful,
but he was persuaded by Odysseus to tell a lie. For not any-
20 body who acts under the influence of pleasure is self-indulgent,
bad, or morally weak, but only those who do so under the influence of a base pleasure.

There is also a type who feels less joy than he should at the
things of the body and, therefore, does not abide by the dictates of reason. The median between this type and the morally
25 weak man is the man of moral strength. For a morally weak
person does not abide by the dictates of reason, because he
feels more joy than he should (in bodily things), but the man
under discussion feels less joy than he should. But a morally
strong man remains steadfast and does not change on either
account. Since moral strength is good, it follows that both
characteristics opposed to it are bad, as they in fact turn out
to be. But since one of the two opposites is in evidence only in
30 a few people and on few occasions, moral strength is generally
regarded as being the only opposite of moral weakness, just as
self-control is thought to be opposed only to self-indulgence.

Since many terms are used in an analogical sense, we have
come to speak analogically of the "moral strength" of a self-
controlled man. (There is a resemblance between the two)
since a morally strong man is the kind of person who does
35 nothing contrary to the dictates of reason under the influence
of bodily pleasures, and the same is true of a self-controlled
1152a man. But while a morally strong man has base appetites, a
self-controlled man does not and is, moreover, a person who

[52] See above, chap. 2, 1146a16-21, with note 13.

finds no pleasure in anything that violates the dictates of reason. A morally strong man, on the other hand, does find pleasure in such things, but he is not driven by them. There is also a similarity between the morally weak and the self-indulgent in that both pursue things pleasant to the body; 5 but they are different in that a self-indulgent man thinks he ought to pursue them, while the morally weak thinks he should not.

10. *Moral weakness and practical wisdom*

It is not possible for the same person to have practical wisdom and be morally weak at the same time, for it has been shown [53] that a man of practical wisdom is *ipso facto* a man of good character. Moreover, to be a man of practical wisdom, one must not only know ⟨what one ought to do⟩, but he must also be able to act accordingly. But a morally weak man is not able so to act. However, there is no reason why a clever man [54] could not be morally weak. That 10 is why occasionally people are regarded as possessing practical wisdom, but as being morally weak at the same time; it is because cleverness differs from practical wisdom in the way we have described in our first discussion of the subject. They are closely related in that both follow the guidance of reason, but they differ in that ⟨practical wisdom alone⟩ involves moral choice.

Furthermore, a morally weak man does not act like a man who has knowledge and exercises it, but like a man asleep or drunk. Also, even though he acts voluntarily—for he knows 15 in a sense what he is doing and what end he is aiming at— he is not wicked, because his moral choice is good,[55] and that makes him only half-wicked. He is not unjust, either,

---

[53] See VI. 13, 1144b1-32.

[54] Underlying this and the following statements is the similarity between cleverness and practical wisdom as discussed in VI. 12, 1144a23-36.

[55] I.e., his basic moral purpose is good, even though it is eventually vitiated by appetite.

for he is no underhanded plotter.[56] ⟨For plotting implies deliberation,⟩ whereas one type of morally weak man does not abide by the results of his deliberation, while the other, the excitable type, does not even deliberate. So we see that a morally weak person is like a state which enacts all the right decrees and has laws of a high moral standard, but does not apply them, a situation which Anaxandrides made fun of: "Thus wills the state, that cares not for its laws." [57] A wicked man, on the other hand, resembles a state which does apply its laws, but the laws are bad.

In relation to the characteristics possessed by most people, moral weakness and moral strength lie at the extremes. For a morally strong person remains more steadfast and a morally weak person less steadfast than the capacity of most men permits.

The kind of moral weakness displayed by excitable people is more easily cured than the moral weakness of those who deliberate but do not abide by their decisions; and those who are morally weak through habituation are more curable than those who are morally weak by nature. For it is easier to change habit than to change nature. Even habit is hard to change, precisely because it resembles nature, as Euenus says:

A habit, friend, is of long practice born,
and practice ends in fashioning man's nature.[58]

We have now completed our definitions of moral strength, moral weakness, tenacity, and softness, and stated how these characteristics are related to one another.

---

[56] Cf. V. 8, 1135b19-25, and VII. 6, 1149b13-20.

[57] Anaxandrides (fl. 382-349 B.C.) migrated from his native Rhodes (or Colophon) to Athens, where he gained fame as a poet of the Middle Comedy. The present quotation is frg. 67 Kock.

[58] Euenus of Paros was a famous Sophist, who lived in the late fifth century B.C., and, as we see here, also wrote rather bad hexameter and elegiac verse. Plato scoffs at him several times in *Apology* 20a-c, *Phaedo* 60d-61a, and *Phaedrus* 267a.

11. *Pleasure: some current views* [59]

It is the role of a political philosopher to study pleasure   1152b
and pain. For he is the supreme craftsman of the end to which
we look when we call one particular thing bad and another
good in the unqualified sense. Moreover, an examination of
this subject is one of the tasks we must logically undertake,
since we established [60] that virtue and vice of character are   5
concerned with pains and pleasures, and most people claim
that happiness involves pleasure. That is why the word
"blessed" is derived from the word "enjoy." [61]

Now, (1) some people believe that no pleasure is good,

[59] One of the most puzzling aspects of the *Nic. Eth.* is that it contains
two elaborate but independent discussions of pleasure. The first of these
begins here and encompasses the last four chapters of Book VII, while
the second is contained in the first five chapters of Book X. The pioneering work toward an understanding of the problems posed by these two discussions was done by A. J. Festugière, *Aristote: Le Plaisir* (Paris, 1936, re-
printed without changes in 1960). Two further studies of the problem
have appeared since the publication of Festugière's work: J. Léonard,
Le bonheur chez Aristote (Brussels, 1948), chap. 3; and G. Lieberg, *Die
Lehre von der Lust in den Ethiken des Aristoteles*, "Zetemata" XIX
(Munich, 1958), which is an expanded version of Lieberg's 1953 doctoral
dissertation.
That the version in Book X is the more mature and definitive word
of Aristotle on the problem of pleasure has been proved by Festugière,
pp. xx-xxiv, beyond the shadow of a doubt. It is also practically certain
that the discussion of pleasure in Book VII of the *Nic. Eth.*, together with
the rest of *Nic. Eth.* V-VII was originally written as part of the earlier
Eudemian Ethics (Festugière, pp. xxv-xliv), and transferred to the *Nic.
Eth.* when Aristotle rewrote his lectures on ethics. (On this point, see
Lieberg, pp. 13-15.) This is not the place to discuss the differences in
philosophical content between these two sections on pleasure, especially
since that has been brilliantly done by Festugière and Lieberg, whose
monographs here cited are recommended to the attention of the reader.
[60] See II. 3, 1104b8-1105a13.
[61] We have here another one of Aristotle's fanciful etymologies. He
associates *makarios* ('blessed') with *mala khairein* ('to feel great joy'). An
analogous etymology in English would be to derive '*bless*ed' from
'*pleas*ure.'

either in itself or incidentally, since the good and pleasure are
10   not the same thing.[62] (2) Others hold that, though some pleasures are good, most of them are bad.[63] (3) Then there is a
third view, according to which it is impossible for pleasure
to be the highest good, even if all pleasures are good.[64]

⟨The following arguments are advanced to support (1) the
contention that⟩ pleasure is not a good at all: (a) All pleasure
is a process or coming-to-be leading to the natural state ⟨of
the subject⟩ and perceived ⟨by the subject⟩; but no process is
of the same order as its ends, e.g., the building process is not
of the same order as a house.[65] Further, (b) a self-controlled
15   man avoids pleasures. Again, (c) a man of practical wisdom
does not pursue the pleasant, but what is free from pain.[66]
Moreover, (d) pleasures are an obstacle to good sense: the
greater the joy one feels, e.g., in sexual intercourse, the greater
the obstacle; for no one is capable of rational insight while
enjoying sexual relations.[67] Also, (e) there is no art of pleasure;
yet every good is the result of an art. Finally, (f) children and
beasts pursue pleasures, ⟨whereas they do not know what is
good⟩.

20   ⟨The arguments for the view (2) that⟩ not all pleasures are
good are: (a) Some pleasures are disgraceful and cause for
reproach; and (b) some pleasures are harmful, for there are
pleasant things that may cause disease.[68]

---

[62] This view seems to have been propounded by Speusippus, Plato's
nephew and disciple, who succeeded him as head of the Academy from
347-339 B.C. A similar view had been espoused by Antisthenes (ca. 455-
ca. 360 B.C.), the friend of Socrates and precursor of the Cynic School.

[63] This is probably a reference to the view stated by Plato in *Philebus*
13b.

[64] No particular proponents of this view can be identified, but they
are also discussed in Plato's *Philebus* 53c-55c.

[65] The relation of this argument to those presented in Plato's *Philebus*
(especially 31b-32a, 33d-e, and 54a-d) is unmistakable.

[66] Arguments (b) and (c) had probably been used by Speusippus and
before him perhaps by Antisthenes.

[67] This argument may come from Archytas, a Pythagorean philosopher,
mathematician, ruler of Tarentum, and friend of Plato, in the first
half of the fourth century B.C.; cf. DK[6] 47A 9, lines 10-34.

[68] Cf. especially Plato, *Philebus* 46a-47b.

⟨And the argument in favor of (3), the contention that⟩ pleasure is not the highest good, is that it is not an end but a process or coming-to-be.[69] These are roughly the views put forward.

12. *The views discussed: (1) Is pleasure a good thing?*

But the following considerations will show that the argu-   25
ments we have enumerated do not lead us to the conclusion that (1) pleasure is not a good, or (3) that it is not the highest good. In the first place, ⟨to answer argument (1a) and (3),⟩ we use the word "good" in two senses: a thing may be good in the unqualified sense, or "good" for a particular person. Hence the term has also two meanings when applied to natural states and characteristics ⟨of persons⟩, and conse-quently also when applied to their motions and processes. This means that motions and processes which are generally held to be bad are partly bad without qualification, but not bad for a particular person, and even desirable for him; and   30
partly not even desirable for a particular person except on occasion and for a short time, though they are not desirable in an unqualified sense. Others again are not even pleasures, but only appear to be, for example, all processes accompanied by pain and undergone for remedial purposes, such as the proc-esses to which the sick are subjected.

Secondly, the good has two aspects: it is both an activity and a characteristic. Now, the processes which restore us to our natural characteristic condition are only incidentally pleasant; but the activity which is at work when our appetites ⟨want to see   35
us restored⟩ is the activity of that part of our characteristic con-dition and natural state which has been left unimpaired. For that matter, there are pleasures which do not involve pain and appetite (e.g., the activity of studying) [70] and we experi-   1153a
ence them when there is nothing deficient in our natural state.[71] ⟨That processes of restoration are only incidentally

---

69 See the passages cited on p. 204, note 65.
70 I follow K[b] in reading ἡ τοῦ θεωρεῖν ἐνέργεια.
71 The most concise explanation of this condensed and elliptic para-

pleasant) is shown by the fact that the pleasant things which give us joy while our natural state is being replenished are not the same as those which give us joy once it has been restored. Once restored, we feel joy at what is pleasant in the unqualified sense, but while the replenishment goes on, we enjoy even
5   its opposite: for instance, we enjoy sharp and bitter things, none of which are pleasant either by nature or in the unqualified sense. Consequently, the pleasures (derived from them, too, are not pleasant either by nature or in the unqualified sense), for the difference that exists between various pleasant things is the same as that which is found between the pleasures derived from them.

In the third place, there is no need to believe that there exists something better than pleasure which is different from it, just as, according to some, the end is better than the process which leads to it. For pleasures are not processes, nor do all
10 pleasures involve processes: they are activities and an end, and they result not from the process of development we undergo, but from the use we make of the powers we have. Nor do all pleasures have an end other than themselves; that is only true of the pleasures of those who are being led to the perfection of their natural states. For that reason, it is not correct, either, to say that pleasure is a process perceived (by the subject): one should rather call it an "activity of our characteristic condition as determined by our natural state,"

---

graph is Stewart's paraphrase in *Notes on the Nicomachean Ethics*, Vol. II, pp. 230-31:

'Again, the term "good" is applicable to a function and to a state:— the natural state being "good," the motions which restore a man to it are, of course, "good," and "pleasant" derivatively. If these "motions" are what we are to understand by "pleasures," then our opponents have made out their case—no pleasures are "good." But we must not allow them to stop short at the "goodness" *of the mere state.* The "goodness" of *its function* is higher; and when desire for restoration is being satisfied, the state insofar as it remains partly unimpaired, performs a function: it is this function which is the pleasure experienced in the restorative process—not but that there are pleasures without accompanying pain and desire—for instance the functions of thought, proceeding from a state, or faculty, which lacks nothing to the fulness of its nature.'

and instead of "perceived" we should call it "unobstructed." 15
(There are some [72] who believe pleasure to be process on the
ground that it is good in the true sense of the word, for they
think that activity is process, but it is, as a matter of fact,
different.)

The argument (2b) that pleasures are bad, because some
pleasant things may cause disease, is like arguing that wholesome things (are bad, because) some of them are bad for making money. Both pleasant and wholesome things are bad in the
relative senses mentioned, but that does not make them
bad in themselves: even studying is occasionally harmful to   20
health.

Also, (1d) neither practical wisdom nor any characteristic
is obstructed by the pleasure arising from it, but only by alien
pleasures extraneous to it. The pleasures arising from study
and learning will only intensify study and learning, (but they
will never obstruct it).

The argument (1e) that no pleasure is the result of an art
makes good sense. For art never produces any activity at all: 25
it produces the capacity for the activity. Nevertheless, the arts
of perfume-making as well as of cooking are generally regarded as arts of pleasure.

The arguments (1b) that a self-controlled person avoids
pleasure, (1c) that a man of practical wisdom pursues a life
free from pain, and (1f) that children and beasts pursue pleasure, are all refuted by the same consideration. We have
stated [73] in what sense pleasures are good without qualifica-   30
tion and in what sense not all pleasures are good. These last
mentioned are the pleasures which beasts and children pursue,
while a man of practical wisdom wants to be free from the
pain which they imply. They are the pleasures that involve
appetite and pain, i.e., the bodily pleasures—for they are of
this sort—and their excesses, in terms of which a self-indulgent

---

[72] The reference, as Lieberg (*Die Lehre von der Lust in den Ethiken
des Aristoteles*, pp. 66-69) has demonstrated, is probably to members
of Aristotle's own circle.

[73] See the beginning of this chapter, 1152b26-1153a7.

35 man is self-indulgent. That is why a self-controlled man avoids these pleasures. But there are pleasures even for the self-controlled.

13. *The views discussed: (3) Is pleasure the highest good?*

1153b   To continue: there is general agreement that pain is bad and must be avoided. One kind of pain is bad in the unqualified sense, and another kind is bad, because in some way or other it obstructs us. Now, the opposite of a thing to be avoided—in the sense that it must be avoided and is bad—is good. It follows, therefore, necessarily that pleasure is a
5 good. Speusippus tried to solve the question by saying that, just as the greater is opposed both to the less and to the equal, ⟨so pleasure is opposed both to pain and to the good⟩.[74] But this solution does not come out correctly: surely, he would not say that pleasure is essentially a species of evil.[75]

But (2a) even if some pleasures are bad, it does not mean that the highest good cannot be some sort of pleasure, just as the highest good may be some sort of knowledge, even though some kinds of knowledge are bad. Perhaps we must even draw the necessary conclusion that it is; for since each
10 characteristic has its unobstructed activities, the activity of all characteristics or of one of them—depending on whether the former or the latter constitutes happiness—if unobstructed, must be the most desirable of all. And this activity is pleasure. Therefore, the highest good is some sort of pleasure, despite the fact that most pleasures are bad and, if you like, bad in the unqualified sense of the word. It is for this reason that everyone thinks that the happy life is a pleasant life, and
15 links pleasure with happiness. And it makes good sense this way: for no activity is complete and perfect as long as it is

[74] This argument is more fully stated, but without explicit reference to Speusippus, in X. 2, 1173a5-13.
[75] The argument of Speusippus puts pleasure in the position of one of the extremes, and since the good is always a mean for Aristotle, pleasure would thus be an evil.

obstructed, and happiness is a complete and perfect thing. This is why a happy man also needs the goods of the body, external goods, and the goods of fortune, in order not to be obstructed by their absence.

But those who assert [76] that a man is happy even on the rack and even when great misfortunes befall him, provided that he is good, are talking nonsense, whether they know it or not. Since happiness also needs fortune, some people regard good fortune as identical with happiness. But that is not true, for even good fortune, if excessive, can be an obstruction; perhaps we are, in that case, no longer justified in calling it "good fortune," for its definition is determined by its relation to happiness.

Also, the fact that all beasts and all men pursue pleasure is some indication that it is, in a sense, the highest good:

> There is no talk that ever quite dies down,
> if spread by many men. . . . [77]

But since no single nature and no single characteristic condition is, or is regarded, as the best ⟨for all⟩, people do not all pursue the same pleasure, yet all pursue pleasure. Perhaps they do not even pursue the pleasure which they think or would say they pursue, but they all pursue the same ⟨thing⟩, pleasure. For everything has by nature something divine about it. But the bodily pleasures have arrogated the name "pleasure" unto themselves as their own private possession, because everyone tends to follow them and participates in them more frequently than in any others. Accordingly, since these are the only pleasures with which they are familiar, people think they are the only ones that exist.

It is also evident that if pleasure, i.e., the activity ⟨of our faculties⟩, is not good, it will be impossible for a happy man to live pleasantly. For to what purpose would he need pleasure, if it were not a good and if it is possible that a happy man's life is one of pain? For if pain is neither good nor bad, pleas-

[76] The Cynics are probably meant.
[77] Hesiod, *Works and Days* 763-764, translation mine.

5 ure is not, either: so why should he avoid it? Surely, the life
of a morally good man is no pleasanter (than that of anyone
else), if his activities are not more pleasant.

14. *The views discussed: (2) Are most pleasures bad?*

The subject of the pleasures of the body demands the attention of the proponents of the view that, though some pleasures
—for instance, the noble pleasures—are highly desirable, the
pleasures of the body—that is, the pleasures which are the
10 concern of the self-indulgent man—are not. If that is true,
why then are the pains opposed to them bad? For bad has
good as its opposite. Is it that the necessary pleasures are good
in the sense in which anything not bad is good? Or are they
good up to a certain point? For all characteristics and motions
which cannot have an excess of good cannot have an excess of
pleasure, either; but those which can have an excess of good
15 can also have an excess of pleasure. Now, excess is possible
in the case of the goods of the body, and it is the pursuit of
excess, but not the pursuit of necessary pleasures, that makes
a man bad. For all men get some kind of enjoyment from
good food, wine, and sexual relations, but not everyone enjoys
these things in the proper way. The reverse is true of pain:
a bad person does not avoid an excess of it, but he avoids it
20 altogether. For the opposite of an excess is pain only for the
man who pursues the excess.

It is our task not only to say what is true, but also to state
what causes error, since that helps carry conviction. For when
we can give a reasoned explanation why something which appears to be true is, in fact, not true, it makes us give greater
25 credence to what is true. Accordingly, we must now explain
why the pleasures of the body appear to be more desirable.

The first reason, then, is that pleasure drives out pain.
When men experience an excess of pain, they pursue excessive
pleasure and bodily pleasure in general, in the belief that it
will remedy the pain. These remedial (pleasures) become
30 very intense—and that is the very reason why they are pursued

—because they are experienced in contrast with their opposite.

As a matter of fact, these two reasons which we have stated [78] also explain why pleasure is not regarded as having any moral value: some pleasures are the actions that spring from a bad natural state—either congenitally bad, as in the case of a beast, or bad by habit, as in the case of a bad man —while other pleasures are remedial and indicate a deficient natural state, and to be in one's natural state is better than to be moving toward it. But since the remedial pleasures only arise in the process of reaching the perfected state, they are morally good only incidentally.   1154b

The second reason is that the pleasures of the body are pursued because of their intensity by those incapable of enjoying other pleasures. Take, for example, those who induce themselves to be thirsty.[79] There is no objection to this practice, if the pleasures are harmless; but if they are harmful, it is bad. For many people have nothing else to give them joy,   5 and because of their nature, it is painful for them to feel neither ⟨pleasure nor pain⟩. Actually, animal nature is under a constant strain, as the students of natural science attest [80] when they say that seeing and hearing are painful, but ⟨we do not feel the pain because,⟩ as they assert, we have become accustomed to it. Similarly, whereas the growing process ⟨we go   10 through⟩ in our youth puts us into the same ⟨exhilarated⟩ state as that of a drunken man, and ⟨makes⟩ youth the age of pleasure,[81] excitable [82] natures, on the other hand, always need

---

78 See above, chap. 5, 1148b15-19, and chap. 12, 1152b26-33.

79 This was done, according to several commentators, by eating salty food, e.g., salt fish.

80 According to the ancient commentator Aspasius (ca. A.D. 100-150), Anaxagoras is meant here; cf. Theophrastus, De Sensu 29 (DK6 59A 92).

81 The text has literally: "and youth is pleasant," which does not contribute very much to the context. Since the first part of the sentence seems to explain why young men indulge in the pleasures of the body, the context requires an interpretation of καὶ ἡδὺ ἡ νεότης such as we have given. Cf. also the comments of Joachim and Gauthier-Jolif ad loc.

82 The Greek word melancholikos, which we render here and above, in chap. 7, 1150b25, as 'excitable,' literally means 'of black bile.' It was

remedial action: as a result of ⟨the excess of black bile in their⟩ constitutional blend, their bodies are exposed to constant gnawing sensations, and they are always in a state of vehement desire. Now, since pain is driven out by the pleasure opposed
15 to it or by any strong pleasure at all,[83] excitable people become self-indulgent and bad.

Pleasures unattended by pain do not admit of excess. The objects of these pleasures are what is pleasant by nature and not what is incidentally pleasant. By "things incidentally pleasant" I mean those that act as remedies. For since it is through some action of that part of us which has remained sound that a cure is effected, the remedy is regarded as being pleasant. But ⟨pleasant by nature it is not⟩: pleasant by nature
20 are those things which produce the action of an unimpaired natural state.

There is no single object that continues to be pleasant forever, because our nature is not simple but contains another natural element, which makes us subject to decay. Consequently, whenever one element does something, it runs counter to the nature of the other; and whenever the two elements are in a state of equilibrium, the act performed seems neither painful nor pleasant. If there is a being with a
25 simple nature, the same action will always be the most pleasant to him. That is why the divinity always enjoys one single and simple pleasure: [84] for there is not only an activity of motion but also an activity of immobility, and pleasure consists in rest rather than in motion. But "change in all things is pleasant," as the poet has it,[85] because of some evil in us.

----

not until the theory of the four temperaments by the physician Galen (A.D. 129-?199) that the term assumed the connotations of 'melancholy' which it still has. The earlier medical writers, whom Aristotle follows, believed an excess of black bile to produce a very tense and excitable kind of disposition.

[83] According to Aspasius, the point is that, for example, hunger may be driven out by the pleasures of music.

[84] Cf. the famous description of the Unmoved Mover in *Metaphysics* Λ. 7.

[85] Euripides. *Orestes* 234.

For just as a man who changes easily is bad, so also is a nature
that needs to change. The reason is that such a nature is not
simple and not ⟨entirely⟩ good.

This completes our discussion of moral strength and moral
weakness, and of pleasure and pain. We have stated what each
of them is and in what sense some of them are good and some
bad. It now remains to talk about friendship.

BOOK VIII

1. *Why we need friendship* [1]

Continuing in a sequence, the next subject which we shall have to discuss is friendship. For it is some sort of excellence or virtue, or involves virtue, and it is, moreover, most indis-
5 pensable for life. No one would choose to live without friends, even if he had all other goods. Rich men and those who hold office and power are, above all others, regarded as requiring friends. For what good would their prosperity do them if it did not provide them with the opportunity for good works? And the best works done and those which deserve the highest
10 praise are those that are done to one's friends. How could prosperity be safeguarded and preserved without friends? The

[1] The human relation of 'friendship' forms the subject of this book and the next. As we shall see, the connotations of *philia* are considerably wider than those of 'friendship.' *Philia* is best summed up in the Greek proverb: κοινὰ τὰ τῶν φίλων, "friends hold in common what they have." It designates the relationship between a person and any other person(s) or being which that person regards as peculiarly his own and to which he has a peculiar attachment. For example, in Homer the adjective φίλος, 'dear,' is frequently used of a person's heart or mind, and also to describe the relation to one's wife and children. In neither sense would we speak of 'friendship' in English. But of course, as in English, the term also expresses (from Hesiod on) the relationship to a person to which one feels especially attached, i.e., to a 'friend.' On the other side of the scale, *philia* constitutes the bond that holds the members of any association together, regardless of whether the association is the family, the state, a club, a business partnership, or even the business relation between buyer and seller. Here again, we would not use the term 'friendship' in English, but expressions such as 'harmony' or 'good will.'
But for the Greek, it is the bond that gives different people something 'in common' that counts in *philia*, and it is for that reason, and especially for its importance in social and political matters, that a discussion of it is given more space than is given to any other problem in the *Nic. Eth.*

greater it is the greater are the risks it brings with it. Also, in poverty and all other kinds of misfortune men believe that their only refuge consists in their friends. Friends help young men avoid error; to older people they give the care and help needed to supplement the failing powers of action which infirmity brings in its train; and to those in their prime they give the opportunity to perform noble actions. ⟨This is what is meant when men quote Homer's verse:⟩ "When two go together 15 . . .": [2] friends enhance our ability to think and to act. Also, it seems that nature implants friendship in a parent for its offspring and in offspring for its parent, not only among men, but also among birds and most animals. ⟨Not only members of the same family group but⟩ also members of the same race feel it for one another, especially human beings, and that is why we praise men for being humanitarians or "lovers of their fellow 20 men." Even when traveling abroad one can see how near and dear and friendly every man may be to another human being.

Friendship also seems to hold states together, and lawgivers apparently devote more attention to it than to justice. For concord seems to be something similar to friendship, and concord is what they most strive to attain, while they do their 25 best to expel faction, the enemy of concord. When people are friends, they have no need of justice, but when they are just, they need friendship in addition. In fact, the just in the fullest sense is regarded as constituting an element of friendship. Friendship is noble as well as necessary: we praise those who love their friends and consider the possession of many friends 30 a noble thing. And further, we believe of our friends that they are good men.

There are, however, several controversial points about friendship. Some people [3] define it as a kind of likeness, and say that friends are those who are like us; hence, according to them, the proverb: "Like to like," [4] "Birds of a feather flock to-

2 Homer, *Iliad* X. 224, tr. Richmond Lattimore.
3 For this view, cf. Plato, *Lysis* 214a-215d, to which much of the remainder of this paragraph seems to be indebted.
4 From Homer, *Odyssey* XVII. 218, also quoted by Plato, *loc. cit.*

35 gether," [5] and so forth. On the other side there are those who
say that when people are alike they quarrel with one another
1155b like potters.[6] There are also more profound investigations
into the matter along the lines of natural science: Euripides
speaks of the parched earth as loving the rain while the ma-
5 jestic heaven, filled with rain, loves to fall upon the earth;[7]
Heraclitus says that opposites help one another, that different
elements produce the most beautiful harmony, and that everything comes into being through strife;[8] while Empedocles[9]
and others express the opposite view that like strives for like.

Let us leave aside problems which are an aspect of natural
science—for they are not germane to our present field of study
—and investigate those which pertain to man and are relevant
10 to character and the emotions. For example, can friendship
develop in all men, or is it impossible for those who are
wicked to be friends? Is there only one kind of friendship, or
are there more than one? Those who think that there is only
one kind on the ground that friendship admits of degrees
rely on insufficient evidence: things different in kind also
15 admit of degrees. But these matters have been discussed before.[10]

[5] This proverb, which is attested only in Aristotelian writings but is
no doubt much older, means literally, "jackdaw to jackdaw."
[6] An allusion to Hesiod, *Works and Days* 25-26, as tr. here by Richmond Lattimore:

> Then potter is potter's enemy, and
> craftsman is craftsman's
> rival; tramp is jealous of tramp,
> and singer of singer.

Plato, *loc. cit.*, also mentions these lines.
[7] A paraphrase of four lines from an unknown play of Euripides; cf.
frg. 898 (Nauck[2]), lines 7-10.
[8] Heraclitus, frgg. B 8 and 80 (DK[6]).
[9] Empedocles, frgg. B 22 (DK[6]), lines 4-5; 62, line 6; and 90, lines 1-2.
[10] The reference is probably to the discussion of degrees in *Categories*
7, 6b20-27.

2. The three things worthy of affection

The answers to these questions will perhaps become clear once we have ascertained what is the object worthy of affection.[11] For, it seems, we do not feel affection for everything, but only for the lovable, and that means what is good, pleasant, or useful. However, since we regard a thing as useful when it serves as a means to some good or pleasure, we can 20 say that as ends ⟨only⟩ the good and the pleasant are worthy of affection. Which good, then, is it that men love? Is it the good ⟨in general⟩ or is it what is good for them? For there is sometimes a discrepancy between these two, and a discrepancy also in the case of what is pleasant. Now it seems that each man loves what is good for him: in an unqualified sense it 25 is the good which is worthy of affection, but for each individual it is what is good for him. Now in fact every man does not love what is really good for him, but what appears to him to be good. But that makes no difference ⟨for our discussion⟩. It simply follows that what appears good will appear worthy of affection.

While there are three causes of affection or friendship, we do not speak of "friendship" to describe the affection we feel for inanimate objects, since inanimate objects do not reciprocate affection and we do not wish for their good. It would surely be ridiculous to wish for the good of wine: if one wishes it at all, it is that the wine may keep, so that we can have it 30 ourselves. But men say that we ought to wish for the good of our friend for the friend's sake. When people wish for our good in this way, we attribute good will to them, if the same wish is not reciprocated by us. If the good will is on a reciprocal basis,

11 The Greek *philētos* is usually rendered 'lovable.' However, since 'love' is too strong a word for the noun *philia* ('friendship,' 'affection'), I prefer to use object or thing 'worthy of affection' whenever English usage permits, and 'lovable' whenever 'object worthy of affection' seems awkward. Similarly, the verb *philein* is here translated either as 'to feel affection' or as 'to love,' depending on the context.

it is friendship. Perhaps we should add: "provided that we are aware of the good will." For many people have good will toward persons they have never seen, but whom they assume to be decent and useful, and one of these persons may well reciprocate this feeling. Accordingly, the two parties appear to have good will toward one another; but how can they be called "friends" when they are unaware how they are disposed toward one another? We conclude, therefore, that to be friends men must have good will for one another, must each wish for the good of the other on the basis of one of the three motives mentioned, and must each be aware of one another's good will.

3. *The three kinds of friendship*

These three motives differ from one another in kind, and so do the corresponding types of affection and friendship. In other words, there are three kinds of friendship, corresponding in number to the objects worthy of affection. In each of these, the affection can be reciprocated so that the partner is aware of it, and the partners wish for each other's good in terms of the motive on which their affection is based.[12] Now, when the motive of the affection is usefulness, the partners do not feel affection for one another *per se* but in terms of the good accruing to each from the other. The same is also true of those whose friendship is based on pleasure: we love witty people not for what they are, but for the pleasure they give us.

So we see that when the useful is the basis of affection, men love because of the good they get out of it, and when pleasure is the basis, for the pleasure they get out of it. In other words, the friend is loved not because he is a friend, but because he is useful or pleasant. Thus, these two kinds are friendship only incidentally, since the object of affection is not loved for being the kind of person he is, but for providing some good or pleasure. Consequently, such friendships are easily dissolved when the partners do not remain unchanged: the affection

12 E.g., if the basis of their affection is the pleasant, they try to contribute each to the pleasure of the other.

ceases as soon as one partner is no longer pleasant or useful to
the other. Now, usefulness is not something permanent, but
differs at different times. Accordingly, with the disappearance
of the motive for being friends, the friendship, too, is dissolved, since the friendship owed its existence to these motives.

Friendships of this kind seem to occur most commonly
among old people, because at that age men do not pursue the   25
pleasant but the beneficial. They are also found among young
men and those in their prime who are out for their own
advantage. Such friends are not at all given to living in each
other's company, for sometimes they do not even find each
other pleasant. Therefore, they have no further need of this
relationship, if they are not mutually beneficial. They find
each other pleasant only to the extent that they have hopes   30
of some good coming out of it. The traditional friendship
between host and guest is also placed in this group.

Friendship of young people seems to be based on pleasure.
For their lives are guided by emotion, and they pursue most
intensely what they find pleasant and what the moment
brings. As they advance in years, different things come to be
pleasant for them. Hence they become friends quickly and
just as quickly cease to be friends. For as another thing be-   35
comes pleasant, the friendship, too, changes, and the pleasure
of a young man changes quickly. Also, young people are prone   1156b
to fall in love, since the greater part of falling in love is a
matter of emotion and based on pleasure. That is why they
form a friendship and give it up again so quickly that the
change often takes place within the same day. But they do
wish to be together all day and to live together, because it is
in this way that they get what they want out of their friend-   5
ship.

The perfect form of friendship is that between good men
who are alike in excellence or virtue. For these friends wish
alike for one another's good because they are good men, and
they are good *per se*, ⟨that is, their goodness is something
intrinsic, not incidental⟩. Those who wish for their friends'
good for their friends' sake are friends in the truest sense,   10

since their attitude is determined by what their friends are and not by incidental considerations. Hence their friendship lasts as long as they are good, and ⟨that means it will last for a long time, since⟩ goodness or virtue is a thing that lasts. In addition, each partner is both good in the unqualified sense and good for his friend. For those who are good, i.e., good without qualification, are also beneficial to one another. In the same double sense, they are also pleasant to one another:

15 for good men are pleasant both in an unqualified sense and to one another, since each finds pleasure in his own proper actions and in actions like them, and the actions of good men are identical with or similar to one another. That such a friendship is lasting stands to reason, because in it are combined all the qualities requisite for people to be friends. For, ⟨as we have seen,⟩ every friendship is based on some good or on

20 pleasure—either in the unqualified sense or relative to the person who feels the affection—and implies some similarity ⟨between the friends⟩. Now this kind of friendship has all the requisite qualities we have mentioned and has them *per se,* that is, as an essential part of the characters of the friends. For in this kind of friendship the partners are like one another,[13] and the other objects worthy of affection—the unqualified good and the unqualified pleasant—are also found in it, and these are the highest objects worthy of affection. It is, therefore, in the friendship of good men that feelings of affection and friendship exist in their highest and best form.

25 Such friendships are of course rare, since such men are few. Moreover, time and familiarity are required. For, as the proverb has it, people cannot know each other until they have eaten the specified ⟨measure of⟩ salt together. One cannot extend friendship to or be a friend of another person until each partner has impressed the other that he is worthy of affection, and until each has won the other's confidence. Those

30 who are quick to show the signs of friendship to one another are not really friends, though they wish to be; they are not true

---

13 Following the manuscripts, I read ὅμοιοι in place of the ὅμοια of Bywater and Aspasius.

friends unless they are worthy of affection and know this to be so. The wish to be friends can come about quickly, but friendship cannot.

4. *Perfect friendship and imperfect friendship*

This, then, is perfect and complete friendship, both in terms of time and in all other respects, and each partner receives in all matters what he gives the other, in the same or in a similar form; that is what friends should be able to count on. 35

Friendship based on what is pleasant bears some resem- 1157a blance to this kind, for good men are pleasant to one another. The same is also true of friendship based on the useful, for good men are useful to one another. Here, too, friendships are most durable when each one receives what he gives to the other, for example, pleasure, and not only that: he must also receive it from the same source, as happens, for example, 5 in friendships between witty people, but not in the case of lover and beloved. For lover and beloved do not find pleasure in the same objects: the lover finds it in seeing his beloved, while the beloved receives it from the attention paid to him by his lover. But when the bloom of youth passes, the friendship sometimes passes, too: the lover does not find the sight pleasant ⟨any more⟩, and the beloved no longer receives the attentions of the lover. Still, many do remain friends if, 10 through familiarity, they have come to love each other's characters, ⟨discovering that⟩ their characters are alike. But when it is the useful-and not the pleasant that is exchanged in a love affair, the partners are less truly friends and their friendship is less durable. Those whose friendship is based on the useful dissolve it as soon as it ceases to be to their advantage, since they were friends not of one another but of what was 15 profitable for them.

To be friends with one another on the basis of pleasure and usefulness is, accordingly, also possible for bad people, just as it is for good men with bad, and for one who is neither good nor bad with any kind of person at all. But it is clear that good men alone can be friends on the basis of what they are, for bad people do not find joy in one another, unless they see some material advantage coming to them.

20   Also, only the friendship of good men is proof against slander. For a man does not easily trust anyone's word about a person whom he has himself tried and tested over a long period of time. The friendship of good men implies mutual trust, the assurance that neither partner will ever wrong the other, and all other things that we demand of true friendship. In the other kinds of friendship, however, there is no 25   safeguard against slander and lack of trust.

⟨When we say "other kinds of friendship," we do so⟩ because people call "friends" even those whose relation is based on usefulness, just as states speak of other states as "friendly." (⟨The analogy holds⟩ because alliances between states seem to be motivated by their mutual advantage.) Similarly, those who like one another for the pleasure they get are called "friends," as children are "friends" with one another. In view of that, we, too, should perhaps call such persons "friends" 30   and posit several kinds of friendship: in the primary and proper sense of the word, we call "friendship" that which exists between good men as good men. The other kinds are "friendship" on the basis of the similarity ⟨they bear to the primary kind⟩. In this sense, people are friends to the extent that ⟨their relationship is based upon⟩ some good and something similar to ⟨the basis of the primary kind of friendship⟩. Thus to pleasure-lovers the pleasant is a good. But these two kinds of friendship are very unlikely to coincide: the same persons do not become friends on the basis of usefulness and on the 35   basis of what is pleasant. For things which are related only incidentally are not usually found coupled together.

1157b   These are the kinds into which friendship is divided. Accordingly, bad men will be friends on the basis of pleasure or usefulness, since these are the respects in which they are like each other, while good men will be friends on the basis of what they are, that is, because they are good. The good are friends in the unqualified sense, but the others are friends

only incidentally and by reason of the similarity they bear
to the former.

5. *Friendship as a characteristic and as an activity*

As in the case of virtues, some men are called "good" because   5
of a characteristic they have and others because of an activity
in which they engage, so in the case of friendship there is a
distinction ⟨between the activity of friendship and the lasting
characteristic⟩. When friends live together, they enjoy each
other's presence and provide each other's good. When, however, they are asleep or separated geographically, they do not
actively engage in their friendship, but they are still characterized by an attitude which could express itself in active
friendship. For it is not friendship in the unqualified sense but   10
only its activity that is interrupted by distance. But if the
absence lasts for some time, it apparently also causes the friendship itself to be forgotten. Hence the saying: "Out of sight, out
of mind." [14]
Neither old nor sour people are apparently disposed to
forming friendships. There is only little pleasure one can get
from them, and no one can spend his days in painful or un-   15
pleasant company: we see that nature avoids what is painful
more than anything else and aims at what is pleasant. Those
who extend friendship to one another without living together
are more like men of good will than like friends. For nothing
characterizes friends as much as living in each other's company. Material advantage is desired by those who stand in   20
need, but company is something which is wanted even by men
who are supremely happy, for they are the least suited to live
in isolation. But it is impossible for men to spend their time
together unless they are pleasant ⟨in one another's eyes⟩ and
find joy in the same things. It is this quality which seems
typical of comradeship.
The highest form of friendship, then, is that between good   25

[14] The author of this hexameter verse is unknown. A more literal translation is: "A lack of converse spells the end of friendships."

men, as we have stated repeatedly. For what is good or pleasant without qualification is regarded as an object of affection
and of choice, while for each individual it is·what is good or
pleasant to him. But for a good man, a good man is the object
of affection and of choice for both these reasons.

Now, affection resembles an emotion, while friendship is
rather a characteristic or lasting attitude. For it is equally
possible to feel affection for inanimate objects, (which can-
30 not reciprocate the affection,) but mutual affection involves
choice, and choice springs from a characteristic. Also, men
wish their friends' good for the sake of those for whom they
feel friendship, and this attitude is not determined by an
emotion but by a characteristic. Also, in loving a friend they
love their own good. For when a good man becomes a friend
he becomes a good to the person whose friend he is. Thus,
35 each partner both loves his own good and makes an equal
return in the good he wishes for his partner and in the pleasure he gives him. Now friendship is said to be equality,[15]
and both those qualities inhere especially in the relationship
1158a between good men.

6. *Additional observations on the three kinds of friendship*

Friendship does not arise easily among the sour and the
old, inasmuch as they are rather grouchy and find little joy in
social relations. For a good temper and sociability are regarded
as being most typical of and most conducive to friendship.
That is why young men become friends quickly and old men
do not: people do not become friends of those in whom they
5 find no joy. (This also applies to the sour.) Such men do, however, display good will toward one another, since one may wish
for another's good and be ready to meet his needs. But they
are not really friends, because they do not spend their days

---

[15] According to Diogenes Laertius VIII. 1. 10, this expression, probably
in the reverse form "Equality is friendship," goes back to Pythagoras.
The word for 'friendship' used here is *philotēs* rather than *philia*, because
of its assonance with *isotēs* ('equality').

together and do not find joy in one another, and these seem to
be the chief marks of friendship.   10

To be friends with many people, in the sense of perfect
friendship, is impossible, just as it is impossible to be in love
with many people at the same time. For love is like an extreme, and an extreme tends to be unique. It does not easily
happen that one man finds many people very pleasing at the
same time, nor perhaps does it easily happen that there are
many people who are good. Also, one must have some experience of the other person and have come to be familiar   15
with him, and that is the hardest thing of all. But it is possible
to please many people on the basis of usefulness and pleasantness, since many have these qualities, and the services they
have to offer do not take a long time ⟨to recognize⟩.

Of these two kinds of friendship, the one that is based on
what is pleasant bears a closer resemblance to ⟨true⟩ friendship, when both partners have the same to offer and when
they find joy in one another or in the same objects. Friendships of young people are of this kind. There is a greater   20
element of generosity in such friendships, whereas friendships based on usefulness are for hucksters. Also, those who
are supremely happy have no need of useful people, but they
do need pleasant ones: they do wish to live in the company
of others, and, though they can bear what is painful for a
short time, no one could endure it continually—in fact, no
one could continually endure the Good itself,[16] if that were   25
painful to him. It is for this reason that they seek friends
who are pleasant. They should, however, look for friends who
are good as well as pleasant, and not only good, but good for
them; for in this way they will have everything that friends
should have.

People in positions of power seem to keep their various
friends in separate compartments. One group of friends is
useful to them and another pleasant, but rarely do the same
men belong in both groups. For these potentates do not seek
friends who are both pleasant and virtuous nor friends who   30

[16] This seems to be a joke at the expense of the Academy.

are useful for the attainment of noble objects. On the contrary, when their aim is to get something pleasant they seek witty people, ⟨and when they want what is useful, they seek⟩ men who are clever at carrying out their orders, and these qualities are hardly ever found in the same person. Now, as we have stated,[17] it is the good man who is pleasant and useful at the same time. But such a man does not become the friend of someone whose station is superior to his own, unless that person is also superior to him in virtue. Unless that is the case, his friendship will not be based on ⟨proportionate⟩ equality, since he will not be surpassed ⟨by a virtue⟩ proportionate ⟨to the surpassing power⟩.[18] But potentates of this sort are not often found.

1158b   In sum, the friendships we have so far discussed are based on equality; both partners receive and wish the same thing from and for one another, or they exchange one thing for another, for instance, pleasure for material advantage. That these kinds of friendship are inferior to and less lasting ⟨than true friendship⟩ has already been stated.[19] Because of their resemblance and dissimilarity to the same thing, ⟨namely, to true friendship,⟩ they are regarded both as being and as not being friendship. They appear to be friendship in that they

[17] See above, chaps. 3, 1156b13-15, and 4, 1157a1-3.

[18] The difficulty about this sentence is that Aristotle has not yet explained what he means by "proportion" in friendship. That explanation will come in the next chapter. The point here is that friendship with a ruler can only be based on a proportionate—not on absolute—equality: the ruler, by virtue of his position, bestows more benefits on those inferior to him than he receives from them, and the inferior, in turn, owe more affection to the ruler than he does to them. Now, since true friendship is based on the virtue of the partners, the potentate, in order to deserve this excess of friendship, must have an excess virtue, so that the good man, in addition to the affection he owes him as his ruler, can also give him the love due to a friend. Accordingly, if the ruler's virtue is equal to his superiority in power, the benefits he will give as a friend will be exactly as great as those he will give as a ruler, and the good man will proportionately add to his affection for his ruler exactly the same amount of love for him as his friend. In this way, proportionate equality is established between the two.

[19] See above, chaps. 3, 1156a16-24, and 4, 1157a20-33.

are like the friendship which is based on virtue or excellence:
one of these friendships has what is pleasant and the other
has what is useful, and both these elements are inherent in
friendship based on virtue. But since friendship based on
virtue is proof against slander and lasting, while these kinds
—besides many other differences—change quickly, they do not   10
appear to be friendships, because of their dissimilarity.

7. Friendship between unequals

There exists another kind of friendship, which involves the
superiority of one of the partners over the other, as in the
friendship between father and son, and, in general, between
an older and a younger person, between husband and wife,
and between any kind of ruler and his subject. These kinds
of friendship are different (not only from those which involve
equality, but) also from one another: the friendship which
parents have for their children is not the same as that which   15
a ruler has for his subjects, and even the friendship of a father
for his son is different from that of the son for his father, and
the friendship of a husband for his wife differs from that of
a wife for her husband. For in each of these cases, the virtue
or excellence and the function of each partner is different,
and the cause of their affection, too, is different. Therefore,
the affection and friendship they feel are correspondingly different. It is clear that the partners do not receive the same   20
thing from one another and should not seek to receive it. But
when children render to their parents what is due to those
who gave them life, and when parents render what is due to
their children, the friendship between them will be lasting
and equitable. In all friendships which involve the superiority
of one of the partners, the affection, too, must be proportionate: the better and more useful partner should receive more   25
affection than he gives, and similarly for the superior partner
in each case. For when the affection is proportionate to the
merit of each partner, there is in some sense equality between
them. And equality, as we have seen, seems to be part of
friendship.

But the term "equal" [20] apparently does not have the same meaning in friendship as it does in matters of justice. In
30 matters of justice, the equal is primarily proportionate to merit, and its quantitative sense, ⟨i.e., strict equality,⟩ is secondary; in friendship, on the other hand, the quantitative meaning ⟨of strict equality⟩ is primary and the sense of equality proportionate to merit is secondary. This becomes clear if there is a wide disparity between the partners as regards their virtue, vice, wealth, or anything else. For then they are no longer friends or even expect to be friends. The most strik-
35 ing example of this is the gods, for their superiority in all good things is exceeding. But the same point is clear in the
1159a case of kings. Persons much inferior to them in station do not expect to be friends with kings, nor do insignificant people expect to be friends with the best and wisest men. There is no exact line of demarcation in such cases to indicate up to what point ⟨of inequality⟩ men can still be friends. The friendship can still remain even when much is taken away, but when one partner is quite separated from the other, as in the
5 case of the divinity, it can remain no longer. This raises the question whether or not we wish our friends the greatest of all goods, namely, to be gods. For ⟨if that wish were fulfilled,⟩ they would no longer be our friends, and, since friends are something good, we would have lost this good. Accordingly, if our assertion [21] is correct that a man wishes his friend's good
10 for his friend's sake, the friend would have to remain the man he was. Consequently, one will wish the greatest good for his friend as a human being. But perhaps not all the greatest goods, for each man wishes for his own good most of all.

8. Giving and receiving affection

Most people, because of ambition, seem to wish to receive affection rather than to give it. That is why most men like
15 flattery, for a flatterer is or pretends to be a friend in an in-

20 For the meaning of this term, see p. 117, note 13.
21 See above, chap. 2, 1155b31.

ferior position, who pretends to give more affection than he
receives. Receiving affection is regarded as closely related to
being honored, and honor is, of course, the aim of most
people. But, it seems, they do not choose honor for its own
sake but only because it is incidental to something else. For
most men enjoy being honored by those who occupy positions
of power, because it raises their hopes. They think they will   20
get anything they need from the powerful, and they enjoy the
honor they get as a token of benefits to come. Those, on the
other hand, who desire honor from good and knowing men
aim at having their own opinion of themselves confirmed.
They, therefore, enjoy ⟨the honor they get⟩ because ⟨their belief in⟩ their own goodness is reassured by the judgment of
those who say that they are good. But ⟨unlike honor⟩, affection
is enjoyed for its own sake. Thus, receiving affection would   25
seem to be better than receiving honor, and friendship would
seem to be desirable for its own sake.

Nevertheless, friendship appears to consist in giving rather
than in receiving affection. This is shown by the fact that
mothers enjoy giving affection. Some mothers give their children away to be brought up by others, and though they know
them and feel affection for them they do not seek to receive
affection in return, if they cannot have it both ways. It seems   30
to be sufficient for them to see their children prosper and to
feel affection for them, even if the children do not render
their mother her due, because they do not know her.[22] Since,
then, friendship consists in giving rather ⟨than in receiving⟩
affection, and since we praise those who love their friends, the
giving of affection seems to constitute the proper virtue of   35
friends, so that people who give affection to one another
according to each other's merit are lasting friends and their
friendship is a lasting friendship.   1159b

It is in this way that even unequals are most likely to be

[22] The theme of children lost to their parents through war, shipwreck,
piracy, etc., and growing up not knowing them and unknown to them,
was so common in the comedy of Aristotle's time that it is almost certainly the source of his remark here.

friends, since equality may thus be established between them
⟨by a difference in the amount of affection given⟩. Friendship
is equality [23] and likeness, and especially the likeness of those
who are similar in virtue. Because they are steadfast in themselves, they are also steadfast toward one another; they neither
5   request nor render any service that is base. On the contrary,
one might even say that they prevent base services; for what
characterizes good men is that they neither go wrong themselves nor let their friends do so. Bad people, on the other
hand, do not have the element of constancy, for they do not
remain similar even to themselves. But they do become friends
for a short time, when they find joy in one another's wicked-
10   ness. Friends who are useful and pleasant to one another stay
together for a longer time, for as long as they continue to
provide each other with pleasures or material advantages.

It is chiefly from opposite partners that friendship based
on usefulness seems to come into being, for example, from
the combination of poor and rich, or ignorant and learned.
For a man aims at getting something he lacks, and gives some-
15   thing else in return for it. We might also bring lover and beloved, beautiful and ugly, under this heading ⟨of the union
of opposites⟩. That is why lovers occasionally appear ridiculous, when they expect to receive as much affection as they
give. If they are similarly lovable, they are equally entitled to
expect affection, but if they have nothing lovable about them,
this is a ridiculous expectation.

But perhaps opposites do not aim at each other as such
20   but only incidentally, and perhaps their desire is really for
what is median, since that is a good. The dry, for example,
does not desire to become wet, but to arrive at a middle state,
and similarly with the hot and with all other opposing principles. But let us dismiss these questions, as they belong to
another subject, ⟨namely, physics⟩.

[23] Cf. p. 224, note 15.

9. *Friendship and justice in the state*

As we stated initially,[24] it seems that friendship and the just   25
deal with the same objects and involve the same persons. For
there seems to be a notion of what is just in every community,[25] and friendship seems to be involved as well. Men ad-
dress as friends their fellow travelers on a voyage, their fellow
soldiers, and similarly also those who are associated with them
in other kinds of community. Friendship is present to the
extent that men share something in common, for that is also   30
the extent to which they share a view of what is just. And the
proverb "friends hold in common what they have" is correct,
for friendship consists in community. Brothers and bosom
companions hold everything in common, while all others
only hold certain definite things in common—some more and
others less, since some friendships are more intense than
others. Questions of what is just also differ ⟨with different   35
forms of friendship⟩. What is just is not the same for parents
with regard to their children and for brothers with regard   1160a
to one another, nor is it the same for bosom companions as for
fellow citizens, and similarly in the other kinds of friendship.
There is of course a corresponding difference in what is unjust in each of these relationships: the gravity of an unjust
act increases in proportion as the person to whom it is done
is a closer friend. It is, for example, more shocking to defraud
a bosom companion of money than a fellow citizen, to refuse   5
help to a brother than to refuse it to a stranger, or to strike
one's father than to strike any other person. It is natural that
the element of justice increases with ⟨the closeness of⟩ the
friendship, since friendship and what is just exist in the same
relationship and are coextensive in range.

24 See above, chap. 1, 1155a22-28.
25 See Glossary for explanation of the term *koinōnia*, here translated as
'community or social organism.' It is one of the key concepts of Aristotle's
social and political thought. In view of what has been said in note 1, p.
214, the importance of *philia* ('friendship') in any *koinōnia* is evident.

All communities are like parts of the political community
10 (or state). Men combine with an eye to some advantage or to
provide some of the necessities of life, and we think of the
political community as having initially come together and as
enduring to secure the advantage (of its members). This is indeed the goal which lawgivers aim at, and men call "just"
what is to the common advantage. Now, all other forms of
15 community aim at some partial advantage. Sailors associate for
the advantages seafaring brings in the form of making money
and something of that sort. Soldiers work together for the
advantages war brings and what they desire is money, victory,
or the conquest of a city. Similarly fellow tribesmen and fellow demesmen [26] come together when they offer sacrifice and
hold gatherings for such a purpose, which pays homage to the
gods and provides recreation and pleasure for themselves. For
25 the ancient sacrifices and festive gatherings (of the tribes and
demes) take place after the harvest as a kind of offering of
first fruits, for these were the seasons at which people used to
have most leisure. But all these communities seem to be encom-
passed by the community that is the state; for the political
community does not aim at the advantage of the moment, but
at what is advantageous for the whole of life. Thus all associations seem to be parts of the political community, but the kind
of friendship prevalent in each will be determined by the
30 kind of association it is.

[26] Tribes and demes were political and administrative subdivisions of
the Athenian state and also had certain religious functions. There follow
in the manuscript two lines which are evidently an interpolation made
either by Aristotle himself in a revision of his work or by some later
scholar. For the words which follow the interpolation evidently refer to
the fellow tribesmen and fellow demesmen. The interpolated passage
runs: "Several associations seem to have arisen on the basis of pleasure,
20 e.g., religious guilds and social clubs, which are organized for purposes of
offering sacrifice and of fellowship." The sentence which follows in the
manuscripts seems to belong more properly a few lines further down after
τοῖς καιροῖς, i.e., after the reference to the festivals of demes and tribes,
and I have transposed it there.

10. *The different political systems* [27]

There are three ⟨true⟩ forms of constitution [28] and an equal number of perversions—corruptions, as it were—from these. The ⟨true⟩ constitutions are kingship, aristocracy, and, in the third place, a constitution based on property qualification, to which the description "timocratic" [29] seems appropriate, though most people are used to calling it "constitutional govern-   35 ment." Of these three, kingship is the best and timocracy the worst. The perversion of kingship is tyranny: both are forms   1160b of one-man rule, but the difference between them is very considerable. A tyrant looks out for his own advantage, whereas a king looks out for the advantage of his subjects. For only a person who is self-sufficient and superior ⟨to his subjects⟩ in all good things can be a king. A person such as that needs nothing in addition to what he has, and will, therefore, not   5 look to his own advantage, but to that of his subjects. If he is not a man of this sort, he will be king ⟨in name only and⟩ merely by virtue of the lot. [30] Tyranny is the exact opposite of kingship in that the tyrant pursues his own good. In the case of tyranny, it is even more obvious that it is the worst ⟨form of government than in the case of timocracy, which is still, after all, a constitutional form of government⟩: what is opposite to the best is the worst.

Kingship leads to tyranny. For tyranny is the depraved   10

---

[27] The indebtedness of Aristotle to Plato's account of three true and three corrupt forms of government in the *Statesman* 301a-303b is evident in this chapter, as it is in the identical classification in *Politics* III. 7.

[28] See Glossary, *politeia*.

[29] Contrary to Plato, who in *Republic* VIII. 545a-b derives 'timocracy' from *timē* ('honor'), Aristotle derives it from *timēma* ('property qualification') and means by it a government of property owners, i.e., of those who have a stake in the country by reason of the property they own.

[30] A reference to the Athenian office of the King Archon who, in Aristotle's time, was appointed by lot and had nothing in common with a king except the name. The point here is that a selfish monarch is, like the Athenian magistrate, a king in name only.

form of one-man rule, and a wicked king turns into a tyrant. ⟨Similarly,⟩ aristocracy may change to oligarchy through the vice of its rulers, when they fail to distribute according to merit what the city has to offer, when they take all or most good things for themselves, when they appoint always the same people to public office, and when they value wealth more
15 highly than anything else. The result will be that a few wicked men rule instead of the most honest. ⟨The third process of deterioration is from⟩ timocracy to democracy. These two border on one another. For, ⟨like democracy,⟩ timocracy too tends to be essentially rule of the majority, and all those who meet the property qualifications are equal. ⟨Of the perverted forms,⟩ democracy is the least wicked, since its perver-
20 sion of the constitutional kind of government is only small. These, then, are the ways in which constitutions are most likely to change, since the transition ⟨in these three cases⟩ is shortest and most easily effected.

Resemblances to these forms of government—models, as it were—can be found in the household. The community or association of father and sons has the form of kingship, since
25 the father's concern is for his children. That is precisely the reason why Homer addresses Zeus as "Father," for kingship means paternal rule. Among the Persians, however, the rule of the father is tyrannical, since they treat their sons like slaves. The association of master and slave, too, is tyrannical,
30 since it is the master's advantage which is accomplished in it. Now, while the relationship of slavery appears correct, the Persian tyranny ⟨of the father⟩ is mistaken: different kinds of subjects [31] need different kinds of rule. The association of

[31] Several passages from *Politics* I could be cited to show the precise difference Aristotle has in mind. The most pertinent is probably 1260a9-14, quoted by Burnet in his note on this passage:

The manner in which the free rules over the slave is different from that in which male rules female and a man rules a child. All have the requisite parts of the soul, but they have them in different ways: the deliberative element is completely lacking in the slave; the female has it but without authority; and the child has it but in incomplete form.

husband and wife is evidently aristocratic. For the husband's rule depends on his worth or merit, and the sphere of his rule is that which is proper to a man. Whatever is more suited to a woman he turns over to his wife. But whenever the husband takes the authority over all ⟨household⟩ matters   35 into his hand, he transforms the association into an oligarchy, since in doing so he violates the principle of merit and does not rule by virtue of his superiority. Sometimes the wife rules   1161a because she is an heiress. But of course this kind of rule is not in terms of excellence or virtue, but is based on wealth and power, just as in oligarchies. The association of brothers, on the other hand, resembles timocratic rule: they are equal except to the extent that they differ in age. Therefore, if the   5 difference in age is great, their friendship is no longer of the fraternal kind. Democracy, in turn, is found principally in habitations which have no master, where everyone is on an equal footing, and also in communities where the ruler is weak and everyone can do as he pleases.

11. *Friendship and justice in the different political systems*

Each of these constitutions exhibits friendship to the same   10 extent that it exhibits ⟨a notion of⟩ what is just. The friendship of a king for those who live under his rule depends on his superior ability to do good. He confers benefits upon his subjects, since he is good and cares for them in order to promote their welfare, just as a shepherd cares for his sheep. Hence, Homer spoke of Agamemnon as "shepherd of the people." The friendship of a father ⟨for his children⟩ is of the   15 same kind, but it differs in the magnitude of benefits bestowed. For he is the author of their being, which is regarded as the greatest good, and he is responsible for maintaining and educating them. We also attribute these benefits to our ancestors. Furthermore, it is by nature that a father rules over his children, ancestors over their descendants, and a king over his subjects. These kinds of friendship depend on superiority, and   20 that is why we ⟨do not only love but⟩ also honor our parents. Accordingly, in those relationships the same thing is not just for both partners, but what is just depends on worth or merit, and the same is true for friendship.

The friendship between husband and wife is the same as that in an aristocracy. It is based on excellence or virtue: the superior partner gets a larger share of good, and each gets
25 what is suited to him, and the same relationship holds for what is just.

The friendship of brothers is like friendship among bosom companions. For they are equal and belong to the same age group, and where that is the case, men generally have the same emotions and the same characters. The kind of friendship which we find in a timocratic form of government is also similar to this friendship between brothers. For ⟨in timocratic government⟩ the citizens tend to be equal and decent. They hold office in turn and on an equal footing, and, accordingly, their friendship too is based on equality.
30 In the perverted constitutions, the role of friendship decreases to the same extent as the part played by the just. It is least significant in the worst form: in a tyranny, friendship has little or no place. For where ruler and ruled have nothing in common, there is no friendship ⟨nor any justice⟩, either.
35 Thus there is nothing just in the relation of a craftsman to his tool, of the soul to the body, and of a master to his slave. It is true that in all these cases ⟨the instrument⟩ derives a benefit
1161b from its user, but there can be neither friendship nor anything just in a relationship to inanimate objects. Nor can either exist with a horse or an ox, nor with a slave as slave, since the partners have nothing in common. For a slave is a living tool, and a tool is an inanimate slave. Accordingly,
5 inasmuch as he is a slave, there can be no friendship with him, but there can be friendship with him as a man. For there seems to be some element of justice in any human being's relationship to a man capable of sharing in law and contract. Therefore, friendship, too, is possible with him inasmuch as he is a human being. Consequently, friendship and the just

can play a small part even in tyrannies. In democracies, their
part is larger, since where the citizens are equal, they have   10
many things in common.

12. *Friendship within the family*

All friendship, as we have stated,[32] involves a community
or association. But we should probably consider friendship
between kinsmen and friendship between bosom companions
separately. Friendships between fellow citizens, fellow tribesmen, fellow voyagers, and so forth, ⟨as compared with these,⟩
seem to be determined to a greater extent by the ⟨external⟩   15
community, in that they are evidently based on some sort of
an agreement ⟨to do certain things in common⟩. With these
we might also classify the friendship between host and guest.
There are, apparently, many kinds of friendship among
kinsmen, but all seem to depend upon parental friendship.
For parents love their children as something which belongs to
them, while children love their parents because they owe their
being to them. But parents know better that the offspring is   20
theirs than children know that they are their parents' offspring, and the bond which ties the begetter to the begotten
is closer than that which ties the generated to its author. For
that which has sprung from a thing belongs to its source, for
example, a tooth, a hair, and so forth belongs to its owner,
but the source does not belong at all—or only to a lesser degree
—to that which has sprung from it. Moreover, ⟨there is also a
difference between the love of parents and the love of chil-
dren⟩ in point of time: parents love their children as soon as
they are born, but children their parents only as, with the   25
passage of time, they acquire understanding or perception.
This also explains why affection felt by mothers is greater
⟨than that of fathers⟩.
So we see that parents love their children as themselves:
offspring is, as it were, another self, "other" because it exists
separately. Children love their parents because they were

[32] See above, chap. 5, 1159b29-32.

30 born of them, while brothers love one another because they
were born of the same parents: the identical relation they
have with their parents makes them identical with one another. This is the origin of expressions like "of the same
blood," "of the same stock," and so forth. Brothers are, therefore, in a sense identical, though the identity resides in separate persons. Of great importance to friendship is common
upbringing and closeness in age: "Two of an age ⟨delight each
other⟩" and "familiarity makes for fellowship." [33] That is why

35 friendship between brothers resembles friendship between club
members or bosom companions.[34] The bond between cousins

1162a and between other relations is based on the bond between
brothers, and thus on the fact that they are ⟨ultimately⟩ de-
scended from the same parents. They feel a more or a less
close attachment to one another, depending on how close or
remote the common forebear is.

The friendship of children to their parents and of man

5 to the gods is friendship to what is good and superior. For
⟨parents⟩ are the greatest benefactors ⟨children have⟩: they
are responsible for their being and their nurture, and for their
education once they have been born. But this kind of friendship has also a higher degree of what is pleasant and useful
than does friendship with persons outside the family, inasmuch as the partners have more of their life in common.
Friendship between brothers has elements which are also

[33] Only the first of these two proverbial expressions is attested elsewhere. Plato quotes "two of an age delight each other" in *Phaedrus* 240c
and Aristotle in the *Eudemian Ethics* VII. 2, 1238a34, and in *Rhetoric* I.
11, 1371b15.

[34] The term *hetairos* and its derivative adjective *hetairikos*, which I
have translated as 'bosom companion' throughout this book, may also
have the more technical meaning of 'member of a *hetaireia* or club.'
Such clubs were political in character toward the end of the fifth century,
but when a law, enacted shortly after the restoration of the democracy
in 403 B.C., prevented the formation of such clubs for political purposes,
they became purely social in character. If Aristotle is thinking of such
clubs here, we might compare them to the 'fraternal' organizations prevalent in modern American society and the custom of their members to
refer to each other as 'brothers.'

found in friendship between bosom companions. It has them 10
in a higher degree when the brothers are good men and, in
general, when they are like one another, inasmuch as they are
more closely linked together and have been loving one another
since birth, and inasmuch as children of the same parents,
who have been brought up together and have received a
similar education, are more alike in character. Also, there is
the test of time to which brothers are subjected more thoroughly and reliably than anyone else. The friendly relationships among other relatives are analogous, ⟨that is, they vary 15
in proportion to the closeness of their kinship⟩.

The friendship between man and wife [35] seems to be inherent in us by nature. For man is by nature more inclined
to live in couples than to live as a social and political being,
inasmuch as the household is earlier [36] and more indispensable
than the state, and to the extent that procreation is a bond
more universal to all living things ⟨than living in a state⟩.
In the case of other animals, the association goes no further 20
than this. But human beings live together not merely for
procreation, but also to secure the needs of life. There is division of labor from the very beginning and different functions
for man and wife. Thus they satisfy one another's needs by
contributing each his own to the common store. For that
reason, this kind of friendship brings both usefulness and
pleasantness with it, and if the partners are good, it may even 25
be based on virtue or excellence. For each partner has his
own peculiar excellence and they can find joy in that fact.
Children are regarded as the bond that holds them together,
and that is why childless marriages break up more easily. For

[35] It should be noted that fourth-century Greek did not generally differentiate between "man" and "husband" or between "woman" and "wife."

[36] A temporal priority is of course meant here. In *Politics* I. 2, 1253a19,
where Aristotle is concerned with the logical—and not the chronological—
relation between state and household, he says: "The state is by nature
prior to the household and to each of us individually," because the household and the individual do not reach self-sufficiency, and do not fully
attain their *telos* or goal without the larger community or association to
which they belong.

children are a good common to both partners, and what
people have in common holds them together. How a man is
30 to regulate his life in relation to his wife and, in general, how
a person is to regulate his life in relation to his friend, appears to be tantamount to inquiring what constitutes just
conduct for them. For just behavior between friends is apparently not the same as between strangers, or as between
bosom companions or club members, or between schoolmates.

13. What equal friends owe to one another

There are, as we said at the outset,[37] three kinds of friendship. Within each kind, people may either be friends on the
35 basis of equality or one partner may be superior to the other.
In other words, equally good persons can become friends or
a better man can become the friend of a worse, and, similarly,
1162b those who find each other pleasant or whose relation is based
on usefulness may be equal or unequal in the benefits they
confer upon one another. In view of all this, those who are
equal must respect the principle of equality by giving equal
affection to one another and by establishing equality in other
respects, while those who are unequal must make a return
proportionate to their superiority or inferiority.

5 Complaints and reproaches occur only or chiefly in friendships based on usefulness, as is to be expected. For when
people are friends on the basis of virtue or excellence, they
are eager to do good to one another, since that is a mark of
excellence as well as of friendship. In this kind of competition,
complaints and quarrels do not exist, for no one is annoyed
10 at a person for giving affection and being his benefactor;
on the contrary, a cultivated man retaliates by doing good
in turn. If a person gives more than he receives, he will have
no complaints against his friend, since he accomplishes what
he set out to do: for each one desires ⟨to give as well as re-
ceive⟩ what is good.

Nor do complaints occur very much in friendships based on

[37] See above, chap. 3, 1156a7.

pleasure. For the desire of both partners is fulfilled at the
same time if they enjoy spending time together. In fact, a
man would impress us as ridiculous if he complained that he
did not find his friend delightful, since he is free not to spend   15
his days with him.

However, friendship based on usefulness is subject to complaints. For where material advantage is the purpose of the
relationship, people always want more and think they have
less than they should have; they blame their partners that they
are not getting all they need, though they deserve it. ⟨In this
case,⟩ the benefactors are unable to satisfy the wants of the   20
recipients.

The just, it seems, has two aspects: one is unwritten and the
other laid down by law. Friendship based on usefulness has
two corresponding aspects: one kind seems to be moral and the
other legal. Now, complaints are most liable to arise when the
partners contract their friendship in one of these forms and
dissolve it in terms of the other. A friendship formed on fixed   25
conditions is legal friendship. ⟨It takes two forms:⟩ one is
purely commercial and is an exchange from hand to hand,
while the other is more generous in allowing time for payment, though it is still based on a *quid-pro-quo* agreement. In
this kind of relationship, the obligation is clear and not open to
dispute, and, further, the delay in payment contains an element of friendship. That is why in some places such cases are
not actionable, and the belief is that people who have transacted   30
business with each other in good faith ought to be on good
terms with one another.

The moral kind of friendship, on the other hand, is not
formed on fixed conditions. Gifts are given or favors done to
the partner as a friend, but the giver expects to get back an
equal or greater amount on the assumption that this was not a
gift but a loan. He will complain because he has not contracted his friendship in the same form in which he dissolves
it, ⟨i.e., he acts as if he had contracted it on fixed terms⟩. The
reason for this is that all men or most wish for what is noble,   35
but in fact prefer what is to their material advantage. It is

noble to do good to another person without expecting good in return, but it is profitable to be the recipient of good deeds. Accordingly, if the recipient is able to do so, he ought to return an equivalent of what he received, and he ought to give it willingly.[38] For we must not treat a man as our friend against his will: in other words, we must realize that we went wrong at the beginning when we accepted a good deed from the wrong person. ⟨In this case⟩ the benefactor was not a friend and did not act from a motive of friendship. We ought, therefore, to break off the relationship as if we had been the recipient of a good deed on fixed conditions. ⟨If we had realized at the beginning what the relationship would be,⟩ we would have agreed to make return if able to do so. On the other hand, if we were unable to repay, even the giver would not have expected us to do so. Therefore, we should make return if we can. But one should examine at the beginning by whom the good deed is done and what his conditions are, so that one can accept it on these conditions or reject it.

It is a moot question whether we ought to measure a good deed by the material advantage the recipient derives from it, and make the return commensurate with this advantage, or whether it should be measured by the beneficence of the person who performs it. Recipients minimize the action and say that what they received meant little to their benefactors, and that they might just as well have got it from someone else. Givers, on the contrary, assert that they gave the most valuable thing they had, that it was not available from any other source, and that it was given at a critical moment or in an emergency. Now, since the friendship is based on usefulness the material advantage to the recipient is surely the true measure. It is he who stands in need, while the other satisfies it in the expectation of getting an equivalent return. Accordingly, the value of the assistance is just as great as the amount of benefit received, and, therefore, the recipient must repay the amount of the advantage he reaped from it—or even more, for that would be nobler. In friendship based on excellence

---

[38] I see no cogent reason for following Grant, Bywater, and Burnet in bracketing καὶ ἑκόντι.

or virtue, however, there are no complaints, and the moral
purpose or choice of the giver serves as a kind of measure. For
the decisive factor for virtue and character lies in moral choice.

14. *What unequal friends owe to one another*

In those friendships, too, in which one partner is superior
to the other, disagreements occur. Each partner thinks that he
is entitled to more than the other, and when he gets it the   25
friendship ends. If one partner is better than the other, he
thinks he has more than the other coming to him, since the
larger share ought to be assigned to the good. The same
thing happens when one of the partners is more useful than
the other; people say that a useless man should not have as
large a share (as a useful person). A friendship becomes a
public service [39] if what the man gets out of his friendship is not
what he deserves on the basis of his contribution. The usual   30
view is that a friendship should be like a business partnership: [40] those who contribute more should also take more of
the proceeds. The inferior partner who stands in need takes
the reverse position. It is the mark of a good friend, he argues,
to come to the aid of the needy. What is the use of being a
friend of a man of high moral standards or power, they ask, if   35
you are to get nothing out of it?

Now it seems that both partners are right in their claims: 1163b
each is entitled to get a larger share from the friendship, but
not a larger share of the same thing. The superior partner
ought to be given a larger share of honor and the needy
partner a larger share of profit. For the reward of excellence
a..d beneficence is honor, whereas profit is the (form taken by)
assistance to one in need.

We see the same situation also in political systems. A per-   5
son who contributes nothing good to the common interest is

---

[39] *Leitourgia* is a public service the costs of which are defrayed by a
private individual. Such *leitourgiai* included services such as equipping
a warship, training and costuming a tragic or comic chorus, paying the
expenses of a sacred embassy sent by the state to consult an oracle, etc.
[40] See Glossary, *koinōnia.*

not held in honor. For what belongs to the community is given to him who works for the common good, and this common possession is honor. It is impossible to enrich oneself at the expense of the community and to be honored by the com-
10   munity at the same time. Yet no one can put up with the smaller share in everything. Therefore, if a man sustains financial loss, honor is his reward, and if he is venal, money. For a return proportionate to merit restores equality and preserves the friendship, as we have said.[41]

Accordingly, this is the basis for relations between unequals. The person who has profited in money or in excellence must give honor in return, for in giving that he gives what it is
15   possible for him to give. Friendship demands the possible; it does not demand what the giver deserves. In some cases, in fact, it is impossible to make the kind of return which the giver deserves, for instance, in the honors we pay to the gods and to our parents. Here no one could ever make a worthy return, and we regard a man as good if he serves them to the best of his ability.

That is why it would seem that a son does not have the right to disown his father, whereas a father has the right to
20   disown his son. A debtor must pay his debt, but nothing a son may have done ⟨to repay his father⟩ is a worthy return for everything his father has provided for him, and therefore he will always be in his debt. But a creditor is free to remit the debt, and a father likewise. At the same time it seems unlikely that any father would break off relations with his son, unless the son were exceedingly wicked. For apart from the natural friendship ⟨which a father feels for his son⟩, it is only human not to reject the assistance ⟨which a son may offer in old age⟩. The son, on the other hand, if he is wicked, will
25   regard the task of satisfying his father's needs as something to be avoided or not to be eagerly pursued. For most people wish to be the recipients of good deeds, but avoid performing them because they are unprofitable. So much, then, on this subject.

[41] See above, chaps. 7, 1158b27-28; 8, 1159a33-b3; 13, 1162a34-b4.

BOOK IX

1. *How to measure what friends owe to one another*

Wherever friendships are dissimilar in kind, it is proportion which, as we have stated,[1] establishes equality between the partners and preserves the friendship. In a friendship between fellow citizens, for example, a shoemaker receives an equivalent recompense in exchange for his shoes, and the same is true of a weaver and of the other craftsmen. Now, in these 35 cases money has been devised as a common measure, and, 1164a consequently, money is the standard to which everything is related and by which everything is measured. In the friendship between lovers, on the other hand, the lover sometimes complains that his most passionate affection is not returned, though it may quite well be that there is nothing lovable about him, while frequently the complaint of the beloved is 5 that the lover, who first promised everything, now fulfills none of his promises. Such situations arise when one partner's affection for the beloved is motivated by pleasure, while the other's affection for the lover is motivated by usefulness, and neither of them has the requisite quality ⟨which the other expects to find⟩. If this is the basis on which the friendship rests, the break comes as soon as they do not attain the objective of their affection. For each loved the other not for what he was 10 but for what he had to offer, and that was not something lasting, and, accordingly, such friendships do not last, either. But when friendship is based on character, it does last, as we have

1 The statement has not so far been made in precisely the same form in which Aristotle makes it here. However, he has emphasized the importance of proportion in mutual exchange in V. 5, 1132b31-33, and statements similar to the one made here can be found in VIII. 7, 1158b27-28; 8, 1159a35-b3; 13, 1162a34-b4; and 14, 1163a11-12. What Aristotle means by "friendships dissimilar in kind" are those friendships in which the objectives of the two partners are different, e.g., one partner hopes to get something useful out of the friendship and the other something pleasant.

stated,[2] because it is friendship for its own sake, ⟨in which each partner loves his friend for what he is⟩.

Differences arise when each partner gets something other ⟨than what he had expected⟩ and not what he desires. Not to attain what we aim at is like getting nothing at all. It is as in the story of the man who made a promise to the harper: the better he would sing the more he would pay him. When the next morning the singer demanded fulfillment of the promise, the man replied that he had already repaid the pleasure ⟨he got from the singing⟩ with the pleasure ⟨he gave the singer in making him anticipate a reward⟩.[3] Now all would be well, if this were what each partner wanted; but if one partner wants enjoyment and the other profit, and if one has what the other wants but the other does not, then the terms of their association will not be properly met. For a man concentrates his efforts on whatever he happens to need, and he will give what he has in order to get it.

Which person should have the right of assessing the value of the benefit, the first giver or the first recipient? ⟨The latter,⟩ since the giver seems to be leaving it up to him. We are told that this is what Protagoras used to do: after every course he taught he would tell the student to estimate how much the knowledge gained was worth to him, and that was the amount he would take as his fee.[4] But in cases of this sort, some people like the principle: "Let the hire ⟨that has been promised⟩ to a friend ⟨be made good⟩." [5] When people take the money first

---

[2] See VIII. 3, 1156b9-12.

[3] Plutarch (*On the fortune of Alexander* 333 f) tells this story of Dionysius, tyrant of Syracuse.

[4] Cf. Plato, *Protagoras* 328b-c.

[5] Hesiod, *Works and Days* 370. Aristotle quotes only the first two words of the line which we give here in full in Richmond Lattimore's translation. The lines following this in Hesiod (371-72), also in R. Lattimore's translation, are:

> When you deal with your brother, be pleasant,
>   but get a witness; for too much
> trustfulness, and too much suspicion,
>   have proved men's undoing.

and then do not do any of the things they said they would because their promises were excessive, they of course get involved
in complaints, since they do not fulfill what they had agreed   30
to. The Sophists no doubt are compelled to demand payment
first, because ⟨otherwise⟩ no one would give money for their
kind of knowledge. So when people are paid in advance, they
are naturally involved in complaints if they took their pay
without doing what they were paid to do.

When no agreement has been made regarding the service
to be rendered, there is, as we said,[6] no complaint against   35
a person who gives freely for his partner's sake, since a friendship based on excellence is free from complaints: recompense   1164b
must be made in terms of the giver's purpose or choice, for in a
friend and in virtue it is the purpose that matters. This, it
seems, is also the way it should be when ⟨teacher and student⟩
have studied philosophy together. For money is not the standard by which the worth ⟨of a teacher⟩ can be measured, and
no honor could match what he has given. Still, it is perhaps
sufficient to make what return we can, just as we do in the   5
case of the gods and our parents.

If the gift is not given for the sake of the recipient but on
the understanding that there will be some recompense, the
best thing would of course be that both partners regard the
return as fair. But if they should not reach agreement, it
would seem not only necessary but just that the first recipient
of a benefit assess its value. For if the giver receives in exchange an amount equal to the advantage which has come   10
to the recipient or the amount the recipient would have given
for the pleasure, he will have an equivalent return from the
recipient.

We see the same thing happening when something is offered
for sale,[7] and in some places there are laws which provide
that no legal action can be taken to enforce voluntary contracts, on the ground that when one has had common dealings

---

6 See VIII. 13, 1162b6-13.

7 I.e., the just price is that offered by the buyer who will pay what the
object is worth to him.

with a man in good faith one ought to settle with him in good faith. ⟨The law⟩ holds that it is more just that the value
15 be assessed by the man who has been trusted than by the person who trusted him. For most things do not have the same value in the eyes of those who have them and of those who want to get them: what is a person's own and what he has to offer seems to him to have great value. And yet the recompense given depends on the value assigned by the recipi-
20 ent. But surely the recipient should not assess the object at the value it has in his eyes now that he possesses it, but at the value he attached to it before it came into his possession.

2. *Conflicting obligations*

There is also the following problem: should a person assign all prerogatives to his father and obey him in everything, or should he put his faith in a doctor when he is ill, and vote for a military expert when he must elect a general? Similarly,
25 should he accommodate a friend rather than a good man, and should he render the thanks he owes to his benefactor rather than freely give presents to his bosom companion, if he is not in a position to do both?

Surely, to draw an exact line of demarcation in all these cases is not an easy matter. Many and various considerations make one case different from the next in importance and unimportance as well as in point of what is noble and what is
30 necessary. But it is quite clear that we should not make all our returns to the same person. Moreover, we must, as a general rule, repay good deeds rather than do favors for our bosom companions, just as a loan must be paid back to a creditor before presents can be given to a bosom companion. Perhaps even this does not always hold true: when, for example, a man has been ransomed from robbers, should he
35 ransom his ransomer in return regardless of who he is, ⟨if the ransomer falls into robbers' hands⟩ (or repay ⟨the amount of the ransom⟩, if the ransomer has not been captured but demands
1165a repayment)? Or should he ransom his father? It would seem

that he should ransom his father in preference even to himself. Therefore, as we just said, as a general principle we must repay a debt, but in a situation in which giving is nobler or more necessary ⟨than repayment would be⟩, we must abandon principle and make the gift. For there are times when it would not even be fair and equitable to make recompense for the original benefit, for instance, when A has 5 done a good deed for B, whom he knows to be a good man, and B makes a return to A, despite his belief that A is wicked. There are also occasions when one ought not to make a loan to a man who has previously made us a loan, for example, if A has made the loan in the belief he will get it back, because B is an honest man, while B has no hope of recovering it from A because A is a bad man. Therefore, if this is the true situation, the demand ⟨for a loan in return for a loan previ- 10 ously given⟩ is not fair; but if it is not the true situation, though the second party thinks it is, there would seem to be nothing peculiar in his refusing. So, as we have often stated,[8] discussions about emotions and actions are no more definite than the matter with which they deal.

It is now quite clear that we must not make the same return to everyone and that we should not make all our returns to our father, just as we do not offer every sacrifice to Zeus. 15 Since the returns we owe to parents, brothers, bosom companions, and benefactors are different, we must render what is appropriate and fitting to each. This is what people in fact seem to do: when there is a wedding they invite their relatives, since they have common family ties, and thus also a common interest in family affairs. For the same reason, they think that 20 relatives have a special obligation to get together at funerals. When it comes to providing food it would seem to be our first objective to satisfy the needs of our parents, since we owe it to them and since it is nobler to give this assistance to the authors of our being rather than to ourselves. Honor, too, we owe to our parents, as we owe it to the gods, but not every kind of honor. We do not owe the same honor to our father 25

[8] See I. 3, 1094b11-27; 7, 1098a26-29; II. 2, 1103b34-1104a5.

as we do to our mother, nor again do we owe them the honor
due to a wise man or the honor due to a general; we owe them
the honor due to a father and a mother, respectively. We also
owe to every older person the honor due his age by getting
up for him, by offering him a seat, and so forth. But on the
other hand, in our relations with our bosom companions and
brothers we can say anything we please and can share everything with them. We must also try to render what is ap-
30 propriate to kinsmen, fellow tribesmen, fellow citizens, and
every other person, and compare what each is entitled to in
terms of the closeness of his relation to us and in terms of
his excellence or usefulness. This comparison is fairly easy
when the persons involved belong to the same group, but it
is more troublesome when they belong to different groups.
None the less, this is hardly a sufficient reason to give up the
35 task, and we must differentiate ⟨between the various obliga-
tions⟩ as best we possibly can.

3. *When friendships are dissolved*

A further problem is whether or not a friendship should
1165b be broken off when the friend does not remain what he was.
Surely, there is nothing strange about breaking friendships
based on what is useful or pleasant when the partners no
longer have the qualities of being useful or pleasant. For
they were friends of these qualities ⟨rather than of the persons
of their partners⟩, and it is only reasonable that the affection
should pass with the passing of the qualities. But there is
reason for complaint, if a person loves another for being use-
5 ful or pleasant but pretended to love him for his character.
For as we said at the beginning,[9] differences between friends
arise most frequently when they are not friends in the sense
they think they are. So when a person has erroneously assumed that the affection he got was for his character, though
nothing in his friend's conduct suggested anything of the sort,

9 See VIII. 13, 1162b23-25.

he has only himself to blame. But when he has been deceived   10
by his friend's pretense, he has every right to complain against
the deceiver. In fact, his complaint is more justified than complaints against those who counterfeit money, inasmuch as he
offends against something more valuable.

If we accept a person as a friend assuming that he is good,
but he becomes, and we think he has become, wicked, do we
still owe him affection? Surely, that is impossible, since only
the good—not just anything—is the object of affection. What
is evil neither is nor should be an object of affection, for a   15
man must not be a lover of evil, nor must he become like
what is base. As we have said,[10] like is the friend of like.
Should the friendship, then, be broken off at once? Probably
not in every case, but only when a friend's wickedness has
become incurable. But if there is a chance of reforming him,
we must come to the aid of his character more than to the
aid of his property, inasmuch as character is the better thing
and a more integral part of friendship. But no one would re-   20
gard a person who breaks off such a friendship as acting
strangely, because the man who was his friend was not the
kind of man (he turned out to be): his friend has changed,
and since he is unable to save him, he severs his connections
with him.

But if one partner were to remain as he was, while the
other became better and far outdistanced him in excellence,
ought the latter to treat the former as a friend? Surely, that
is impossible, and that it is becomes most obvious when the
distance between them becomes great, as, for example, in   25
childhood friendships. For if one partner were to remain
mentally a child, while the other has grown to be a man
in the best sense of the word, how could they still be friends,
when they neither like nor feel joy and pain at the same
things? They will not even have the same tastes in regard to
one another, and without that, as we saw,[11] it is impossible

10 See VIII. 1, 1155a32-34; 3, 1156b19-21.
11 See VIII. 5, 1157b22-24.

30 to be friends, since they cannot live together. But we have
    already discussed these matters.¹²
        Should, then, a former friend be treated just as if he had
    never been a friend at all? No; we should remember our past
    familiarity with him, and just as we feel more obliged to do
    favors for friends than for strangers, we must show some
35 consideration to him for old friendship's sake, provided that
    it was not excessive wickedness on his part that broke the
    friendship.

4. *Self-love as the basis of friendship*

1166a   The friendly relations which we have with our neighbours
    and which serve to define the various kinds of friendship
    seem to be derived from our relations to ourselves. We count
    as a friend (1) a person who wishes for and does what is good
    or what appears to him to be good for his friend's sake; or (2)
    a person who wishes for the existence and life of his friend for
5   the friend's sake. This is also the feeling which mothers have
    for their children and which friends who have had a quarrel,
    ⟨but are still friends, have for one another⟩. We regard as a
    friend also (3) a person who spends his time in our company
    and (4) whose desires are the same as ours, or (5) a person who
    shares sorrow and joy with his friend. This quality, too, is most
    frequently found in mothers. By one or another of these senti-
    ments people also define friendship.
10   A good man has all these feelings in relation to himself. All
    others have them to the extent to which they regard them-
    selves as good; and the measure ⟨of excellence⟩ in particular
    instances seems to be virtue and a man of high moral stand-
    ards, as we have said.¹³ For (4) a good man remains consistent
    in his judgment, and he desires the same objects with every
    part of his soul. He, therefore, (1) wishes for and does what
15 is good for himself and what appears good to him—for the
    mark of a good man is to work hard to achieve the good—and he

¹² *Ibid.*, 1157b17-24 and 7, 1158b33-35.
¹³ See III. 4, 1113a22-33.

does so for his own sake, for he does it for the sake of the
intellectual part of himself, which of course is thought to
constitute what each person really is. Further, (2) he wishes
for his own life and preservation, and he wishes it especially
for that part of him with which he thinks. For to a man of
high moral standards existence is good. Everyone ⟨—not a
morally good man alone—⟩ wishes good things for himself;
⟨but he wishes only for what is good for himself as a man:⟩
no one would choose to become another kind of being and to   20
have that other being [14] possess everything good. ⟨In other
words, no one would choose to become a god,⟩ for the divinity
already possesses the good, anyway, ⟨and does not have to
wish for it⟩. A person ⟨wishes good for himself⟩ as long as
he remains whatever kind of being he actually is, and it is
the thinking part of each individual that constitutes what
he really is or constitutes it in a greater degree than anything
else. A man like that also (3) wishes to spend his time with
himself, for he does so with pleasure. The memory of his
achievements gives him delight, and his hopes for the future   25
are good; and such memories and hopes are pleasant. Moreover, his mind has an ample supply of subjects for study. (5)
No one shares with himself his own sorrows and pleasures more
than he does. The same thing is at all times painful and
the same thing is at all times pleasant to him, and not different at different times. He is, one might say, a person who
knows no regrets.

Since a good man has every one of these sentiments toward   30
himself, and since he has the same attitude toward his friend
as he does toward himself, for his friend really is another self,
therefore friendship, too, is regarded as being one or other of
these sentiments, and those who harbor them are regarded as
friends. We may dismiss for the moment the question whether
or not friendship with oneself is possible.[15] On the basis of

---

[14] I see no need for Bywater's bracket around ἐκεῖνο τὸ γενόμενον.
The best commentary on this rather elliptical passage is Stewart's. With
the content of this passage, cf. VIII. 7, 1159a5-11.

[15] This question will be taken up in chap. 8 below.

what we have said, friendship would seem to be possible to
the extent that a man is composed of two or more elements,
and because the extreme degree of friendship can be likened
to self-love.

Most people, however ordinary they may be, appear to have
the attributes just discussed. Now, do men share in these
sentiments to the extent that they are satisfied with themselves
and assume themselves good? ⟨That seems to be the case,⟩
since no one who is thoroughly base and reprobate harbors
them, or even gives the appearance of harboring them. One
might almost say that base people do not even share them,
for (4) they are at variance with themselves and have appetite
for one thing and wish for another, as morally weak people
do: instead of what seems to be good to them they choose
what is pleasant and actually harmful, and others again, from
cowardice and laziness, refrain from doing what they think
is best for them. Those who have committed many shocking
crimes and are hated for their wickedness (2) run away from life
and do away with themselves. Wicked men seek the company of
others with whom to spend their days, but (3) they avoid their
own company. For when they are by themselves they remember
many events that make them uneasy, and they anticipate
similar events for the future, but when they are with others,
they can forget. Further, since there is nothing lovable about
them, (1) their relations with themselves are not friendly. Therefore, such people (5) do not share their joys and sorrows with
themselves, for their soul is divided against itself, and while
one part, because of its wickedness, feels sorrow when it abstains from certain things, another part feels pleasure: one
part pulls in one direction and the other in another as if to
tear the individual to pieces. If a man cannot feel pain and
pleasure at the same time, he can at least after a little while
feel pain for having felt pleasure at a certain object, and he
can wish that it had not been pleasant to him. Bad people are
full of regrets.

We see, therefore, that a bad man's disposition is not friendly

even toward himself, because there is nothing lovable about
him. Accordingly, if to be such a person means utter misery,
we must strain all our efforts to avoid wickedness and must try
to be good. For in this way, a person can have a friendly attitude toward himself and can become the friend of another.

5. Friendship and good will

Good will looks like a friendly relationship, but friendship it   30
is not. For we can have good will toward people we do not know
and the fact that we have it may remain unnoticed, but there
can be no friendship in such circumstances. That has already
been stated.[16] But good will is not even affection: it lacks
intensity and desire, the qualities which ⟨always⟩ accompany
affection. Further, affection involves familiarity, whereas good
will can arise on the spur of the moment, as it does, for ex-   35
ample, toward competitors in a contest: a spectator may come
to have good will for a competitor and side with him without   1167a
giving him any active assistance. For, as we said, the good will
comes on the spur of the moment and the love is superficial.
So it seems that good will is the beginning of friendship,
just as the pleasure we get from seeing a person is the beginning of falling in love. For no one falls in love who has
not first derived pleasure from the looks of the beloved. But
if someone finds joy in the looks of another, he is not in love   5
with him for all that: ⟨he is in love only⟩ if he longs for the
beloved when he is away and craves his presence. Thus, it is
likewise impossible to be friends without first feeling good will
toward one another, but people who have good will for one
another do not therefore feel mutual affection. For they
only wish for the good of those toward whom they have good
will, without giving them active assistance in attaining the
good and without letting themselves be troubled in their be-   10
half. Hence one might call good will "friendship" in an extended sense, but it is inactive friendship. But if it goes on

16 See VIII. 2, 1155b32-1156a5.

for a long time and reaches the point of familiarity, it becomes friendship—not a friendship which is motivated by what is useful or by what is pleasant, for these factors are not the basis of good will. When a person has been the recipient of a good deed, he gives his good will in return for what he has received,
15 and in doing so he does what is just. But if someone wishes to do good to another in the hope of gaining advancement through him, he does not seem to have good will for that person, but rather for himself, just as a man is not another's friend if he caters to him for the use he can get out of him.

In general, some sort of excellence and moral goodness are the basis on which good will arises when a person strikes us as
20 beautiful, brave, or something similar, as we said when mentioning the competitors in a contest.

6. *Friendship and concord*

Concord,[17] too, appears to be a friendly relation. That is why it is not simply an identity of opinion, for even people who do not know one another might hold the same opinions. Nor is concord attributed to people who have the same judgment on any subject whatever it may be. ⟨We do not attribute it,⟩ for example, to those who have the same judgment about
25 the heavenly bodies, since to be of the same mind in these matters does not constitute a friendly relation. But we do attribute concord to states, when the citizens have the same judgment about their common interest, when they choose the same things, and when they execute what they have decided in common. In other words, concord is found in the realm of action, and in the realm of action in matters of importance and in those matters in which it is possible for both partners
30 or all partners to attain their goals. For example, there is concord in a state when all citizens decide that the offices should be elective, or that an alliance should be concluded with the

17 *Homonoia* is primarily a political concept. Literally, it designates the quality of 'being of the same mind,' 'thinking in harmony.'

Spartans, or that Pittacus should govern them at the time
when Pittacus himself was willing to do so.[18] But when each
of two persons wishes himself to be the ruler, as, e.g., ⟨Eteocles
and Polyneices in Euripides'⟩ *Phoenician Women,* there is
faction. For concord does not consist in two persons having
identical thoughts of any kind at all, but in having them in
relation to the same person, e.g., when both the common   35
people and the better classes [19] wish that the best men should   1167b
rule. For in this way only does everyone attain his goal. We
see, consequently, that concord is friendship among fellow
citizens, and that is indeed the common use of the term. For
its sphere is what is in the common interest and what is important for life.

Now, this kind of concord exists among good men. They are   5
of the same mind each with himself and all with one another,
since—to use the expression—they never shift their position: [20]
the wishes of people like this remain constant and do not flow
this way and that, as the Euripus does.[21] They wish for what
is just and what is in the common interest, and these are their
common goals. Bad men, on the other hand, cannot live in
concord, except to a small extent, any more than they can be   10
friends. They aim at more than their share when material

18 Pittacus was elected sole ruler (*aisymnētēs*) of his native Mytilene
early in the sixth century B.C. in order to reform the government. He
resigned from his rule after ten years, despite the requests of the My-
tileneans that he continue in office. That is the reason why Aristotle adds
the clause: "at the time when Pittacus himself was willing to do so." For
when Pittacus refused, there was one dissenting opinion, that of Pittacus,
and the concord was broken.

19 For *epieikēs,* see Glossary. The connotations in this context are obviously social and political.

20 The exact significance of the proverbial expression ἐπὶ τῶν αὐτῶν
ὄντες, which means literally "being on the same things," is not known,
and the translation here aims only at giving the approximate sense.

21 As F. Dirlmeier, *Aristoteles: Nikomachische Ethik* (Darmstadt, 1956),
in his note on this passage has shown, the Euripus straits between Boeotia
and Euboea at Chalcis are meant here. The Euripus is still famous for its
irregular, violent current, which changes direction every few hours.

advantages are to be gotten, but fall short when it comes to exertion and to the performance of public services.[22] Each of them has these wishes only for himself; on his neighbor he keeps a jealous eye and prevents him ⟨from getting what he wants⟩. For unless they are on guard ⟨against one another⟩, the common good goes to ruin. So faction comes to be rife among 15 them, when they force one another to do what is just, though they are themselves unwilling to do it.

7. *Good deeds and affection*

It is thought that benefactors have a greater affection for those they benefit than recipients do for those who have done some good to them, and since this seems to be unreasonable, people look for an explanation. In the view of the majority, 20 the explanation is that one partner is a debtor and the other a creditor. In case of a loan the debtor wishes that his creditor did not exist, while the giver of the loan is actually concerned for the debtor's safety, so similarly men who have done a good deed wish for the existence of its recipients in order to receive their gratitude in return, whereas the recipients have no in- 25 terest in making a return. Epicharmus would probably say that those who give this explanation "look at a thing only from the bad side," [23] but ⟨actually⟩ it seems to be ⟨no more than⟩ human: most people's memories are short, and they want to have good done to themselves rather than do it to an- other.

But, it would seem, the true cause lies more deeply in the nature of things, and the case of the lender is not even analo- 30 gous. There is no affection between creditor and debtor, but only the wish for the preservation of the other, in order that something may be got out of him. But benefactors have affec- tion and love for those they have benefited, even if they are

22 For the meaning, see p. 243, note 39.

23 Epicharmus was a Sicilian comic poet who lived early in the fifth cen- tury B.C. The precise significance of this quotation (frg. 146 Kaibel) is not known.

not useful to them at the moment and are unlikely to be
useful at a later time. The same is also true of craftsmen: every
craftsman loves the work of his own hands more than he
would be loved by it, if it were to come to life. Perhaps poets   35
have this attitude more intensely than anyone. For they exag-   1168a
gerate their attachment to their own poems, and love them as
if they were their children. It is with this kind of attitude that
the sentiment of benefactors is comparable: the recipient of
their benefaction is the work of their own hands, and, accordingly, they love their handiwork more than it loves its
maker. The reason for this is that existence is for all men   5
desirable and worthy of affection; but we exist in activity, i.e.,
by living and acting, and in his activity the maker is, in a
sense, the work produced. He therefore loves his work, because
he loves existence. And this lies in the nature of things: what a
thing is potentially is revealed in actuality by what it produces.[24]

At the same time, to the benefactor, that which depends
on his action is noble, with the result that the object of his   10
action gives him joy. But the recipient finds nothing noble
in the giver; at most, he finds some advantage in him, but
advantage is less pleasant and less lovable. Pleasant is only the
activity of the present, the hope of the future, and the memory
of the past; and what activity gives us is the pleasantest and
the most lovable, too. Now, the work has permanence for him   15
who achieved it, since what is noble lasts for a long time; but
the use the recipient gets from it is transitory. And while the
memory of noble acts is pleasant, the memory of useful things
is unlikely to be pleasant, or is so to a less degree, though the
reverse seems to be true of anticipation.

Also, affection is something active, while getting affection
is passive; and affection and friendly feelings are the attributes   20
of the more active of the two partners. Moreover, we all love
a thing more if we got it through effort. For example, those
who have earned their own money love it more than those
who have inherited it. To receive a good deed seems to take no

---

[24] See Glossary, *dynamis* and *energeia*.

effort, but to do a good deed involves labor. That is, by the
25 way, the reason why mothers love their children more ⟨than
fathers do⟩: birth involves a greater effort on the mother's
part, and she knows more clearly that the child is hers. The
same would also seem to apply to benefactors.

8. Self-love

A further problem is whether a person should love himself or someone else most of all. People decry those who love
30 themselves most, and use the term "egoist" in a pejorative
sense. Only a base man, it is thought, does everything for his
own sake, and the more wicked he is the more selfishly he
acts. He is, therefore, criticized, for example, for never doing
anything unless he is made to do it. A good man, on the
other hand, is regarded as acting on noble motives, and the
better he is the nobler his motives are: he acts for his friend's
35 sake and neglects his own affairs.

However, the facts are not in harmony with these argu-
1168b ments, and that is not surprising. It is said that we should
love our best friend best, and the best friend is he who, when
he wishes for someone's good, does so for that person's sake
even if no one will ever know it. Now, a man has this sentiment primarily toward himself, and the same is true of all
5 the other sentiments by which a friend is defined. For, as we have
stated,²⁵ all friendly feelings toward others are an extension
of the friendly feelings a person has for himself. Furthermore,
all proverbs express a similar opinion, e.g., "⟨friends have⟩
one soul," "friends hold in common what they have," "friendship is equality," and "charity begins at home." ²⁶ All these
sentiments will be found chiefly in a man's relation to himself,
since a man is his own best friend and therefore should have
10 the greatest affection for himself. Accordingly, it is under-

²⁵ In chap. 4 above.
²⁶ The Greek has: "The knee is closer than the shin," for which Ross
(*Ethica Nicomachea*), whose rendering I here borrow, uses the more
familiar English equivalent.

standable that there should be a problem which of these two
views we ought to follow, since both are plausible.

When there is a difference of opinion of this sort, we should
perhaps differentiate the arguments from one another and
define the extent and the sense in which each contains truth.
Consequently, if we were to take the sense in which each side
uses the word "egoist," we should probably clarify the matter.
Now those who use "egoist" as a term of opprobrium apply it   15
to people who assign to themselves the larger share of material
goods, honors, and bodily pleasures. For these are the objects
which most people desire, and which they zealously pursue as
being supremely good, and for this reason, too, they fight to
get them. Those, therefore, who try to get more than their
share of these things, gratify their appetites, their emotions in
general, and the irrational part of their souls, and most peo-   20
ple are of this kind. Hence, the ⟨pejorative⟩ use of the term is
derived from the fact that the most common form of self-love
is base, and those who are egoists in this sense are justly criticized. That most people usually apply the word "egoist" to
persons who assign to themselves the large share of things of
this sort, is quite clear. If a man were always to devote his attention above all else to acting justly himself, to acting with   25
self-control, or to fulfilling whatever other demands virtue
makes upon him, and if, in general, he were always to try to
secure for himself what is noble, no one would call him an
egoist and no one would find fault with him.

However, it would seem that such a person is actually a
truer egoist or self-lover. At any rate, he assigns what is supremely noble and good to himself, he gratifies the most sover-   30
eign part of himself, and he obeys it in everything. Just as a
state and every other organized system seems to be in the truest
sense identical with the most sovereign element in it, so it is
with man. Consequently, he is an egoist or self-lover in the
truest sense who loves and gratifies the most sovereign element
in him. Moreover, when we call a person "morally strong" or
"morally weak," depending on whether or not his intelligence
is the ruling element ⟨within him⟩, we imply that intelligence   35

is the individual. And also, we regard a man as being an inde-
1169a pendent and voluntary agent in the truest sense when he has
acted rationally. Thus it is clear that a man is—or is in the
truest sense—the ruling element within him, and that a good
man loves this more than anything else. Hence, it is he who
is in the truest sense an egoist or self-lover. His self-love is
different in kind from that of the egoist with whom people
find fault: as different, in fact, as living by the guidance of
5 reason is from living by the dictates of emotion, and as different as desiring what is noble is from desiring what seems to be
advantageous. Those, then, whose active devotion to noble actions is outstanding win the recognition and praise of all; and
if all men were to compete for what is noble and put all their
efforts into the performance of the noblest actions, all the
needs of the community will have been met, and each individ-
10 ual will have the greatest of goods, since that is what virtue is.

Therefore, a good man should be a self-lover, for he will
himself profit by performing noble actions and will benefit
his fellow men. But a wicked man should not love himself,
since he will harm both himself and his neighbors in following
15 his base emotions. What a wicked man does is not in harmony
with what he ought to do, whereas a good man does what he
ought to do. For intelligence always chooses what is best for itself, and a good man obeys his intelligence.

It is also true that many actions of a man of high moral
standards are performed in the interest of his friends and of
his country, and if there be need, he will give his life for them.
20 He will freely give his money, honors, and, in short, all good
things that men compete for, while he gains nobility for himself. He would rather choose to experience intense pleasure for
a short time than mild pleasure for a long time; he would
rather live nobly for one full year than lead an indifferent existence for many; and he would rather perform one great and
25 noble act than many insignificant ones. People who die for a
cause achieve this perhaps, and they clearly choose great nobility for themselves. A good man would freely give away his

money if it means that his friends would get more, for ⟨in this way⟩ the friend's gain is wealth, while his own is nobility, so that he assigns the greater good to himself. He acts in the same way when it comes to honor and public office: he will give these freely to his friend, since that will bring him nobility 30 and praise. No wonder, then, that he is regarded as a man of high moral standards, since he chooses nobility at the cost of everything else. It is even possible that he lets his friend perform actions ⟨which he intended to perform himself⟩, and that he actually finds it nobler to be the cause of his friend's action than to act himself. So we see that in everything praiseworthy a man of high moral standards assigns himself the larger share 35 of what is noble. It is in this sense, then, as we said, that he ought to be an egoist or self-lover, but he must not be an 1169b egoist in the sense in which most people are.

9. *Friendship and happiness*

A further problem is whether or not a happy man will need friends. It is said that supremely happy and self-sufficient people do not need friends, since they already have the good things 5 of life. Therefore, ⟨it is argued,⟩ since they are self-sufficient, they have no need of anything further; ⟨we need⟩ a friend, who is another self, only to provide what we are unable to provide by ourselves; hence the verse: "When fortune smiles, what need is there of friends?" [27] However, it seems strange that we should assign all good things to a happy man without attributing friends to him, who are thought to be the greatest of ex- 10 ternal goods. Also, if the function of a friend is to do good rather than to be treated well, if the performance of good deeds is the mark of a good man and of excellence, and if it is nobler to do good to a friend than to a stranger, then a man of high moral standards will need people to whom he can do good. This raises the further question whether we need friends more in good or in bad fortune, and by raising it we imply

27 Euripides, *Orestes* 667.

15 that in misfortune a man needs someone who will do good to
him, and in good fortune he will need someone to whom he
may do good.

It is perhaps also strange to make a supremely happy man
live his life in isolation. No one would choose to have all good
things all by himself, for man is a social and political being
and his natural condition is to live with others. Consequently,
even a happy man needs society. Since he possesses what is by
20 nature good, it is obviously better for him to spend his days
with friends and good men than with any stranger who comes
along. It follows that a happy man needs friends.

What, then, do the proponents of the first view mean and to
what extent is their view true? ⟨The reason why they hold this
view is probably⟩ that most people understand by friends those
who are useful. Now, a supremely happy man will have no
need of this kind of friend, since he already has the good
25 things of life. Nor will he need a friend for the pleasantness
⟨of his company⟩, or, if so, only to a small extent, for his own
life is so pleasant that he needs no extraneous pleasure. And
since he does not need useful or pleasant friends, people think
that he needs no friends at all.

But that is certainly not true. We stated at the beginning [28]
that happiness is some kind of activity, and an activity clearly
is something that comes into being and not something we can
30 take for granted like a piece of property. ⟨From the propositions: (1)⟩ being happy consists in living and in being active,
and, as we stated at the beginning,[29] the activity of a good man
is in itself good and pleasant; (2) what is our own is a pleasant thing to us; (3) we are better able to observe our neighbors than ourselves, and their actions better than our own;
35 and (4) the actions of persons who have a high moral standard
are pleasant to those good men who are their friends, in that
1170a they possess both qualities which are pleasant by nature, ⟨i.e.,
they are good and they are their own⟩; it follows that a supremely happy man will need friends of this kind. His moral

28 See I. 7, 1098a16, and 8, 1098b31-1099a7.
29 See I. 8, 1099a14-15 and 21.

purpose or choice is to observe actions which are good and which are his own, and such are the actions of a good man who is his friend.

Also, it is thought that the life of a happy man ought to be pleasant. Now, ⟨if a happy man lived⟩ in isolation, his life would be hard. For it is not easy to be continuously active all 5 by oneself; it is easier in the company of and in relation to others. Accordingly, when an activity is in itself pleasant, as it must be in the case of a supremely happy person, it will be more continuous ⟨if we engage in it together with friends⟩. For a morally good man, inasmuch as he is a morally good man, finds joy in actions that conform to virtue and is displeased by actions which display vice, just as an expert in music feels pleasure when he hears beautiful tunes, and pain when he 10 hears bad tunes. We may also get some sort of training in virtue or excellence from living together with good men, as Theognis says.[30]

If we examine the matter ⟨more profoundly⟩ along the lines of natural science, a morally good man seems to be by nature desirable as a friend for a morally good man. For we have stated [31] that what is by nature good is good and pleasant in 15 itself to a morally good man. Now, in the case of animals, life is defined by their capacity for sense perception, and in the case of man by the capacity for sense perception or for thought. But a capacity is traced back to its corresponding activity, and it is the activity that counts.[32] Consequently, life in the true sense is perceiving or thinking. Life is one of the

[30] Theognis, line 35 (Diehl [3]): "You will learn noble things from noble people." Theognis, an elegiac poet, flourished soon after the middle of the sixth century B.C.

[31] See I. 8, 1099a7-11, and III. 4, 1113a25-33.

[32] For 'capacity' (*dynamis*) and 'activity' (*energeia*), see Glossary. The meaning here is that a capacity makes sense only in terms of the activity in which it results and which makes it what it is. Cf. *Metaphysics* Θ. 8, 1050a8-11: "The objective of a thing is its first principle, and the objective of coming-into-being is the end. And activity is the end, and for its sake do we acquire the capacity: animals do not see in order to have sight, but they have sight in order to see."

20   things which are good and pleasant in themselves, since it is
determinate and what is determinate belongs to the nature of
the good. But what is by nature good is also good to the good
man, and that is why life seems to be a pleasant thing in the eyes
of all men. Still, we must not take "life" to be a wicked and corrupt existence, nor a life spent in pain; for such an existence
is as indeterminate as its foundations, ⟨vice and pain,⟩ are. The
25   point about pain will be clarified in the sequel.[33]

Life is in itself good and pleasant. We can see that from the
very fact that everyone desires it, especially good and supremely happy men: for them life is the most desirable of all
things, and their existence is the most blessed. Moreover, when
a person sees, he perceives that he sees; when he hears, he
perceives that he hears; when he walks, he perceives that he
30   walks; and similarly in all other activities there is something
which perceives that we are active. This means that, in perception, we perceive that we perceive, and in thinking we
perceive that we think. But to perceive that we are perceiving
or thinking means that we exist, since, as we saw, existence is
1170b   perceiving or thinking. Now, to perceive that we are living
is something pleasant in itself, for existence is by nature good,
and to perceive that that good thing is inherent in us is pleasant.
Further, life is desirable especially for good men, because existence is good and pleasant to them: they are pleased when they
5   are conscious of the presence in them of what is in itself good.
Also, the attitude of a morally good man is the same toward
himself as it is toward his friend, since a friend is another self.
From all this it follows that just as one's own existence is desirable for each man, so, or nearly so, is his friend's existence
also desirable for him. Now as we saw, his existence is desirable because he perceives his own goodness, and this kind
10   of perception is in itself pleasant. Consequently, he must also
include his friend's existence in his consciousness, and that
may be accomplished by living together with him and by sharing each other's words and thoughts. For this would seem to be

[33] See X. 1-5.

the meaning of living together when said of human beings: it does not mean feeding in the same place as it does in the case of cattle.

If, therefore, existence is in itself desirable to a supremely happy man, since it is by nature good and pleasant, and if   15 his friend's existence is almost as desirable to him, we may conclude that a friend is something desirable. But what is desirable for a happy man he must have, or else he will be deficient in that respect (and, consequently, not supremely happy). It follows that, in order to be happy, a man needs morally good friends.

10. *How many friends should we have?*

Ought we to make as many friends as possible? Or will the   20 *mot juste* about hospitality, "not too many guests, nor yet none," [34] also fit friendship in the sense that a person should neither be friendless nor have an excessive number of friends? The saying would seem to fit exactly those who become friends with a view to their (mutual) usefulness. To accommodate many people in return for what they have done to us is troublesome, and life is not long enough to do that. Accord-   25 ingly, more friends than are sufficient for one's own life are superfluous and are an obstacle to the good life, so that there is no need of them. To give us pleasure a few friends are sufficient, just as it takes little to give food the right amount of sweetness.

But, as regards morally good men, should we have as many in number as possible as our friends? Or is there some limit   30 to the number of friendly relations a person can have, just as there is a limit to the size of a city-state? Ten persons do not make a city-state, and when there are a hundred thousand it is no longer a city-state.[35] The right number is perhaps not

[34] Hesiod, *Works and Days* 715.

[35] Although Aristotle uses the generic term *anthrōpos* ('human being') here, there can be no doubt that his numbers refer only to adult males who are the only full-fledged citizens. According to the most recent cal-

some specific number, but anything that lies between certain fixed limits. The number of our friends, is, accordingly, also

1171a limited. Perhaps it is the largest number with whom a man might be able to live together, for, as we noticed,[36] living together is the surest indication of friendship; and it is quite obvious that it is impossible to live together with many people and divide oneself up among them. Furthermore, one's friends should also be the friends of one another, if they are all going

5 to spend their days in each other's company; but it is an arduous task to have this be the case among a large number of people. It is also difficult to share the joys and sorrows of many people as intensely as if they were one's own, for it might well happen that one would have to share the joy of one friend and the grief of another all at the same time.

So the right course is perhaps not to seek to have as many friends as possible, but as many as are sufficient for living to-

10 gether. In fact, it would even seem to be impossible to be an intimate friend of many. For that very reason it is also impossible to be in love with many people: being in love means to have something like an excess of friendship, and that is only possible toward one person. Accordingly, intimate friendship is only possible with a few people.

This seems to be corroborated by the way things are. In friendships of bosom companions not many people are included, and the friendships celebrated in stories are ⟨always⟩

15 between two people.[37] Those who have many friends and are

---

culations, Athens had about 258,000 inhabitants in Aristotle's time, of whom about 28,000 were adult males; 112,000 if the wives and children of the citizens are included in the count; 12,000 resident aliens or 42,000 if their families are included; and 104,000 slaves. Cf. Victor Ehrenberg, *The Greek State* (Oxford, 1960), p. 33. Plato in *Laws* V. 737e wants his city to consist of 5,040 land-owning citizens, a number which Aristotle in *Politics* II. 6, 1265a13-17, considers too large. In his own discussion of the proper size of a city, in *Politics* VII. 4, 1326a5-b25, Aristotle does not commit himself to any particular number.

[36] See VIII. 5, 1157b17-24; and 6, 1158a8-10.

[37] Such famous friendships are those, for example, of Achilles and Patroclus, and Orestes and Pylades.

on familiar terms with any chance acquaintance are thought
to be friends to none, except in the sense in which there is
friendship among fellow citizens. They are also called "obsequious." Now, in the kind of friendship that exists among
fellow citizens, it is actually possible to be friends with many
people without being obsequious and while remaining a truly
good man. But to be a friend of many people is impossible,
if the friendship is to be based on virtue or excellence and
on the character of our friends. We must be content if we
find even a few friends of this kind.   20

11. *Friendship in good and in bad fortune*

Is the need of friends greater in good fortune or in bad?
Men seek them in both: in bad fortune they need their assistance, and in good fortune they need people with whom to
live together and to whom they will be able to do good, since
men wish to be beneficent. Accordingly, friends are more
indispensable in bad fortune; and that is why the useful kind   25
of friend is needed in such situations. But it is nobler to have
friends in good fortune, and for that reason people look for
good men (as their friends when they are well off), because
it is more desirable to do good to them and to spend one's
time with them.

The very presence of friends is pleasant in both good and
bad fortune. Pain is alleviated when friends share the sorrow.
In this connection, the question might be raised whether   30
friends share a burden, as it were, or whether the truth is
rather that the pain is reduced by the pleasantness which their
presence brings, and by the thought that they are sharing the
sorrow. Let us dismiss the question whether the alleviation is
brought about by these or by some other factors. At any rate,
it is evident that ⟨friendship⟩ brings about what we have said
it does.

It seems that the presence of friends consists in a mixture   35
of several factors. The very sight of friends is pleasant, especially at a time of misfortune, and it provides some relief from   1171b

pain. For, if a friend is tactful, seeing him and talking to him are a source of comfort, since he knows our character and the things which give us pleasure or pain. But on the other hand, it is painful to see him pained by our misfortunes, for everyone tries to avoid being the cause of a friend's pain. For that reason, manly natures take scrupulous care not to let their friends share their pain, and, unless a man is extremely insensitive to pain,[38] he cannot bear the pain which ⟨sympathy for him⟩ gives his friends. In general, such a person does not let others join in his lamentations, because he himself is not given to lamenting. But womenfolk and womanish men enjoy it when others join their mourning, and they feel affection for them as being their friends and sharers of their sorrow. Still, it is the better type of man whom we must obviously imitate in all matters.

In good fortune, the presence of friends brings with it a pleasant way of passing one's time and the pleasant thought that they are pleased by the good we are enjoying. This is a reason for thinking that we ought to be eager to invite our friends to share our good fortunes, since it is noble to do good, and to be reluctant to ask our friend to share our misfortunes, since one should let others participate as little as possible in what is evil. Hence the saying: "That I'm unfortunate is enough." [39] We should invite our friends to come to our side chiefly when a little trouble on their part will mean a great benefit to us.

Conversely, it is perhaps fitting for a man to go unasked and eagerly to a friend in misfortune: doing good is the mark of a friend, and especially to do good to those in need without being asked, since that is nobler and more pleasant for both

[38] The text of the manuscripts here is somewhat peculiar. In following most translators and commentators, I have strained the usual sense of *alypia*, 'absence of pain,' to mean 'insensitivity to pain.' Apelt's emendation of ἀτυχίᾳ to read ἀλυπίᾳ avoids this difficulty, and gives the meaning: "and, unless his misfortune is extreme, he cannot bear the pain which ⟨sympathy for him⟩ gives his friends."

[39] The author of this saying is unknown.

partners. It is also fitting to join eagerly in the activities of a
friend who is enjoying good fortune, for here, too, friends are
needed; but we should take our time in going to enjoy the
fruits of their good fortune, for to be eager to receive a bene-   25
fit is not noble. Still, we should perhaps scrupulously avoid
the reputation of being disagreeable in rejecting their kind-
nesses, for that happens occasionally. So we see that the
presence of friends is desirable in all circumstances.

12. *Friends must live together*

What lovers love most is to see one another, and they prefer
sight to all the other senses, because love exists and is gener-   30
ated by sight more than by any other sense. Is it, similarly,
true of friends that the most desirable thing for them is to live
together? (Apparently, yes;) for friendship is an association or
community, and a person has the same attitude toward his
friend as he has toward himself. Now, since a man's perception that he exists is desirable, his perception of his friend's
existence is desirable, too. But only by living together can the
perception of a friend's existence be activated, so that it stands   35
to reason that friends aim at living together. And whatever   1172a
his existence means to each partner individually or whatever
is the purpose that makes his life desirable, he wishes to pursue it together with his friends. That is why some friends
drink together or play dice together, while others go in for
sports together and hunt together, or join in the study of philosophy: whatever each group of people loves most in life, in   5
that activity they spend their days together. For since they
wish to live together with their friends, they follow and share
in those pursuits which, they think, constitute their life together.

Thus, the friendship of base people becomes wicked, because, unsteady as they are, they share in base pursuits, and by
becoming like one another they become wicked. But the   10
friendship of good men is good, and it increases with (the fre-
quency of) their meetings. Also, it seems, they become better

as they are active together and correct one another: from the mould of the other each takes the imprint of the traits he likes, whence the saying: "Noble things from noble people." [40] Let this be enough of our treatment of friendship. Our next 15 task is a discussion of pleasure.

[40] See p. 265, note 30.

BOOK X

1. *The two views about pleasure*

After this, a discussion of pleasure is no doubt our next task.[1] Pleasure is considered to be deeply ingrained in the human race. and that is why in educating the young we use 20 pleasure and pain as rudders with which to steer them straight. Moreover, to like and to dislike what one should is thought to be of greatest importance in developing excellence of character. For in view of the fact that people choose the pleasant and avoid the painful, pleasure and pain pervade the whole of life and have the capacity of exerting a decisive influence for a life of excellence or virtue and happiness. Surely, a subject 25 as important as this ought not to be omitted, especially since it is very controversial.

One school asserts that pleasure is the good,[2] and another the opposite view that it is utterly base.[3] While some of the latter school are no doubt convinced that pleasure is actually bad, others think that it is conducive to living a better life to 30 create an impression that pleasure is a base thing even if it is not: most people, they argue, gravitate toward pleasure and become slaves to it, so that they ought to be driven in the opposite direction, in order thus to reach the median.

But surely this view cannot be correct. When it comes to emotions and actions, what is said is less reliable than what is 35 done; and, consequently, when words clash with perceived facts, they are scorned and bring the truth into discredit be- 1172b

1 Here begins the second and more mature discussion of pleasure. For its relation to the earlier discussion, see p. 203, note 59.

2 Eudoxus and his followers are meant; see I. 12, 1101b27-34, and chap. 2 below.

3 Speusippus, who succeeded Plato as head of the Academy, is meant. Though he is mentioned by name in connection with this theory in VII. 13, 1153b5, his name is not mentioned in the discussion of his theory in chap. 2 below.

sides. For if a man who ⟨constantly⟩ disparages pleasure is once seen pursuing it, people will take his lapse to mean that he really considers all pleasure desirable; for drawing fine distinctions is not the strong point of most people. So it seems that true assertions are not only most useful for knowledge,
5 but also for life. For since they are in harmony with the facts, they gain credence, and so induce those who have understanding to guide their lives by them. But enough of this, and on to the various views on pleasure.

2. *Eudoxus' view: pleasure is the good*

Eudoxus [4] believed that pleasure is the good ⟨for the follow-
10 ing reasons⟩. He saw that all things, rational and irrational, strive for pleasure, and that in all situations what is good is desirable, and that which is most desirable is best. The fact that everything strives for the same goal indicated to him that this goal is the best for all. He believed that each individual finds what is good for himself just as he finds his proper food; but what is good for all and for which all strive, that is the
15 supreme good. Eudoxus' arguments gained credence more because of his excellent character than on their own merit. As he had the reputation of being a man of unusual self-control, people thought that he was propounding his theories not because he was addicted to pleasure, but because what he said was actually true.

Eudoxus thought that the same conclusion followed just as plainly from an examination of the opposite of pleasure. Since pain, he argued, is as such avoided by all, pleasure, its oppo-
20 site, is conversely desirable. Again, he held that a thing is most desirable when we choose it not on account of or for the sake

4 Eudoxus of Cnidus (*ca.* 408-355 B.C.) was primarily a mathematician and astronomer, but also made contributions to medicine, geography, and philosophy. After a brief visit to Athens, in the course of which he made the acquaintance of Plato, he transferred his school from Cyzicus to Athens in 368 B.C. For his work, see T. L. Heath, *A History of Greek Mathematics*, Vol. I (Oxford, 1921), pp. 322-34.

of something else, and that it is pleasure which is generally acknowledged to have this quality: no one ever asks the question for what purpose a man is feeling pleasure, because we assume that pleasure is in itself desirable. Further, ⟨he argued,⟩ the addition of pleasure to any good thing at all, for example, to just action or to self-control, makes that good thing more desirable; but what is good can be increased only by another good thing, ⟨and, therefore, pleasure is good⟩. 25

As for this last argument, it does indeed seem to prove that pleasure is a good thing, but not that it is more of a good thing than any other. For every good thing becomes more desirable when combined with another good than when taken by itself alone. As a matter of fact, Plato uses a similar argument in his refutation of the view that pleasure is the good: [5] a pleasant life, he says, is more desirable when combined with practical wisdom than without it; but if pleasure is better in 30 combination with something else ⟨than alone⟩, it is not the good, since the good cannot become more desirable by the addition of something to it. Obviously, the same would apply to things other ⟨than pleasure⟩: nothing can be the good, if it becomes more desirable by the addition of some other thing which is intrinsically good. What good is there, then, which does have this quality, and which is, furthermore, a good in which we can share? It is something of that sort that we are 35 looking for.

Those who object that the aim of all things is not ⟨necessarily⟩ good are talking nonsense.[6] For what all believe to be true is actually true; and anyone who challenges that basic 1173a belief will hardly gain more credence by propounding his view. If the desire for ⟨pleasure⟩ were confined to creatures that have no intelligence, the objection would make sense, but how can it make sense when intelligent beings share the same desire? But there is perhaps even in inferior beings some natural good stronger than they are themselves which aims at the 5 good which is properly theirs.

5 Plato, *Philebus* 20e-22e, 27d, 60a-61b, 67a.
6 This was the view of Speusippus; cf. p. 273, note 3.

The objections advanced against ⟨Eudoxus' argument about⟩ the opposite of pleasure do not seem to be sound, either. The point is made that if pain is evil, it does not follow that pleasure is good: one evil can also be opposed to another and both evils can be opposed to something that is neither good nor evil. The argument is not bad, yet as applied to the problem under discussion it is not true. For if both pleasure and pain

10   were evil, both ought to be avoided: if they were both neither good nor evil, neither of them ought to be avoided or one ought to be avoided just as much as the other. But in actual fact, we see that people avoid pain as an evil and choose pleasure as a good; it is, accordingly, as a good and an evil that they are opposed to one another.

3. The view that pleasure is evil

Moreover, if pleasure is not a quality, that does not mean that it is not a good. For the activities which manifest virtue are

15   not qualities either, nor is happiness; ⟨yet both virtuous activities and happiness are good⟩.

The assertion is made that, while the good is something determinate, pleasure is indeterminate because it admits of degrees.[7] If this judgment is based on the view that we feel pleasure with greater or lesser intensity, ⟨it will have to be admitted that⟩ the same also holds true of justice and the other virtues. For when we say of people that they have these virtues, we clearly speak of them as having certain qualities to a greater

20   or lesser degree and as acting more or less virtuously. Some men are more just and more courageous ⟨than others⟩, and there are also degrees in acting justly and with self-control. However, if their judgment is based on the various forms pleasure takes, they allege the wrong cause ⟨of the indeterminateness of pleasure⟩, for ⟨the distinction that ought to be made is that⟩ some pleasures are unmixed and others mixed. Furthermore, is there any reason why pleasure should not be

25   analogous to health which, though determinate, admits of de-

7 For this argument, see Plato, Philebus 24a-25a, 27e-28a, and 31a.

grees? For the proportion ⟨of the various elements, which constitutes health,⟩ is not the same for all persons, nor is it always
the same in the same individual; rather, it can remain the
same up to a point even when it is disintegrating and it can
vary in degree. It is possible, therefore, that the same may also
be true of pleasure.

Again, the assumption is made that the good is something
final and complete, whereas motion and coming-to-be are incomplete, and on that basis they try to prove that pleasure is a   30
motion and a coming-to-be.[8] But to assert that pleasure is a
motion does not seem to be right, either. We think of speed
and slowness as the terms appropriate to all motion; and if a
motion does not in itself ⟨have degrees of velocity⟩—the motion
of the universe does not—all motion has it in relation to something else. But pleasure has neither speed nor slowness. It is
of course possible to become pleased quickly, just as we can
fly into a temper quickly; however, the experience itself of
pleasure is not quick, not even in relation to ⟨the pleasure ex-   1173b
perienced by⟩ some other person, while all such motions as
walking and growing ⟨can be quicker in one case than they are
in another⟩. In short, although it is possible to pass into a state
of pleasure quickly or slowly, speed and slowness are not involved in the active exercise of pleasure, that means, in being
pleased. Also, in what sense can pleasure be considered as a
coming-to-be? It seems that a thing cannot come to be out of   5
just any chance thing, but it is resolved again into that from
which it comes to be. This means that what comes to be through
pleasure passes away through pain.

A further argument of theirs [9] is that pain is a deficiency of
our natural condition, while pleasure is its replenishment. But
deficiency and replenishment are bodily affects. Thus, if pleasure is the replenishment of our natural condition, we will feel
pleasure in that part of us in which the replenishment takes   10
place, and that is the body. However, that is not what is generally held to be true. Consequently, pleasure is not a replen-

8 Cf. *ibid.*, 53c-54d.
9 *Ibid.*, 31e-32b, 35e-36c, and 51b.

ishment, although of course we do feel pleased while the replenishment is going on, just as an operation performed on us
gives us, ⟨but is not,⟩ pain. The opinion that pleasure is replenishment seems to have been suggested by the pleasures and pains
connected with food. For when hunger has made us deficient
15 and we have suffered its pain, we later find pleasure in replenishment. But that does not apply to all pleasures: the pleasures
of gaining knowledge involve no pain, nor do, among the
pleasures of our senses, those that come through smell, through
many sounds and sights, memories and hopes. What is there,
then, that these pleasures cause to be? There has been no de-
20 ficiency of which they could be the replenishment.

When culpable pleasures are cited ⟨to support the contention that pleasure is bad⟩, one might reply (1) that these are
not actually pleasant. If something is pleasant to a person
whose disposition is bad, we must not think that it is actually.
pleasant to anyone other than him, just as we would deny that
that is actually healthy, sweet, or bitter which is so to the invalid, or that that is white which appears white to a man with
25 an ailment of the eyes. (2) Another answer might be that, even
though pleasures are desirable, they are not desirable when
they come from sources such as these, just as wealth is desirable, but not wealth won by treason, and health is desirable,
but not if it means eating anything and everything. (3) Or one
might retort that pleasures are different in kind. There is a
difference between pleasures that come from noble sources and
pleasures that come from base sources, and the pleasure of a
30 just man cannot possibly be felt by someone who is not just,
nor the pleasure of music by someone who is not musical, and
so forth.

That pleasure is not a good or that pleasures differ in kind
seems also to be evinced by the difference between a friend
and a flatterer. We think of a friend's company as having the
good as its aim, but of the company of a flatterer only as giving us pleasure; and, while flattery brings reproach, a friend
1174a is praised for associating with us for different purposes. No
one would choose to live his entire life with the mentality of a

child, even if he were to enjoy to the fullest possible extent what children enjoy; nor would he choose to find his joy in doing something very base, even though he were to escape any painful consequences. Also, there are many things for which we would exert our efforts even if they would not entail any pleasure, for example, sight, memory, knowledge, and the possession of the virtues. It makes no difference whether pleasures necessarily accompany these things, for we would choose them even if we were to get no pleasure from them.

The obvious conclusion, then, seems to be that pleasure is not the good, and that not all pleasures are desirable, and further that some pleasures, which differ one from the other in kind or in their source, are desirable in themselves. So much for the current views on pleasure and pain.

4. *The true character of pleasure*

What pleasure is or what sort of thing it is will emerge more clearly if we take up the problem from the beginning.

We regard an act of vision as complete [10] at any given moment: it lacks nothing which has to develop later in order to make complete the specific form that constitutes seeing.[11] Something similar seems to be true of pleasure also: it is a whole, and one cannot at a given moment find a pleasure whose specific form will be brought to completion only if the

[10] Although we translate *teleios* as 'complete' throughout most of this chapter and the next, the word also has the connotation of 'perfect'; see Glossary.

[11] What is here rendered as 'specific form' or simply 'form' (*eidos*) is that set of qualities which a scientific definition (*logos*) analyzes into its constituent parts. Each thing is a composite of matter (*hylē*) and form (*eidos*); e.g., a tree is composed of wood, the matter, and "treeness," the specific form without which the matter would remain unintelligible. To analyze this form into its constituent parts (in the case of the tree, having a bark, leaves, certain definite proportions, etc.) is to define the tree. For an excellent and clear discussion of the concept of form, especially of its significance for the *Ethics*, see H. H. Joachim, *Aristotle: The Nicomachean Ethics*, pp. 179-89.

pleasure lasts longer. That is precisely why pleasure is not motion. For all motion—take building, for example—takes
20 place in time and is directed at an end; it is complete only when it has accomplished that at which it aims. In other words, it is complete either in the whole time it takes or at the moment ⟨when the end is reached⟩. The parts and individual moments of any motion are incomplete and each is different in its specific form from the whole and from the others. Fitting the stones together is not the same as fluting the columns, and both differ from the construction of the temple. The construction of the temple is the complete motion, since,
25 in terms of the whole project, it lacks nothing; but the motions of laying the foundation and of making the triglyph are incomplete, since each constitutes a part. Accordingly, these motions are different in form, and it is impossible to find a motion which is complete in its form at any given moment, but, if at all, only in the whole time it takes.

The same is true of walking and every other motion. For
30 if locomotion is motion from one point to another, it, too, takes different forms, such as flying, walking, jumping, and so forth. More than that, there are even differences in walking: for the point from which the motion starts and the point to which it proceeds are not the same for an entire racecourse and for a part of it, and the terminal points of one part are different from those of another; nor is passing along one line the same as passing along another, for you do not just pass
1174b along *a* line, but a line that is in a ⟨definite⟩ place, and one line is in a different place from another. We have dealt with the subject of motion in greater detail in another work; [12] however, it seems that motion is not complete at any given moment, but that the many motions ⟨which make up the whole⟩ are incomplete and different in form, since the termi-
5 nal points determine the form. Yet the specific form which constitutes pleasure is complete at any given moment So pleasure and motion are obviously different things, and pleasure is something whole and complete.

[12] In *Physics* VI-VIII.

This is also shown by the fact that while motion is possible only in time, pleasure is not in time. For what takes place in a moment is a whole. This further shows that those people are wrong who assert that pleasure is motion or coming-to-be. For these terms cannot be applied to everything, but only to what has parts and is not a whole. There is no coming-to-be of an act of vision nor of a point nor of a unit: none of these is motion or coming-to-be, and the same is, accordingly, true of pleasure, since it is a whole.

All sense perception is actively exercised in relation to its object, and is completely exercised when it is in good condition and its object is the best of those that can be perceived by the senses. For something like that seems to come very close to being complete activity, assuming that it makes no difference whether we say that the sense perception or the organ in which it resides is actively exercised. From all this it follows that in any sense perception that activity is best whose organ is in the best condition and whose object is the best of all the objects that fall within its range, and this activity will be the most complete and the most pleasant. For each sense, and similarly all thought and study, has its own pleasure and is pleasantest when it is most complete; but it is most complete when the organ is in good condition and the object the worthiest of all that fall within its range; pleasure completes the activity. Still, pleasure does not complete the activity in the same way in which the perceived object and sense perception do, when both are good, just as health and a physician are not in the same sense the cause of a man's healthy state.

That there is a pleasure for each sense is obvious, for we speak of sights and sounds as being pleasant. It is also obvious that the pleasure is greatest when the sense perception is keenest and is exercised upon the best object. As long as this is the condition of the perceived object and the perceiving subject the pleasure will last on, since there is something to act and something to be acted upon.

Pleasure completes the activity not as a characteristic completes an activity by being already inherent in it, but as a

completeness that superimposes itself upon it, like the bloom of youth in those who are in their prime. So long, then, as the object of thought or of sense perception and the discriminating or studying subject are in their proper condition, there
1175a will be pleasure in the activity. For as long as that which is acted upon and that which acts remain unchanged in themselves and in their relation to one another, the same result must naturally follow.

How is it, then, that no one feels pleasure continuously? Do we get tired? ⟨That seems to be the correct answer;⟩ for whatever is human is incapable of continuous activity. Conse-
5 quently, pleasure is not continuous, either, since it accompanies activity. And for the same reason, some things which delight us when they are new, give us less delight later on: at first our thinking is stimulated and concentrates its activity upon them. To take sight as an example, people are engrossed in what they see, but afterwards the activity is not the same but is relaxed, and as a result the pleasure loses its edge.
10

One is led to believe that all men have a desire for pleasure, because all strive to live. Life is an activity, and each man actively exercises his favorite faculties upon the objects he loves most. A man who is musical, for example, exercises his hearing upon tunes, an intellectual his thinking upon the sub-
15 jects of his study, and so forth. But pleasure completes the activities, and consequently life, which they desire. No wonder, then, that men also aim at pleasure: each man finds that it completes his life, and his life is desirable.

We need not discuss for the present the question whether we choose life for the sake of pleasure or pleasure for the sake of life. For the two are obviously interdependent and
20 cannot be separated: there is no pleasure without activity, and every activity is completed by pleasure.

5. *The value of pleasure*

This also suggests that pleasures differ in kind. For when things differ in kind we believe that their completion is

brought about by something correspondingly different. We
see that this is so in the case of the products of nature as well
as those of art, for example, in the case of animals and trees,
a painting and a statue, a house and a piece of furniture.
We likewise think of activities which differ in kind as attain- 25
ing their completion through the agency of things which
differ in kind. Now, the activities of thought differ in kind
from the activities of the senses and from one another, so that
the pleasures which complete them are correspondingly different.

This is corroborated by the fact that each pleasure is in-
timately connected with the activity which it completes. For 30
an activity is increased by the pleasure proper to it. People
who engage in an activity with pleasure are more perceptive
in the judgment and accurate execution of particulars; those
who enjoy doing geometry become geometers and understand
the particular facts of geometry more readily, and similarly
those who are fond of music, building, and so forth, become
proficient each in his own proper line of work through the joy 35
he derives from it. Pleasures increase activities, and what
increases a thing is proper to it. But when things differ in
kind there must be a corresponding difference in kind in what 1175b
is proper to them.

This seems to emerge even more clearly from the fact that
the pleasures arising from one activity obstruct those caused
by other activities. Devotees of flute music, for example, are
incapable of paying attention to a discussion if they suddenly
hear someone playing the flute, because they derive greater
joy from flute-playing than from the activity in which they 5
are engaged. Accordingly, the pleasure which flute-playing
brings destroys the activity concerned with discussion. The
same thing also happens in other cases when a person is
engaged in two activities at the same time: the pleasanter
activity crowds out the other; and if the pleasure it gives is
much greater, it crowds out the other all the more to the
point where one engages in it no longer. Therefore, when we
enjoy something very much, we hardly do anything else at all; 10

and when something we do gives us only slight satisfaction, we turn to something else, for example, people who eat candy in the theater do so especially when the actors are bad. So, since an activity is made more precise, more enduring, and better by the pleasure proper to it, but spoiled by pleasures
15 not proper to it, it is clear that there is a great difference between them. One might almost say that alien pleasures have the same effect as a pain that comes with a given activity. For a pain that comes with an activity destroys it; if, for example, writing or doing sums is unpleasant and irritating for a person, he does not write or do sums, because the activity is pain-
20 ful. It is, therefore, true that an activity is affected in opposite ways by the pleasures and by the pains proper to it; and the pleasures and pains proper to it are those which accompany the activity itself. Alien pleasures, as we have said, are very close to pain in their effect: they destroy activity, but not in the same way.

Now, activities differ from one another in goodness and
25 badness. Some are desirable, others should be avoided, and others again are indifferent. The same is also true of pleasures, since each activity determines its own proper pleasure. The pleasure proper to a morally good activity is good, the pleasure proper to a bad activity evil. For appetites deserve praise when their objects are noble, but blame when they are base. But
30 the pleasures inherent in the activities are more truly proper to these activities than are the desires. The desires are distinct from the activities in time as well as in their nature, whereas pleasure is so closely linked to activity and so little distinguished from it that one may dispute whether ⟨or not⟩ activity is identical with pleasure. At any rate, pleasure seems to be neither thought nor again sense perception—that would be
35 absurd; but because they are never found apart, some people get the impression that they are identical.

So we see that differences in activities make for corresponding differences in pleasures. Now, sight is superior in purity
1176a to touch, and hearing and smell are superior to taste, and, accordingly, their respective pleasures also differ from one an-

other. The pleasures of thought, in turn, are superior to the
pleasures of the senses, and there are further differences within
each class.

Each animal is thought to have its own proper pleasure, just
as each has its own function, for the activity determines the
pleasure. This is shown if we study particular animals: the   5
pleasure of a horse differs from that of a dog and of a man. As
Heraclitus says, an ass would prefer chaff to gold,[13] for food
gives asses more pleasure than gold. Accordingly, as animals
differ in kind, so do their pleasures differ in kind, and it makes
sense that there should be no difference in the pleasures when
animals do not so differ. But as regards men, there is consider-   10
able variation. The same things give delight to some and pain
to others, are painful and hateful to some and pleasant and
agreeable to others. We find this also true of sweetness: the
same things do not seem sweet to a man in fever and to a
healthy person. Nor is the same thing hot to an invalid and to
a man in good condition. The same is true also of other cases.   15

But in all matters of this sort we consider that to be real and
true which appears so to a good man. If this is right, as it
seems to be, and if virtue or excellence and the good man, insofar as he is good, are the measure of each thing, then what
seem to him to be pleasures are pleasures and what he enjoys
is pleasant. It is not surprising that some things which are disagreeable to him are pleasant to someone else; for there are   20
many ways in which men can become corrupted and perverted.
Still, such things are not actually pleasant, but are so only to
persons of this kind, that is, to persons who have this kind of
disposition.

It is, accordingly, clear that we cannot call pleasures those
which are admittedly base; they are pleasures only to corrupt
people. But of the pleasures which are regarded as decent,
what sort or which particular pleasure are we to claim as being
truly proper to man? Surely, this is shown by the activities in   25
which he engages, since it is these that the pleasures accompany. Those pleasures, therefore, which complete the activities

[13] Heraclitus, frg. B 9 (DK[6]).

of a perfect or complete and supremely happy man, regardless
of whether these activities are one or several, can be called in
the true sense the pleasures proper to man. All the rest are
human pleasures only in a secondary and even less than secondary sense, as are the activities ⟨which they accompany⟩.

6. Happiness and activity

30   Now that we have completed our discussion of the virtues,
and of the different kinds of friendship and pleasure, it remains to sketch an outline of happiness, since, as we assert, it
is the end or goal of human ⟨aspirations⟩. Our account will be
more concise if we recapitulate what we have said so far.

We stated, then, that happiness is not a characteristic; [14] ⟨if
it were,⟩ a person who passes his whole life in sleep, vegetating
35   like a plant, or someone who experiences the greatest misfortunes could possess it. If, then, such a conclusion is unaccept-
1176b able, we must, in accordance with our earlier discussion,[15] classify happiness as some sort of activity. Now, some activities are
necessary and desirable only for the sake of something else,
while others are desirable in themselves. Obviously, happiness
must be classed as an activity desirable in itself and not for the
5   sake of something else. For happiness lacks nothing and is self-
sufficient. Activities desirable in themselves are those from
which we seek to derive nothing beyond the actual exercise of
the activity. Actions in conformity with virtue evidently constitute such activities; for to perform noble and good deeds is
something desirable for its own sake.

Pleasant amusements, too, ⟨are desirable for their own sake⟩.
We do not choose them for the sake of something else, since
10   they lead to harm rather than good when we become neglect-
ful of our bodies and our property. But most of those who are
considered happy find an escape in pastimes of this sort, and
this is why people who are well versed in such pastimes find
favor at the courts of tyrants; they make themselves pleasant

[14] See I. 5, 1095b31-1096a2; 8, 1098b31-1099a7.
[15] I. 7, 1098a5-7.

by providing what the tyrants are after, and what they want is   15
amusement. Accordingly, such amusements are regarded as being conducive to happiness, because men who are in positions
of power devote their leisure to them. But perhaps such persons cannot be ⟨regarded as⟩ evidence. For virtue and intelligence, which are the sources of morally good activities, do not
consist in wielding power. Also, if these men, who have never
tasted pure and generous pleasure, find an escape in the pleas-   20
ures of the body, this is no sufficient reason for thinking that
such pleasures are in fact more desirable. For children, too,
think that what they value is actually the best. It is, therefore,
not surprising that as children apparently do not attach value
to the same things as do adults, so bad men do not attach
value to the same things as do good men. Accordingly, as we
have stated repeatedly,[16] what is valuable and pleasant to a   25
morally good man actually is valuable and pleasant. Each individual considers that activity most desirable which corresponds to his own proper characteristic condition, and a morally good man, of course, so considers activity in conformity
with virtue.

Consequently, happiness does not consist in amusement. In
fact, it would be strange if our end were amusement, and if
we were to labor and suffer hardships all our life long merely
to amuse ourselves. For, one might say, we choose everything   30
for the sake of something else—except happiness; for happiness
is an end. Obviously, it is foolish and all too childish to exert
serious efforts and toil for purposes of amusement. Anacharsis [17] seems to be right when he advises to play in order to be
serious; for amusement is a form of rest, and since we cannot
work continuously we need rest. Thus rest is not an end, for   35
we take it for the sake of ⟨further⟩ activity. The happy life is   1177a

16 See I. 8, 1099a13; III. 4, 1113a22-33; IX. 4, 1166a12-13; 9, 1170a13-16;
X. 5, 1176a15-22.

17 Anacharsis, who is said to have lived early in the sixth century B.C.,
was a Scythian whose travels all over the Greek world brought him a
reputation for wisdom. He allegedly met Solon at Athens and was num-
bered in some ancient traditions among the Seven Wise Men.

regarded as a life in conformity with virtue. It is a life which involves effort and is not spent in amusement.

Moreover, we say that what is morally good is better than what is ridiculous and brings amusement, and the better the organ or man—whichever may be involved in a particular case 5 —the greater the moral value of the activity. But the activity of the better organ or the better man is in itself superior and more conducive to happiness.

Furthermore, any person at all, even a slave, can enjoy bodily pleasures no less than the best of men. But no one would grant that a slave has a share in happiness any more than that he lives a life of his own.[18] For happiness does not consist in 10 pastimes of this sort, but in activities that conform with virtue, as we have stated earlier.[19]

7. *Happiness, intelligence, and the contemplative life*

Now, if happiness is activity in conformity with virtue, it is to be expected that it should conform with the highest virtue, and that is the virtue of the best part of us. Whether this is intelligence or something else which, it is thought, by its very nature rules and guides us and which gives us our notions of 15 what is noble and divine; whether it is itself divine or the most divine thing in us; it is the activity of this part (when operating) in conformity with the excellence or virtue proper to it that will be complete happiness. That it is an activity concerned with theoretical knowledge or contemplation [20] has already been stated.[21]

18 The reason is that a slave, as slave, is an instrument to be used by another and accordingly cannot dispose of himself. Cf. also VIII. 11, 1161b4-8 and *Politics* III. 9, 1280a32-34.

19 See I. 7, 1098a16-17; and in this chapter, 1176a35-b9.

20 *Theōria* is the activity of the mind for its own sake as applied either to reality as such or to the objects of nature (*physis*) including astronomy, cosmology, biology, etc., or to mathematics. It is, in other words, the characteristic activity of the "intellectual"—as opposed to the "moral"—virtues. While most translations conventionally render the noun by 'contemplation,' the present translation has preferred 'theoretical knowledge'

This would seem to be consistent with our earlier statements as well as the truth. For this activity is not only the highest—for intelligence is the highest possession we have in us, and the objects which are the concern of intelligence are the highest objects of knowledge—but also the most continuous: we are able to study continuously more easily than to perform any kind of action. Furthermore, we think of pleasure as a necessary ingredient in happiness. Now everyone agrees that of all the activities that conform with virtue activity in conformity with theoretical wisdom is the most pleasant. At any rate, it seems that ⟨the pursuit of wisdom or⟩ philosophy holds pleasures marvellous in purity and certainty, and it is not surprising that time spent in knowledge is more pleasant than time spent in research. Moreover, what is usually called "self-sufficiency" will be found in the highest degree in the activity which is concerned with theoretical knowledge. Like a just man and any other virtuous man, a wise man requires the necessities of life; once these have been adequately provided, a just man still needs people toward whom and in company with whom to act justly, and the same is true of a self-controlled man, a courageous man, and all the rest. But a wise man is able to study even by himself, and the wiser he is the more is he able to do it. Perhaps he could do it better if he had colleagues to work with him, but he still is the most self-sufficient of all. Again, study seems to be the only activity which is loved for its own sake. For while we derive a greater or a smaller advantage from practical pursuits beyond the action itself, from study we derive nothing beyond the activity of studying. Also, we regard happiness as depending on leisure; for our purpose in being busy is to have leisure, and we wage war in order to have peace. Now, the practical virtues are activated in political and military pursuits, but the actions in-

20

25

30

1177b

5

---

or 'study.' However, it is difficult to avoid translating the adjective *theorētikos* by 'contemplative' when it describes the kind of life which is devoted to *theōria*.

21 Actually, this has not yet been stated, but it may be inferred from I. 5, 1095b14-1196a5; VI. 7, 1141a18-b3; 12, 1143b33-1144a6; 13, 1145a6-11.

volved in these pursuits seem to be unleisurely. This is completely true of military pursuits, since no one chooses to wage
10   war or foments war for the sake of war; he would have to be
utterly bloodthirsty if he were to make enemies of his friends
simply in order to have battle and slaughter. But the activity
of the statesman, too, has no leisure. It attempts to gain advantages beyond political action, advantages such as political
power, prestige, or at least happiness for the statesman himself
and his fellow citizens, and that is something other than polit-
15   ical activity: after all, the very fact that we investigate politics
shows that it is not the same ⟨as happiness⟩. Therefore, if we
take as established (1) that political and military actions surpass all other actions that conform with virtue in nobility and
grandeur; (2) that they are unleisurely, aim at an end, and are
not chosen for their own sake; (3) that the activity of our intelligence, inasmuch as it is an activity concerned with theoretical knowledge, is thought to be of greater value than the
20   others, aims at no end beyond itself, and has a pleasure proper
to itself—and pleasure increases activity; and (4) that the qualities of this activity evidently are self-sufficiency, leisure, as
much freedom from fatigue as a human being can have, and
whatever else falls to the lot of a supremely happy man; it follows that the activity of our intelligence constitutes the complete happiness of man, provided that it encompasses a com-
25   plete span of life; for nothing connected with happiness must
be incomplete.

However, such a life would be more than human. A man who
would live it would do so not insofar as he is human, but because there is a divine element within him. This divine element
is as far above our composite nature [22] as its activity is above the
active exercise of the other, ⟨i.e., practical,⟩ kind of virtue. So if
30   it is true that intelligence is divine in comparison with man,
then a life guided by intelligence is divine in comparison with
human life. We must not follow those who advise us to have
human thoughts, since we are ⟨only⟩ men, and mortal thoughts,

---

[22] Man, consisting of soul and body, i.e., of form and matter, is a
composite being, whereas the divine, being all intelligence, is not.

as mortals should; on the contrary, we should try to become immortal as far as that is possible and do our utmost to live in accordance with what is highest in us. For though this is a small portion ⟨of our nature⟩,[23] it far surpasses everything else in power and value. One might even regard it as each man's true self, since it is the controlling and better part. It would, therefore, be strange if a man chose not to live his own life but someone else's.

1178a

Moreover, what we stated before [24] will apply here, too: what is by nature proper to each thing will be at once the best and the most pleasant for it. In other words, a life guided by intelligence is the best and most pleasant for man, inasmuch as intelligence, above all else, is man. Consequently, this kind of life is the happiest.

5

8. *The advantages of the contemplative life*

A life guided by the other kind of virtue, ⟨the practical,⟩ is happy in a secondary sense, since its active exercise is confined to man. It is in our dealings with one another that we perform just, courageous, and other virtuous acts, when we observe the proper kind of behavior toward each man in private transactions, in meeting his needs, in all manner of actions, and in our emotions, and all of these are, as we see, peculiarly human. Moreover, some moral acts seem to be determined by our bodily condition, and virtue or excellence of character seems in many ways closely related to the emotions. There is also a close mutual connection between practical wisdom and excellence of character, since the fundamental principles of practical wisdom are determined by the virtues of character, while practical wisdom determines the right standard for the moral virtues. The fact that these virtues are also bound up with the emotions indicates that they belong to our composite nature, and the virtues of our composite nature are human virtues; consequently, a life guided by these virtues and the happiness ⟨that

10

15

20

23 Literally, "for though this is small in bulk."
24 See IX. 9, 1169b30-1170a4; X. 6, 1176b26-27.

goes with it are likewise human⟩. The happiness of the intelligence, however, is quite separate ⟨from that kind of happiness⟩. That is all we shall say about it here, for a more detailed treatment lies beyond the scope of our present task.

It also seems that such happiness has little need of external trimmings, or less need than moral virtue has. Even if we grant
25 that both stand in equal need of the necessities of life, and even if the labors of a statesman are more concerned with the needs of our body and things of that sort—in that respect the difference between them may be small—yet, in what they need for the exercise of their activities, their difference will be great. A generous man will need money to perform generous acts,
30 and a just man will need it to meet his obligations. For the mere wish to perform such acts is inscrutable, and even an unjust man can pretend that he wishes to act justly. And a courageous man will need strength if he is to accomplish an act that conforms with his virtue, and a man of self-control the possibility of indulgence. How else can he or any other virtuous man make manifest his excellence? Also, it is debatable
35 whether the moral purpose or the action is the more decisive element in virtue, since virtue depends on both. It is clear of
1178b course that completeness depends on both. But many things are needed for the performance of actions, and the greater and nobler the actions the more is needed. But a man engaged in study has no need of any of these things, at least not for the active exercise of studying; in fact one might even go so far as to say that they are a hindrance to study. But insofar as he
5 is human and lives in the society of his fellow men, he chooses to act as virtue demands, and accordingly, he will need externals for living as a human being.

A further indication that complete happiness consists in some kind of contemplative activity is this. We assume that the gods are in the highest degree blessed and happy. But
10 what kind of actions are we to attribute to them? Acts of justice? Will they not look ridiculous making contracts with one another, returning deposits, and so forth? Perhaps acts of courage—withstanding terror and taking risks, because it is

noble to do so? Or generous actions? But to whom will they give? It would be strange to think that they actually have currency or something of the sort. Acts of self-control? What would they be? Surely, it would be in poor taste to praise them for not having bad appetites. If we went through the whole list we would see that a concern with actions is petty and unworthy of the gods. Nevertheless, we all assume that the gods exist and, consequently, that they are active; for surely we do not assume them to be always asleep like Endymion.[25] Now, if we take away action from a living being, to say nothing of production, what is left except contemplation? Therefore, the activity of the divinity which surpasses all others in bliss must be a contemplative activity, and the human activity which is most closely akin to it is, therefore, most conducive to happiness.

This is further shown by the fact that no other living being has a share in happiness, since they all are completely denied this kind of activity. The gods enjoy a life blessed in its entirety; men enjoy it to the extent that they attain something resembling the divine activity; but none of the other living beings can be happy, because they have no share at all in contemplation or study. So happiness is coextensive with study, and the greater the opportunity for studying, the greater the happiness, not as an incidental effect but as inherent in study; for study is in itself worthy of honor. Consequently, happiness is some kind of study or contemplation.

But we shall also need external well-being, since we are only human. Our nature is not self-sufficient for engaging in study: our body must be healthy and we must have food and generally be cared for. Nevertheless, if it is not possible for a man to be supremely happy without external goods, we must not think that his needs will be great and many in order to be happy; for self-sufficiency and moral action do not consist in an excess (of possessions). It is possible to perform noble

15

20

25

30

35

1179a

[25] Supposedly the most beautiful of men, Endymion was loved by the Moon, who cast him into a perpetual sleep that she might descend and embrace him each night.

5 actions even without being ruler of land and sea; a man's
actions can be guided by virtue also if his means are moderate.
That this is so can be clearly seen in the fact that private individuals evidently do not act less honorably but even more
honorably than powerful rulers. It is enough to have moderate
means at one's disposal, for the life of a man whose activity
is guided by virtue will be happy.

10 Solon certainly gave a good description of a happy man,
when he said that he is a man moderately supplied with
external goods, who had performed what he, Solon, thought
were the noblest actions, and who had lived with self-control.[26]
For it is possible to do what one should even with moderate
possessions. Also Anaxagoras, it seems, did not assume that
a happy man had to be rich and powerful.[27] He said that he
would not be surprised if a happy man would strike the com-
15 mon run of people as strange, since they judge by externals
and perceive nothing but externals. So it seems that our
account is in harmony with the opinion of the wise.

Now, though such considerations carry some conviction, in
the field of moral action truth is judged by the actual facts of
life, for it is in them that the decisive element lies. So we must
20 examine the conclusions we have reached so far by applying
them to the actual facts of life: if they are in harmony with
the facts we must accept them, and if they clash we must
assume that they are mere words.

A man whose activity is guided by intelligence, who culti-
vates his intelligence and keeps it in the best condition, seems
to be most beloved by the gods. For if the gods have any con-
25 cern for human affairs—and they seem to have—it is to be expected that they rejoice in what is best and most akin to them,
and that is our intelligence; it is also to be expected that they
requite with good those who most love and honor intelligence,
as being men who care for what is dear to the gods and who

[26] Solon's views are found in his famous conversation with Croesus,
reported by Herodotus (I. 30-32).
[27] Anaxagoras, in DK6, 59 A 30.

act rightly and nobly. That a wise man, more than any other, has all these qualities is perfectly clear. Consequently, he is the 30 most beloved by the gods, and as such he is, presumably, also the happiest. Therefore, we have here a further indication that a wise man attains a higher degree of happiness than anyone.

9. *Ethics and politics*

Now that we have given an adequate outline of these matters, of the virtues, and also of friendship and pleasure, can we regard our project as having reached its completion? Must 35 we not rather abide by the maxim that in matters of action the end is not to study and attain knowledge of the particular 1179b things to be done, but rather to do them? Surely, knowing about excellence or virtue is not enough: we must try to possess it and use it, or find some other way in which we may become good.

Now, if words alone would suffice to make us good, they would rightly "harvest many rewards and great," as Theognis 5 says,[28] and we would have to provide them. But as it is, while words evidently do have the power to encourage and stimulate young men of generous mind, and while they can cause a character well-born and truly enamored of what is noble to be possessed by virtue, they do not have the capacity to turn the common run of people to goodness and nobility. For the 10 natural tendency of most people is to be swayed not by a sense of shame but by fear, and to refrain from acting basely not because it is disgraceful, but because of the punishment it brings. Living under the sway of emotion, they pursue their own proper pleasures and the means by which they can obtain them, and they avoid the pains that are opposed to them. But they do not even have a notion of what is noble and truly 15

---

[28] Theognis, lines 432-434 (Diehl[3]), which are, incidentally, also quoted by Plato, *Meno* 95e, read in full: "If a god had granted to the descendants of Asclepius to cure wickedness and the destruction-bent mind of men, they would harvest many great rewards."

pleasant, since they have never tasted it. What argument indeed can transform people like that? To change by argument
what has long been ingrained in a character is impossible or,
at least, not easy. Perhaps we must be satisfied if we have
whatever we think it takes to become good and attain a modi-
cum of excellence.

20   Some people believe that it is nature that makes men good,
others that it is habit, and others again that it is teaching.
Now, whatever goodness comes from nature is obviously not
in our power, but is present in truly fortunate men as the
result of some divine cause. Argument and teaching, I am
afraid, are not effective in all cases: the soul of the listener
25   must first have been conditioned by habits to the right kind
of likes and dislikes, just as land ⟨must be cultivated before
it is able⟩ to foster the seed. For a man whose life is guided
by emotion will not listen to an argument that dissuades him,
nor will he understand it. How can we possibly persuade a
man like that to change his ways? And in general it seems that
emotion does not yield to argument but only to force. There-
30   fore, there must first be a character that somehow has an
affinity for excellence or virtue, a character that loves what is
noble and feels disgust at what is base.

To obtain the right training for virtue from youth up is
difficult, unless one has been brought up under the right laws.
To live a life of self-control and tenacity is not pleasant for
most people, especially for the young. Therefore, their upbringing and pursuits must be regulated by laws; for once they
35   have become familiar, they will no longer be painful. But it
80a   is perhaps not enough that they receive the right upbringing
and attention only in their youth. Since they must carry on
these pursuits and cultivate them by habit when they have
grown up, we probably need laws for this, too, and for the
whole of life in general. For most people are swayed rather
5   by compulsion than argument, and by punishments rather
than by ⟨a sense of⟩ what is noble. This is why some believe
that lawgivers ought to exhort and try to influence people

toward ⟨a life of⟩ virtue because of its inherent nobility, in
the hope that those who have made good progress through
their habits will listen to them.[29] Chastisement and penalties,
they think, should be imposed upon those who do not obey
and are of an inferior nature, while the incorrigible ought
to be banished abroad.[30] A good man, they think, who orients   10
his life by what is noble will accept the guidance of reason,
while a bad man, whose desire is for pleasure, is corrected by
pain like a beast of burden. For the same reason, they say that
the pains inflicted must be those that are most directly opposed to the pleasures he loves.

Accordingly, if, as we have said, a man must receive a good
upbringing and discipline in order to be good, and must   15
subsequently lead the same kind of life, pursuing what is
good and never involuntarily or voluntarily doing anything
base, this can be effected by living under the guidance of a
kind of intelligence and right order which can be enforced.
Now, a father's command does not have the power to enforce
or to compel, nor does, in general, the command of a single
man, unless he is a king or someone in a similar position.   20
But law does have the power or capacity to compel, being
the rule of reason derived from some sort of practical wisdom
and intelligence. While people hate any men who oppose,
however rightly, their impulses, the law is not invidious when
it enjoins what is right.

But, with a few exceptions, Sparta is the only state in which   25
the lawgiver seems to have paid attention to upbringing and
pursuits. In most states such matters are utterly neglected,
and each man lives as he pleases, "dealing out law to his
children and his wife" as the Cyclopes do.[31] Now, the best
thing would be to make the correct care of these matters a   30
common concern. But if the community neglects them, it

29 This is advocated by Plato in his *Laws* IV. 722d-723d.
30 This is the view attributed by Plato to Protagoras in *Protagoras* 325a.
31 Homer, *Odyssey* IX. 114-115. The Cyclopes, according to Homer,
were savage one-eyed giants.

would seem to be incumbent upon every man to help his
children and friends attain virtue. This he will be capable of
doing, or at least intend to do.[32]

It follows from our discussion that he will be better capable
of doing it if he knows something about legislation. For clearly
matters of common cencern are regulated by laws, and good
35 concerns by laws which set high moral standards. Whether
1180b the laws are written or unwritten would seem to make no
difference, nor whether they give education to one person or
many, just as it makes no difference in the case of mental or
physical training or any other pursuit. For just as legal traditions and ⟨national⟩ character prevail in states, so paternal
5 words and ⟨ancestral⟩ habits prevail in households—and the
latter have an even greater authority because of the tie of
kinship and of benefits rendered, ⟨for members of a house-
hold⟩ have the requisite natural affection and obedience ⟨to-
ward the father⟩ to start with. Furthermore, individual treatment is superior to group treatment in education as it is in
medicine. As a general rule, rest and abstaining from food
are good for a man with a fever, but perhaps they are not good
10 in a particular case. And an expert boxer perhaps does not
make all his pupils adopt the same style of fighting. It seems
that each particular is worked out with greater precision if private attention is given, since each person has more of an opportunity to get what he needs.

But a physician, a physical trainer, or any other such person
can take the best care in a particular case when he knows the
general rules, that is, when he knows what is good for everyone or what is good for a particular kind of person; for the
15 sciences are said to be, and actually are, concerned with what
is common to particular cases. Of course, there is probably
nothing to prevent even a person with no scientific knowledge from taking good care of a particular case, if he has
accurately observed by experience what happens in a particular case, just as there are some who seem to be their own

32 I accept Bywater's suggestion to transpose καὶ δρᾶν αὐτὸ δύνασθαι
from line 30 to line 32.

best physicians, even though they are incapable of giving aid
to another. Nevertheless, if a man wants to master a skill or   20
art or some theoretical knowledge, he ought, one would think,
probably to go on to a universal principle, and to gain knowledge of it as best as possible. For, as we have stated, it is with
this that the sciences are concerned.

Moreover, a man who wants to make others better by devoting his care to them—regardless of whether they are many
or few—should try to learn something about legislation, if
indeed laws can make us good. To inculcate a good disposi-   25
tion in any person, that is, any person who presents himself,
is not a job for just anyone; if anyone can do it, it is the man
who knows, just as it is in medicine and in all other matters
that involve some sort of care and practical wisdom.

Is it not, then, our next task to examine from whom and
how we can learn to become legislators? Is it not, as always,
from the experts, in this case the masters of politics? For, as   30
we saw,[33] legislation is a part of politics. Or does politics not
appear to be like the rest of the sciences and capacities? [34]
In the other sciences and faculties we find that the people
who transmit the capacity are at the same time actively engaged in practicing what they know, as, for example, physicians and painters. The Sophists, on the other hand, profess   35
to teach social and political matters, but none of them practices them. That is done by the politicians, whose practice,   1181a
it would seem, owes more to some sort of native capacity and
to experience than to thought. We find that they neither
discuss nor write about these matters—though that would
certainly be nobler than making speeches for the law courts
and the assemblies—nor again that they have succeeded in
making masters of politics of their own sons or any of their   5
friends. But one would expect that they would have done so,
had they been able; for they could not have left a better be-
quest to their cities, nor is there anything they would rather

[33] VI. 8, 1141b24-26.
[34] The same point is made by Plato, *Meno* 91a-100c and *Protagoras*
319d-320b.

choose to have for themselves, and thus also for those dearest
to them, than a capacity of this kind. Nonetheless, experience
10　does seem to make no mean contribution; for they would not
have become masters of politics simply through their familiarity with political matters. This is why those who aim at a
knowledge of politics also seem to need experience.

But, as we can see, those Sophists who profess to teach
politics are very far from teaching it.[35] By and large, they do
not even know what sort of thing it is or with what kind of
subjects it deals. For ⟨if they did,⟩ they would not have classi-
15　fied it as identical with or even inferior to rhetoric; nor would
they have believed that it is easy to legislate by collecting
the most highly regarded laws.[36] They think that it is possible to

[35] The whole of this paragraph (1181a12-b12) is aimed at Isocrates
(436-338 B.C.), who founded a school of rhetoric at Athens which competed
with Plato's Academy. Aristotle's special target here seems to be Isocrates'
Antidosis, written in 354-353 B.C., in which Isocrates states his views on
education.

[36] The passage is full of verbal reminiscences of Isocrates, *Antidosis*
79-83:

Now I think that all would agree that our laws are responsible for
⟨having contributed⟩ a very large number of the greatest goods to the
life of mankind. But the use of these laws is naturally confined to the
interest of the affairs of our city and the dealings we have with one
another. If, however, you were to be persuaded by my arguments, you
might administer the whole of Greece well, justly, and in a manner advantageous to our state. Sensible people ought to devote their efforts
to both ⟨our city and to Greece⟩, but should attach greater value to the
greater and more worthy of these two. Moreover, they ought to recognize that, although tens of thousands of Greeks as well as non-Greeks
are endowed with what talents are needed to enact laws, there are not
many people who are capable of discussing matters of public interest
in a manner worthy of our city and of Greece.

That is why men who make it their business to invent discussions of
this sort must be held in higher esteem than those who enact and
write laws, inasmuch as they are rarer, harder ⟨to find⟩, and require
greater intellectual qualities. This is particularly true of the present.
For when the human race first came to be and began to settle in cities,
all searched for much the same thing as a matter of course. But since
we have reached the point where the arguments advanced and the laws
enacted are innumerable, and where we praise the oldest laws and the
newest arguments, this is no longer a task of a single intelligence: those
who have made it their purpose to enact laws have at their disposal

select the best laws, as if the very selection were not an act
of understanding and as if correct judgment were not the
most important thing here, as it is in matters of music. In
every field, it is those who are experienced that judge its products correctly, and are privy to the means and the manner in   20
which they were accomplished and understand what combinations are harmonious. The inexperienced, on the other hand,
must be satisfied if they do not fail to recognize whether the
work has been produced well or badly. That is the case, for
example, in painting. Laws are, as it were, the products of
politics. Accordingly, how can a man learn from them to
become a legislator or to judge which are the best? We do not   1181b
even find men becoming medical experts by reading textbooks.
Yet medical writers try at least not only to describe the treatments, but also how particular patients, whom they distinguish by their various characteristics, can be cured and how the
treatments are to be applied. Though their books seem useful
for experienced people, they are useless for those who do   5
not have the requisite knowledge. So also collections of laws
and constitutions [37] may perhaps be of good use to those who
have the capacity to study them and judge what enactments
are good and which are not, and what kind of measures are
appropriate to what circumstances. But those who go through
such collections without the trained ability [38] ⟨to do so⟩ do

the multitude of laws already enacted. There is no need for them to
seek out new laws, but they must try to collect those laws which are
highly regarded elsewhere; anyone who wants to can easily do this.
But the opposite is true of those who make speaking their business, because most subjects have been pre-empted; for if they say the same
things that have been said before they will impress their audience as
shameless babblers, and if they look for novel ways, they will have
trouble in finding them. That is why I said that though it is right that
both be praised, those who are able to accomplish the harder task deserve much higher praise.

[37] Aristotle is referring to the collection of 158 constitutions of Greek
and non-Greek states which was undertaken under his supervision. The
Constitution of Athens, discovered on papyrus in 1890 and now in the
British Museum, is the only one of these to have come down to us.

[38] See Glossary, *hexis.*

10 not have the requisite good judgment, unless they have it spontaneously, though they may perhaps gain a deeper understanding of these matters.

Accordingly, since previous writers have left the subject of legislation unexamined, it is perhaps best if we ourselves investigate it and the general problem of the constitution of a state,
15 in order to complete as best we can our philosophy of human affairs.[39] First of all, then, let us try to review any discussion of merit contributed by our predecessors on some particular aspect; and then, on the basis of our collection of constitutions, let us study what sort of thing preserves and what destroys states, what preserves and destroys each particular kind of constitution, and what the causes are that make some states
20 well administered and others not. Once we have studied this, we shall perhaps also gain a more comprehensive view of the best form of constitution, of the way in which each is organized, and what laws and customs are current in each. So let us begin our discussion.

[39] This final paragraph of the *Nic. Eth.* leads us back to the point made at the opening of the work in I. 2: the study of ethics is a part of politics. At the same time, this paragraph serves as a general introduction to the *Politics*, even though the outline given here does not correspond to the order of the *Politics* as it has come down to us.

GLOSSARY OF TECHNICAL TERMS *

akōn, akousion (ἄκων, ἀκούσιον): See *hekōn*.

akratēs (ἀκρατής): A MORALLY WEAK MAN. See *sōphrōn*.

anisos (ἄνισος): See *isos*.

archē (ἀρχή): In its most concrete sense, BEGINNING or STARTING POINT. It designates that which stands at the head or at the beginning, without which everything that follows would not be what it is. Thus, in addition, the term may denote any kind of SOURCE, BEGINNING, or FOUNDATION: it may describe public OFFICE, RULING, or GOVERNMENT over a people, the STARTING POINT of an argument as well as of a foot race, the BASIS or FOUNDATION of a conviction, which might then become the CAUSE or INITIATING MOTIVE of an action, or the irreducible FIRST PRINCIPLE or FUNDAMENTAL PRINCIPLE of realities apprehended by the intelligence.

aretē (ἀρετή): Of fundamental importance in all Greek ethical systems. This term, which is the noun corresponding to the adjectives *agathos*, 'good,' *aristos*, 'best,' originally denoted the excellence of a brave or noble warrior; in Homer, *aretē* is almost a synonym for courage, and *agathos* generally means 'brave' or 'of noble birth.' This military and aristocratic sense of the word underlies the later usage, although, within the structure of the *polis*, *aretē* came to signify 'civic virtue' and moral qualities other than courage which distinguish the outstanding citizen. The full history of the term would involve a history of Greek moral ideas, but it is important to realize that *aretē* was eventually generalized to denote the functional excellence of any person, animal, or thing. For example,

* The English terms used in the translation are set off in capital letters in this Glossary.

the *aretē* of a shoemaker is that quality which makes him produce good shoes; in a race horse, it is the quality which will make the horse run to victory; and the *aretē* of a musical instrument will make it respond well and correctly to the manipulations of the player. In other words, *aretē* is that quality which enables its possessor to perform his own particular function well. It is against this background that any Greek discussion of the *aretē* of man as man has to be seen: his *aretai* or 'virtues' are those qualities which make him function well in relation to his fellow men, that is, the qualities which make him play his part in human society well. This means that the overtone of divine sanction of human morality, which is the cornerstone of any Judaeo-Christian system of ethics, is absent from the Greek. The value of *aretē* is that it is an end in itself, realized in living human society: there is no promise of a Kingdom of Heaven as the reward for virtuous conduct. The English translation 'virtue' seems too narrow, though often inescapable, and we use, accordingly, EXCELLENCE, GOODNESS, VIRTUE, or a combination of these, depending on the context.

dianoia (διάνοια): THOUGHT or UNDERSTANDING. It is used both as the most general term to describe the MIND, or a MENTALITY, and in a narrower sense to describe the discursive THINKING which is involved in any act of reasoning or understanding.

dikaiosynē (δικαιοσύνη): The usual translation is JUSTICE. Though Aristotle often uses *dikaiosynē* in the narrow English sense of 'justice,' he remains ever conscious of the wider connotations of the term: 'justice' is for him the same as 'righteousness,' HONESTY. It is, in short, the virtue which regulates all proper conduct within society, in the relations of individuals with one another, and to some extent even the proper attitude of an individual toward himself.

dynamis (δύναμις): Fundamentally, POWER, FORCE, STRENGTH, ABILITY. But Aristotle uses the word and its derivatives in the very narrow sense of a power which is only inherent in something without as yet manifesting itself. In order to be made manifest, *energeia*, 'active exercise,' 'activity,' 'actuality,' is needed. For example, a man who knows the art of building possesses the *dynamis*, CAPACITY or 'potentiality,' of building a house; but this capacity is only something latent in him until he actively exercises it (*energeia*) by actually building a house. Similarly, the various parts of the soul, the seats, respectively, of nutrition, perception, desire, locomotion, and thought, are called *dynameis*, 'capacities,' in *De Anima* II. 3, 414a31, because they exist only potentially until actively exercised. Similarly, too, the *technai* or 'arts' are regarded as *dynameis* as long as they are not yet translated into activities. For a full definition of *dynamis* and its relation to *energeia*, see *Metaphysics* Δ. 12, 1019a15-32, and Θ (entire).

eidos (εἶδος): Translated as SPECIFIC FORM or simply FORM, *eidos* is that set of qualities which a scientific definition (*logos*) analyzes into its constituent parts. Each thing is a composite of matter (*hylē*) and form (*eidos*); e.g., a tree is composed of wood, the matter, and "treeness," the specific form without which the matter would remain unintelligible. To analyze this form into its constituent parts (in the case of the tree, having bark, leaves, certain definite proportions, etc.) is to define the tree. *Eidos* is also the KIND or SPECIES into which a *genos* ('genus') is divided.

eirōneia (εἰρωνεία): SELF-DEPRECIATION is perhaps the least inaccurate rendering of *eirōneia*, from which English 'irony' is derived. But the partly humorous, partly malicious connotation of 'irony' is not inherent in the Greek term. *Eirōneia* is the exact opposite of boastfulness and involves qualities such as understatement, pretending ignorance, mock modesty and the like, but sometimes also has overtones of slyness.

eleutheriotēs (ἐλευθεριότης): Frequently translated 'liberality,' because, like the Latin *liberalitas*, it denotes the quality of a free man as opposed to a slave. However, by the fourth century B.C., the term was so restricted to money matters that it seems advisable to use the more idiomatic GENEROSITY in preference to the somewhat antiquated term 'liberality.'

energeia (ἐνέργεια): The noun *energeia*, ACTIVITY, ACTIVE EXERCISE, does not occur in Greek literature before Aristotle. The adjective *energos*, however, is found in the meaning of 'active,' 'at work,' and refers, for example, to men or material in active use, or to fields under active cultivation as opposed to those lying fallow. Aristotle uses the noun and its cognate verb form *energein* in two ways. (1) In its widest sense, *energeia* denotes the state of 'being busy' or 'active,' regardless of whether the activity has a palpable result (as it does, for example, in the case of a craftsman) or whether it is self-contained (as, for example, the activity or active exercise of seeing, hearing, etc.). In this sense, *energeia* has a wider range than either *praxis*, 'action,' i.e., 'acting' or 'doing something to' another human being, or *poiēsis*, 'production,' which always results in a product accessible to the senses. (2) In a narrower and more technical sense, *energeia* ('actuality') is the opposite of *dynamis* ('potentiality'). But even this technical sense is closely related to the ordinary use of *energos* mentioned above. See *dynamis*.

enkratēs (ἐγκρατής): A MORALLY STRONG MAN. See *sōphrōn*.

epagōgē (ἐπαγωγή): INDUCTION. Cf. *Topics* I. 12, 105a13-16: "Induction is the procedure which leads from particulars to universals, e.g., if the best helmsman and the best charioteer are those who have knowledge, it is true as a general rule that in each particular field the best is he who has knowledge."

epieikēs (ἐπιεικής): Describes a person whose actions are always seemly, fair, right, EQUITABLE, DECENT, HONEST and the like. Aristotle seems to use the word as a less precise and less scientific way of saying GOOD. In V. 10 the word and its derivatives also carry the notion of 'equity,' i.e., of those questions of justice and injustice, right and wrong, that cannot be determined by formula, but only by some sense of fair play.

epistēmē (ἐπιστήμη): In the strict sense, disinterested, objective, and SCIENTIFIC KNOWLEDGE, thus also translated as SCIENCE or PURE SCIENCE, which differs from *technē* in that it is knowledge for its own sake. Aristotle, however, occasionally uses the term in a loose way for KNOWLEDGE of any kind, even if that knowledge is a means to an end other than itself.

ergon (ἔργον): The literal and most basic meaning is WORK, both in a functional sense, e.g., the 'work' of a hammer is to drive in nails, and in the concrete sense in which we speak of the 'works' of a poet, sculptor, or craftsman. Accordingly, the term has to be translated differently in different contexts. In using PRODUCT, we take that word in a slightly wider sense than good English usage permits; for Aristotle also calls, for example, health the *ergon* of medicine. In other contexts, translations such as FUNCTION, RESULT, or ACHIEVEMENT are more appropriate.

eudaimōn (εὐδαίμων): HAPPY, usually in the sense of a happiness attained by man through his own efforts. Cf. *makarios*.

eupraxia (εὐπραξία): One of the key concepts in Aristotle's ethical theory. It is a noun formation of an adverb-verb combination that means not only 'to act well,' GOOD ACTION, but also 'to fare well,' 'to be successful,' 'to be happy.' In other words, as the principal ingredient in the GOOD LIFE, the noun is practically equivalent to 'happiness.'

gnōmē (γνώμη): The most common use describes a particular 'insight' or JUDGMENT, especially as it is related to matters affecting the conduct of one's life. But the term may denote both a particular judgment and a man's ability to pass good judgments in general, i.e., what we might call his GOOD SENSE or 'sound understanding.' In addition, a *gnōmē* is the equivalent of 'maxim,' 'adage.' In VI. 11 Aristotle relates *gnōmē* to several cognates, such as *syngnōmē*, 'forgiveness,' 'pardon,' 'sympathetic understanding' (literally 'judgment with' or 'on the side of' another person), and *eugnōmōn*, 'well-judging' in the sense of 'kindly,' 'well disposed.'

hekōn, hekousion (ἑκών, ἑκούσιον): An agent is described as *hekōn* when he has consented to perform the action he is performing. This consent may range from mere passive acquiescence to intentional and deliberate conduct. Conversely, an *akōn* is a man who has not given his consent to his action, regardless of whether he acts unconsciously, inadvertently, or even against his own will. The action performed in each case is the neuter *hekousion*, VOLUNTARY ACTION, and *akousion*, INVOLUNTARY ACTION.

hetairos (ἑταῖρος): With derivative adjective *hetairikos*, translated as BOSOM COMPANION, but may also have the more technical meaning of 'member of a *hetaireia* or club.' Such clubs were political in character toward the end of the fifth century B.C., but when a law, enacted shortly after the restoration of the democracy in 403 B.C., prevented the formation of such clubs for political purposes, they became purely social in character.

hexis (ἕξις): CHARACTERISTIC, also TRAINED ABILITY, CHARACTERISTIC CONDITION, CHARACTERISTIC ATTITUDE. A noun related to the verb *echein*, 'to have,' 'hold,' 'hold as a possession,' 'be in a certain condition,' designating a firmly fixed possession of the mind, established by repeated and habitual action. Once attained, it is ever present, at least in a potential form. The Latin interpreters of Greek philosophy rendered the term by *habitus,* a word which well retains the original relation with *habēre = echein.* Hence 'habit' has often been used as an English equivalent.

homonoia (ὁμόνοια): CONCORD, primarily a political concept. Literally, it designates the quality of 'being of the same mind,' 'thinking in harmony.'

isos (ἴσος): *Isos* and *anisos* are translated as EQUAL and UN-EQUAL, respectively. But they have a much wider sense than their English equivalents, especially when referring to a share assigned in a distribution; in this sense the terms correspond to FAIR and UNFAIR.

kalokagathia (καλοκαγαθία): For the Greeks, what the ideal of the 'gentleman' is for the British, though the two terms are far from identical in meaning. The noun combines the adjectives *kalos* and *agathos,* which express external and internal excellence, respectively. In other words, the term, translated as GOODNESS and NOBILITY, combines qualities of good appearance, good bearing, good manners and the like with moral qualities such as honesty, courage, self-control, etc.

koinōnia (κοινωνία): One of the key concepts of Aristotle's social and political thought, and one of his most profound contributions to political philosophy is his definition of the state as a form of *koinōnia* in Book I of the *Politics.* *Koinōnia* is any kind of group whose members are held together by something they have 'in common' with each other, i.e., by some kind of common bond. The size of the group or the nature of the bond is immaterial: at its largest, mankind might be described as a *koinōnia,* held together by the common bond of humanity; a state is a *koinōnia* in that it is held together by the common inter-est of its citizens; similarly, a club, a village, or even as small a unit as the family are spoken of as different kinds of *koinōnia.* ASSOCIATION perhaps comes closest to rendering the concept in English, but it fails to bring out the bond so prominent in the Greek. COMMUNITY, SOCIETY, HUMAN RELATIONS, SOCIAL ORGANISM, and PARTNERSHIP are also used in this translation, depending on the context.

leitourgia (λειτουργία): A PUBLIC SERVICE, the costs of which are defrayed by a private individual. Such *leitourgiai* included services such as equipping a warship, training and costuming a tragic or comic chorus, paying the expenses of a sacred embassy sent by the state to consult an oracle, etc.

logos (λόγος): Fundamental meaning is SPEECH, STATEMENT, in the sense that any speech or statement consists of a coherent and rational arrangement of words. From this derives the wider application of the term to a RATIONAL PRINCIPLE or REASON underlying a great variety of things. In this sense it may be translated rational ACCOUNT, EXPLANATION, ARGUMENT, TREATISE, or DISCUSSION. *Logos* is also used in a normative sense, describing the human faculty of REASON which comprehends and formulates rational principles and thus guides the conduct of a good and reasonable man.

makarios (μακάριος): BLESSED or SUPREMELY HAPPY, to describe god-given happiness. Cf. *eudaimōn*.

megaloprepeia (μεγαλοπρέπεια): MAGNIFICENCE seems to be the closest English equivalent. Literally, the term means 'greatness befitting (an occasion).' This virtue involves the kind of public spirit that was exhibited in Athens by the so-called "liturgies" (see *leitourgia*), i.e., the financing of dramatic productions, of the equipment of warships, etc.

megalopsychia (μεγαλοψυχία): Literally means 'greatness of soul' and was translated into Latin as *magnanimitas*, from which English 'magnanimity' is derived. However, since the connotations of *megalopsychia* are much wider than the modern meaning of 'magnanimity,' HIGH-MINDEDNESS seems better suited to rendering the pride and confident self-respect inherent in the concept.

mousikē (μουσική): Though the concept includes MUSIC, it actually encompasses all the artistic and intellectual activities over which the Muses preside. Accordingly, it ranges from the writing and reciting of poetry to dancing, astronomy, etc.

pathos (πάθος): In its most rudimentary sense, *pathos* is the opposite of *praxis*, 'action,' and denotes anything which befalls a person or which he experiences. In most cases, EMOTION comes closest to what Aristotle means; but when the connotations of this are too narrow or misleading, AFFECT is used, in Spinoza's sense of *affectus*.

phantasia (φαντασία): A noun derived from *phainō*, 'bring to light,' 'make appear,' and usually translated IMAGINATION. Aristotle defines it in *De Anima* III. 3, 429a1-2 as "a motion engendered by the exercise of sense perception." In other words, the data assembled by sense perception create a certain image in the mind, which then forms the basis of memory, action, and thought. Inasmuch as sense perception can be true or false, and its survival in the mind more or less accurate, so *phantasia* may be more or less accurate.

philētos (φιλητός): Usually rendered LOVABLE. However, since 'love' is too strong for the noun *philia* ('friendship,' 'affection'), to which it is related, object WORTHY OF AFFECTION is preferred; 'lovable' is used whenever the former seems awkward. Similarly, the verb *philein* is translated either as 'to feel affection' or as 'to love,' depending on the context.

philia (φιλία): Though usually translated FRIENDSHIP, the connotations of the Greek term are wider. *Philia* describes

(1) the human relation that is 'friendship,' (2) the characteristic most conducive to the establishment of friendship, i.e., FRIENDLINESS, 'amiability,' or (3) sometimes even the emotion underlying friendship, AFFECTION. In general, *philia* is best summed up in the Greek proverb: κοινὰ τὰ τῶν φίλων, "friends hold in common what they have." It designates the relationship between a person and any other person(s) or being(s) which that person regards as peculiarly his own and to which he has a peculiar attachment. This includes the bond holding the members of any association together, regardless of whether the association is the family, the state, a club, a business partnership, or even the business relation between buyer and seller.

phronēsis (φρόνησις): *Phronēsis* and *sophia* may both be translated as 'wisdom,' and are normally used as synonyms in the dialogues of Plato. But Aristotle, in working toward a more precise terminology, prefers to distinguish them. His usage takes account of the fact that *phronēsis* tends to imply wisdom in action, and hence a moral intelligence, PRACTICAL WISDOM, while *sophia* originally indicated technical competence and artistic skill (e.g., in poetry or handicraft), but came to be used for scientific competence and theoretical wisdom (as in *philosophia*, the 'love of wisdom'). For a detailed discussion of these terms, see VI. 5 and 7.

politeia (πολιτεία): An abstract noun, derived from *politēs*, 'citizen,' itself derivative of *polis*, 'city-state.' It designates the peculiar bond that unites citizen to citizen to form the state, and, in fact, it is *politeia*, or the nature of this bond, that gives the state its identity. CONSTITUTION or POLITICAL SYSTEM are perhaps the closest English approximations to this concept. But in addition, Aristotle gives *politeia*, both in *Nic. Eth.* VIII. 10 and in *Politics* III-VI, a normative meaning to describe one of the three good forms of government to which a corrupt form (which is in this sense not a *politeia*) corresponds. Although the normative sense can often be rendered by 'constitution,' CONSTITUTIONAL GOVERNMENT shall occasionally have to be substituted for it.

politikē (πολιτική): Implicit in the term is the etymological connection with the *polis*, the 'city-state,' and with the *politēs*, 'citizen,' who was a free member of the *polis*. Accordingly, *politikē* (*technē*) is the science of the city-state and its members, not merely in our narrow sense of POLITICS or POLITICAL WISDOM, but also in the sense that the *polis*, according to Plato and Aristotle, is the only form of civilized human existence. Thus the term *polis* also covers our concept 'society' (for which the Greeks had no independent word), and *politikē* is the science of society as well as the science of the state.

proairesis (προαίρεσις): CHOICE, or MORAL CHOICE, one of the key terms in Aristotle's ethical system. The word is a compound of *pro-* 'before,' and *hairesis,* 'a taking,' 'a choosing,' and thus literally means 'a choosing ahead,' 'preference.' Accordingly, the noun describes the act of making up one's mind as a result of deliberation prior to undertaking a particular course of action. See III. 2.

sophia (σοφία): See *phronēsis*. Aristotle understands by *sophia* the highest intellectual, and especially philosophical, excellence of which the human mind is capable, and which is the result of studying nature for its own sake; in this sense it is translated THEORETICAL WISDOM. In a more current and general sense, it is simply equivalent to our WISDOM.

sōphrōn (σώφρων): A *sōphrōn* is a person aware of his limitations in a positive as well as a negative sense: he knows what his abilities and nature do and do not permit him to do. He is a SELF-CONTROLLED MAN in the sense that he will never want to do what he knows he cannot or should not. Aristotle differentiates him from the *enkratēs,* a man who also knows what his abilities and nature permit and do not permit, but who, though feeling drawn to what he cannot or should not do, has the moral fiber to resist temptation and follow the voice of reason instead. (His opposite, the *akratēs,* or 'morally weak man,' succumbs to temptation.) These terms refer not only to different virtues, but also to essentially different types of personality. A *sōphrōn* is well-balanced through and through; he gives the impression of self-control without effort or strain. The *enkratēs,* on the other hand, has an intense and passionate nature which he is, indeed, strong enough to control, but not without a struggle. He is 'morally strong' in his victory; the *sōphrōn,* on the other hand, is not even tempted.

sōphrosyne (σωφροσύνη): Literally translated, means 'soundness of mind,' and describes the full knowledge of one's limitations in a positive as well as negative sense: the *sōphrōn,* who possesses this virtue, knows what he is capable of as well as what he is incapable of doing. 'Temperance,' which is often used to translate this concept, is entirely negative, and is nowadays almost exclusively applied to abstention from alcoholic beverages, a connotation entirely uncharacteristic of the Greek word; 'moderation,' too, has largely negative connotations and has, in addition, a flabbiness that is alien to the Greek term. Though SELF-CONTROL is also more negative than positive in modern usage, if the word is taken more literally than it usually is, i.e., if 'control' is not merely taken as 'restraint' but also as 'mastery,' it comes closer to *sōphrosyne* than most alternative renderings.

spoudaios (σπουδαῖος): Literally, 'serious man,' whom Aristotle frequently invokes for purposes similar to those which make modern laws invoke the "reasonable man." However, Aristotle's stress is less on the reasonableness of a man under particular circumstances than on a person who has a sense of the importance of living his life well and of fulfilling his function in society in accordance with the highest standards. OF HIGH MORAL STANDARD, OF GREAT MORAL

VALUE, MORALLY GOOD and similar expressions are the most appropriate English equivalents, depending upon the context.

synesis (σύνεσις): Translated UNDERSTANDING, denoting primarily the comprehension of what someone else has said; but it also contains the notion of understanding practical problems.

technē (τέχνη): The SKILL, ART, or craft and general know-how, the possession of which enables a person to produce a certain product. The term is used not only to describe, for example, the kind of knowledge which a shoemaker needs to produce shoes, but also to describe the art of a physician which produces health, or the skill of a harpist which produces music. Thus *technē* as an APPLIED SCIENCE concerned with production is often contrasted with *epistēmē,* which is pure scientific knowledge for its own sake. See VI. 4.

teleios (τέλειος): The adjective derived from *telos,* 'end,' 'conclusion.' Its meaning corresponds most closely to Latin *perfectum:* it means 'final' not only in the sense that an end has been reached and completion attained, but also in that this completion constitutes a perfection which (in Aristotle's language) is the complete actuality of a thing (*entelecheia*). To render the term in its various contexts, COMPLETE, FINAL, and PERFECT are used.

theōrein (θεωρεῖν): The literal meaning of this verb is 'to inspect' or 'to keep one's gaze fixed on.' Aristotle used it to describe that activity of the mind most closely associated with *sophia* ('theoretical wisdom'), in which the mind CONTEMPLATES or STUDIES or OBSERVES the knowledge of universal truths which it already possesses. See also *theōria.*

theōria (θεωρία): That kind of mental activity in which we engage for its own sake, or rather for the attainment of truth. It is a contemplation of nature in its widest sense, in which man, as a detached spectator, simply investigates and studies things as they are without desiring to change them. Thus, *theōria* is different, on the one hand, from such practical sciences as ethics and politics, of which the aim is action rather than contemplation, and, on the other hand, from the productive sciences, which aim at the creation of some kind of product. While most translations conventionally render the noun by 'contemplation,' the present translation has preferred THEORETICAL KNOWLEDGE or STUDY. However, it is difficult to avoid translating the adjective *theōrētikos* by 'contemplative' when it describes the kind of life which is devoted to *theōria*.